Philippe Legrain is the author of *Open World: The Truth about Globalisation* (Abacus, 2002). He is a contributing editor to *Prospect* magazine and a freelance writer for a variety of publications such as the *Financial Times*, the *Guardian*, the *New Republic* and *Foreign Policy*. He blogs at www.philippelegrain.com. In 1999, he was highly commended as Young Financial Journalist of the Year in the Harold Wincott Press Awards. He is also a commentator for BBC TV and radio on globalisation and trade. He was previously trade and economics correspondent for *The Economist* and special adviser to World Trade Organization director-general Mike Moore. He has a first-class honours degree in economics and a masters in politics of the world economy, both from the London School of Economics. Philippe is thirty-three and lives in London.

Also by Philippe Legrain

Open World

Immigrants: Your Country Needs Them

Philippe Legrain

Little, Brown

LITTLE, BROWN

First published in Great Britain in 2006 by Little, Brown

A CIP catalogue record for this book is available from the British Library.

ISBN: 978-0-316-73248-2

Typeset in Sabon by M Rules
Printed and bound in Great Britain by
Clays Ltd, St Ives plc

Little, Brown
An imprint of
Little, Brown Book Group
Brettenham House
Lancaster Place
London WC2E 7EN

A Member of the Hachette Livre Group of Companies

www.littlebrown.co.uk

To my mother, with love, and to Pete and Marion,
for always being there for me

Contents

ACKNOWLEDGEMENTS ix

INTRODUCTION
MIGRATION ISN'T JUST FOR THE BIRDS 1
It's time for fresh thinking about immigration

1 WAR ON OUR BORDERS 23
The hidden costs of immigration controls

2 BORDER CROSSING 44
How migrants got to where they are now

3 WHY WE NEED THE HUDDLED MASSES 61
The case for low-skilled migration

4 THE GLOBAL TALENT CONTEST 89
The pros and cons of high-skilled migration

5 COSMOPOLITAN AND RICH 117
The economic benefits of diversity

6 STEALING OUR JOBS? 133
Do immigrants displace local workers?

7 SNOUTS IN OUR TROUGH? 144
Are immigrants a burden on the welfare state?

8 'OUR HEROES' 161
How migration helps poor countries

9 BRAIN DRAIN OR BRAIN GAIN? 179
The costs and benefits of skilled emigration

10 IT NEEDN'T BE FOREVER 198
The case for temporary migration

11 ALIEN NATION? 207
Does immigration threaten national identity?

12 HUNTINGTON AND HISPANICS 226
Is Latino immigration splitting America in two?

13 STRANGER, CAN YOU SPARE A DIME? 245
Does immigration threaten social solidarity?

14 LEARNING TO LIVE TOGETHER 258
How to integrate immigrants into society

15 ILLIBERAL ISLAM? 289
Do Muslim immigrants threaten our security and our way of life?

16 OPEN BORDERS 318
Let them in

NOTES 334

INDEX 360

Acknowledgements

Writing this book was an intensely personal endeavour, but it would not have been possible without the help and support of many other people. Many thanks to Jonny Geller, my agent, and Doug Kean, his assistant at Curtis Brown, as well as to Tim Whiting and Steve Guise, my editors at Little, Brown. I am very grateful to my good friend Gideon Lichfield, who went through the first drafts and suggested many improvements, as well as providing invaluable assistance with my research in Israel. Simon Long was kind enough to read the finished manuscript.

Many people helped me out with my research, but special thanks to Diane Coyle, Elena Muñoz and everyone at Málaga Acoge, Harm Botje in Amsterdam, Patrick and Jeannette Kaltenbach and Alan Riding in Paris, Jander Lacerda in New York, Carlos Salas Porras and his wife Maruca in Ciudad Juárez, Andreas Kluth in Silicon Valley, and Katie Lennon and Linda Pearson in Sydney. Brian Barry gave me valuable advice about Japan. I am very grateful to everyone who took the time to talk to me, not all of whom are mentioned in the book. I also want to thank everyone who has supported me in my career, not least Mike Moore, David Goodhart, Martin Wolf, Pam Woodall and Bill Emmott.

Above all, though, I want to thank my friends and family for their love and support. Lots of love to Mum, Dad, Pierre, Milli and Elizabeth. I am extremely grateful to William DeVine, Jo Turner, Neil Moore and Gemma Crossley for helping me when times were tough. Peter and Marion Doyle will always be in my heart. I am blessed with many good friends, not all of whom I can mention here, but I want to thank in particular Adham Nicola, Allison Gallienne, Chris Foges, Chris Wilkes, Cieppe Nightingale, Colin and Shirley Iles, Daniele Deiana, Dusch Atkinson, Emily Foges, Evan Davis, Frank Paget, Frank Smith, Harry Rich, Hugo Macgregor, Jeff Smith, Jo Malvisi, Johan Nordin, John Cormack, Mark Alefounder, Martyn Fitzgerald, Matt Issitt, Michael Nieuwenhuizen, Paul Bates, Paul Richardson, Richard Scandrett, Rob Gunns and Tim Laxton. Thanks too to Lee Freeman, Mark Westhenry, Malcolm Duffy, Kerri Docherty, Marcus O'Higgins and everyone at Blue Cube.

Last but certainly not least, thank you to David Sanderquist for lighting up my life.

Introduction

Migration Isn't Just for the Birds

It's time for fresh thinking about immigration

> Migration is the oldest action against poverty. It selects those who most want help. It is good for the country to which they go; it helps break the equilibrium of poverty in the country from which they come. What is the perversity in the human soul that causes people to resist so obvious a good?
>
> J. K. Galbraith[1]

Wednesday 6 July 2005 was a day for celebration in London. As the crowds in Trafalgar Square noisily cheered the news that the city would host the 2012 Olympics, a much smaller and more subdued ceremony was taking place a few miles away at Westminster Register Office. Standing beside a framed photograph of Queen Elizabeth II and a large Union Jack, a grey-haired man in a bright red, fur-trimmed robe decked in white gloves and a big gold chain was addressing a room of some forty people of all ages and colours – an old man with a walking stick, a young man in a black fitted shirt, a schoolgirl in her blue-and-yellow uniform, a toddler in his mother's arms, a baby in a cot, one man in a suit and tie.

'Today is a very important day in your lives,' said the Deputy Lord Mayor of Westminster, after apologising for the absence of the Lord Mayor, who was busy touring TV studios welcoming the Olympic decision. 'You are now British citizens and are entitled to vote in this country.' He paused. 'I will try to be as informal as possible. In fact, ceremonies like these have only been going for just over a year.' But almost despite himself, his words rose to the occasion: 'We welcome you here today into this nation and into this community of Westminster. You are now full members of the British family. As British citizens, we hold dear the values of tolerance and respect to others. I trust you will be loyal subjects and observe the law.'

The new British citizens then swore – or affirmed, in the case of non-believers – their allegiance to the Queen, pledged their commitment to the United Kingdom and queued up to be photographed receiving their certificate of citizenship from the Deputy Lord Mayor. Understated yet momentous, it was all over in less than half an hour. As we left, Adriano, my Brazilian – and now British – friend, was grinning from ear to ear. 'I'm like you now,' he beamed.

On 7 July London's joy turned to horror as four British Muslim suicide bombers blew themselves up on a bus and three Tube trains, killing fifty-two people. As Londoners reeled at this callous attack on their way of life, their mayor, Ken Livingstone, captured the public mood: 'This was not a terrorist attack against the mighty and the powerful. It was not aimed at presidents or prime ministers. It was aimed at ordinary, working-class Londoners, black and white, Muslim and Christian, Hindu and

Jew, young and old. It was an indiscriminate attempt to slaughter, irrespective of any considerations for age, for class, for religion, or whatever.' Addressing would-be terrorists directly, he continued: 'In the days that follow look at our airports, look at our sea ports and look at our railway stations and, even after your cowardly attack, you will see that people from the rest of Britain, people from around the world will arrive in London to become Londoners and to fulfil their dreams and achieve their potential.

'They choose to come to London, as so many have come before, because they come to be free, they come to live the life they choose, they come to be able to be themselves. They flee you because you tell them how they should live. They don't want that, and nothing you do, however many of us you kill, will stop that flight to our city where freedom is strong and where people can live in harmony with one another. Whatever you do, however many you kill, you will fail.'

The roll-call of the dead poignantly underscored Mayor Livingstone's words. The fifty-two victims included many foreigners and Britons of foreign descent, whose varied backgrounds highlight London's status as a cosmopolitan city of opportunity. These immigrants were not the lazy, dishonest scroungers of tabloid fare; they were the lifeblood of a diverse and dynamic global city. Among them were: three Polish women – a forty-three-year-old cleaner and a twenty-nine-year-old assistant manager at a postgraduate residential college, both of whom had been living in London for three years, and a recently arrived twenty-four-year-old administrative assistant who had planned to stay in London for only four months while learning English; a forty-six-year-old Romanian dental technician who described London as 'the best place in the world'; a thirty-one-year-old Italian business analyst who had come to London ten years earlier as an au pair and was due to marry her British Muslim fiancé on 11 September 2005;

a twenty-six-year-old Nigerian oil executive; a fifty-year-old cleaner of Ghanaian origin who had spent half her life in London; a thirty-nine-year-old Israeli charity worker who had come to London when she was twenty-one; a twenty-six-year-old New Zealander with dual Irish nationality who had lived in London for three years; a recently arrived thirty-seven-year-old Vietnamese-American; a twenty-seven-year-old accountant from Mauritius who had been in Britain for three years; a twenty-eight-year-old Vietnamese-born Australian working in computing who had lived in London for two years; a thirty-year-old Sri Lankan-born assistant buyer for the Royal Mail, who had come to Britain when she was one; a sixty-year-old retired policeman born in Grenada, who had come to London to retire; a radiographer of Indian origin at Great Ormond Street Hospital for Sick Children; a fifty-six-year-old social worker of Nigerian descent; a twenty-two-year-old shop assistant of Irish origin; a twenty-eight-year-old advertising salesman with Jamaican grandparents; and a thirty-seven-year-old IT manager of Indian descent.

Among the fifty-two victims were also five Muslims: a twenty-four-year-old French computer scientist of Tunisian origin who was working as a waiter in London over the summer while learning English; a twenty-four-year-old Turkish woman, also studying English; a forty-eight-year-old Iranian biomedical officer at Great Ormond Street Hospital; a twenty-four-year-old Afghan man who had come to Britain as a refugee from the Taliban; and a twenty-year-old bank cashier of Bangladeshi origin. The last of them, Shahara Islam, was described as 'a thoroughly modern Muslim, a girl who loved her Burberry plaid handbag and fashionable clothes while at the same time respecting her family's wishes that she sometimes wear traditional *shalwar kameez* at home. She went shopping in the West End of London with friends but would always be seen at the mosque for Friday prayers.'[2] Her short life was an eloquent answer to those on both sides of the divide who claim that Islamic immigrants cannot successfully integrate into Western societies.

A microcosm of the debate

It is a cruel irony that I began writing this book just as my city and everything it stands for came under attack from terrorists who were British-born but of foreign descent. But at the same time, the London bombings have helped crystallise the debate that is at the heart of this book: should we welcome or seek to prevent the unprecedented wave of international migration that is bringing ever greater numbers of people from poor countries to rich countries like Britain, Spain and the United States? Fear of foreigners versus the dynamism of multicultural London: a microcosm of the wider debate about immigration that is raging around the world.

As our societies age and many businesses complain they are short of workers, the pressure to let in immigrants grows, but many people in rich countries remain unconvinced. In the United States, President Bush has sent the National Guard to patrol the border with Mexico to keep out unwanted immigrants, while pundits warn that Hispanic immigration risks splitting America in two. The government tries to juggle its desire to attract talented foreign students and workers with heightened fears about national security since 9/11. As record numbers of Africans risk death on flimsy boats to reach its shores, Spain erects ever higher walls – six metres high at the last count – around its enclaves in North Africa to try to close off Europe's southern gateway. Until recently a country of emigration, Spain now receives more immigrants than any other country in Europe. France's largely immigrant suburbs erupt into riots to protest at poverty and discrimination, while rioters in Sydney launch violent attacks on

Lebanese immigrants. John Howard comes from behind in the polls to win Australia's general election in 2001 by declaring that 'we will decide, and nobody else, who comes to this country' and turning back a boat laden with Afghan refugees. Germans struggle to accept that the children and grandchildren of Turkish guest-workers are German too. The murder in Amsterdam of Theo van Gogh, a top filmmaker critical of Islam, by a Dutch-born Muslim extremist provokes a spate of tit-for-tat burnings of schools, churches and mosques. Meanwhile, the eastward enlargement of the European Union opens the door for Poles, Czechs and others to come to work in Britain, Ireland and Sweden (and more recently Finland, Greece, Portugal and Spain) – and one day the rest of western Europe too.

Do the new arrivals pose a threat to everything we cherish – jobs, the welfare state, our national identity and way of life, even our freedom and security – or does their diversity in fact enrich and invigorate the economy, culture and society of their adopted homes? Could we put a stop to immigration if we wanted to, or is it an inevitable consequence of a globalising world riven between rich and poor? And what should we do to help the immigrants and people of foreign descent who are already living among us fit in better? These questions are not only about Them, and their possible merits and faults, but also about Us – what kind of place, country and world we want to live in; how far our sense of solidarity and justice extends beyond national borders; how much we value diversity and to what extent we fear it clashes with other values we hold dear; and ultimately whether our concept of Us is broad and flexible enough to embrace Them too.

I hope that it is, not least because I feel like one of Them as well as one of Us. My grandparents fled Estonia in 1944 as the Red Army arrived and ended up half a world away building a new life in California. That's where my Estonian-American mother was raised, before moving to New York, where she met and married my French father in 1969. They eventually ended up in London, where I was born in 1973 and grew up. Although the name on my birth certificate, Philippe Legrain, sounds quintessentially French, London is my home and my friends call me Phil. My family history isn't important as such (except to help explain my outlook); it is just one of the many different life stories that we lump together as 'immigration'.

I am in good company. With me are people like George Borjas, a Cuban refugee who has become a professor at Harvard University and an expert on the economics of immigration. Ironically, he advocates that the US should let in only skilled immigrants – a policy that would have denied his family entry to America. Or Stephan Petrusiak, a Polish-Ukrainian who recently returned to Warsaw to complete his medical studies after several years in London working as a nurse for Britain's state-funded National Health Service. He hopes to return to Britain as a fully fledged doctor in 2007. Or Lasso Kourouma, a refugee from the civil war in Côte d'Ivoire who almost drowned trying to get to Spain and spent two years sleeping rough in Malaga. He now has a job as a nightclub bouncer, as well as a lovely wife and a young daughter. Or Jander Lacerda, a Brazilian artist who does odd jobs while trying to establish himself in the New York art world. Or Inmer Omar Rivera, who has made his way illegally from Honduras to the US–Mexican border. He hopes to make it into America and work hard so that his son can afford to study and have a better life. Or Hanna, who was working as a cleaner in London illegally until Poland joined the EU in 2004 and she became entitled to work here. She has now officially registered her cleaning business, pays taxes, regularly sends money back to her mother in Poland and hopes to return there permanently once she has saved enough to secure a better future for her son. Or, for that matter, countless famous and illustrious people who may or may not be representative, but who have certainly made a difference.

Whenever people talk in the abstract about the pros and cons of immigration, one should not forget that immigrants are individual human beings whose lives happen not to fit neatly within national borders – and that like all human beings, they are all different.

How different, though? Different better, or different worse? Such basic questions underlie whether people are willing to accept outsiders in their midst. Are the newcomers perceived to be honest, hard-working people keen to fit in to their new country, or feckless, scrounging layabouts who make no effort to adapt to their adopted society – and might even harbour bad intentions towards it? Perceptions – or prejudice – matter more than reality, since foreigners are strangers and therefore largely unknown. The truth, of course, is that immigrants may be good, bad, or probably a mixture of both. Generally, though, I believe they have two big qualities: they are typically hard-working and enterprising. Why? Because every immigrant is also an emigrant, and it takes courage and enterprise to uproot yourself to a foreign land. You have to be particularly desperate or adventurous to leave behind your family, friends and homeland to take a leap into the unknown and try to start a new life in an alien and potentially hostile country. And once you have made that big leap, you have every incentive to try to better yourself and build a better future for yourself and your children.

Broader questions arise when immigrants arrive in sufficient numbers that they start to change their adopted society. Greens may be concerned that a rising population puts additional strain on the environment. Trade unionists may fear that the newcomers threaten the jobs and wages of marginal workers. Taxpayers may fret about the burden they might impose on the welfare state. Cultural conservatives may worry about their impact on national identity and social mores. Such concerns must be addressed, because even though freer international migration can bring huge economic and cultural benefits, it also requires political consent. Already, as immigration has risen in recent years, it has sparked a backlash in America, Europe and elsewhere.

Fear of foreigners

Around a million people migrate legally to the US each year, and maybe another half a million – nobody knows the exact figure – enter the country illegally.[3] Europe admits some 2.8 million foreigners each year, with another 800,000 or so – again, nobody knows for sure – entering illegally.[4] Canada, with a population of 32 million, admits around 235,000 permanent migrants a year; Australia, with a population of 19 million, around 150,000 (but around 60,000 foreigners leave each year).[5]

These are big numbers, but what makes them especially significant is that people in rich countries are having far fewer babies than ever before. Which means that immigrants account for a rising share of the workforce and population in rich countries – and an even larger share of the population increase. One in ten Europeans and one in eight Americans are now foreign-born. So are one in five Canadians and nearly one in four Australians.[6] Two in five Australians have a parent who was born overseas.[7] Even more strikingly, immigrants accounted for three-quarters of America's population growth in the second half of the 1990s, while Europe's population would have fallen by 4.4 million over the same period were it not for the arrival of 5 million immigrants.

Immigration has already changed the faces of many rich countries. Back in 1970, there were only 10 million foreign-born Americans; now, there are officially over 37 million – plus several million uncounted illegals – and the new faces are mostly Latin American and Asian.[8] In a country fractured by race and fragmented by the unintended consequences of 'affirmative action' (the well-meaning attempt to give blacks and later other minority groups a hand-up through positive discrimination), the new wave of immigration has sparked a fervent debate about the changing face of America.

Peter Brimelow, a British-born but naturalised American financial journalist, sounded the alarm in 1995 in his best-seller, *Alien Nation: Common Sense about America's Immigration Disaster*.[9] He warned that mass immigration was 'so huge and so systematically different from anything that had gone before as to transform – and ultimately perhaps even to destroy – the . . . American nation', adding that 'US government policy is literally dissolving the people and electing a new one'.[10] His argument, in a nutshell, is that 'Race and ethnicity are destiny in American politics. The racial and ethnic balance of America is being radically altered through public policy. This can only have the most profound effects. *Is it what Americans want?*'[11]

In *The Death of the West: How Dying Populations and Immigrant Invasions Imperil Our Country and Civilization*, Pat Buchanan, a right-wing populist who sought the Republican nomination for the presidency in 1992 and 1996 and was the Reform Party's presidential candidate in 2000, shamelessly sought to exploit heightened fears of terrorism in the aftermath of 9/11 to stir up anti-immigrant feelings:

> Suddenly, we awoke to the realization that among our millions of foreign-born, a third are here illegally, tens of thousands are loyal to regimes with which we could be at war, and some are trained terrorists sent here to murder Americans. For the first time since Andrew Jackson drove the British out of Louisiana in 1815, a foreign enemy is inside the gates, and the American people are at risk in their own country. In those days after September 11, many suddenly saw how the face of America had changed in their own lifetimes.[12]

Yearning to turn the clock back to the comforting certainties of the 1950s, he wails that 'Uncontrolled immigration threatens to deconstruct the nation we grew up in and convert America into a conglomeration of peoples with almost nothing in common – not history, heroes, language, culture, faith, or ancestors. Balkanization beckons.'[13]

More recently, Samuel Huntington, the Harvard professor who shot to fame by predicting a global 'clash of civilisations' between Christianity and Islam, has talked up the threat of a domestic clash of civilisations between Latinos and Anglo-Protestant Americans. In *Who Are We? America's Great Debate*, he warns of the risk of a 'bifurcated America, with two languages, Spanish and English, and two cultures, Anglo-Protestant and Hispanic' and the potential for a backlash against this: an 'exclusivist America, once again defined by race and ethnicity and that excludes and/or subordinates those who are not white and European'.[14]

Right on cue, conservative talk-radio stations rail against the Bush administration's unwillingness to deport the nation's illegal residents and fix its 'broken borders'. California's Austrian-born governor, Arnold Schwarzenegger, says the border with Mexico should be closed, although he later recants, claiming (without any sense of irony) that his poor command of English had let him down. Groups of armed vigilantes – who call themselves 'Minutemen', after the shock troops of America's War of Independence – take to patrolling the Arizona desert 'to protect our country from a 40-year-long invasion across our southern border with Mexico'.[15]

An even more vitriolic backlash is sweeping through Europe, where the number of foreign-born residents has soared from 10 million in 1970 to 29 million in 2000. Traditionally Christian Europe – which, unlike the US, has never considered itself a land of immigration – is now home to some 15 million Muslims.

In Britain, tabloid newspapers fan fears about the country being swamped with feral foreigners, accusing them of all manner of ills – stealing jobs, scrounging welfare benefits, spreading disease, committing crime, plotting terrorism and so on. The *Sun* even confected an unsubstantiated but widely believed front-page story – headlined 'Swan Bake' – about immigrants eating the Queen's swans in St James's Park. In the 2005 general election, the opposition Conservative Party made the threat of supposedly out-of-control immigration the centrepiece of its campaign. Although the Tories lost, they prompted the Labour government to harden its stance on immigration.

In France, Jean-Marie Le Pen, the leader of the openly racist National Front, came second in the country's presidential poll in 2002, with a fifth of the vote. When riots erupted in Paris's deprived and largely non-white suburbs in October 2005, interior minister and presidential hopeful Nicolas Sarkozy called the protesters '*racaille*' ('rabble') whom he pledged to sandblast away, while Philippe de Villiers' nationalist Movement for France launched a poster campaign under the banner 'France: Love Her or Leave Her' – in effect calling for the repatriation of disaffected immigrants. Germany is struggling to accept that its Turkish minority is there to stay. The Dutch are questioning their long tradition of multiculturalism. Denmark's coalition government, with the support of the anti-immigration Danish People's Party, has imposed draconian curbs on immigration – and was re-elected with an increased parliamentary majority. Regardless of whether rich countries choose to admit more immigrants, they clearly need to do a better job of integrating those who have already arrived.

A global debate

Migration is increasingly a global issue, yet the debate about it is still mainly conducted along (hostile) national lines – as if each country were an isolated citadel threatened by hordes of barbarian invaders.

When I told my friends I was planning to write a book about migration, they were puzzled: what could I possibly have to say about birds? Most people think of the movement of people across borders as *im*migration, not migration. Which is why, unfortunately, the title of this book refers to immigrants rather than migrants: my publisher (and I) want to be sure that potential readers know what the book is about – although perhaps it would sell better if people mistakenly thought it was about birds.

Of course, nation states still matter, as do the views and interests of their citizens. Much of this book will examine the impact of migration on individual countries, and what they can learn from each other's experiences. But looking at international migration solely from a national perspective gives a distorted and partial view of what is happening. The increase in international migration is not occurring in a vacuum: it is part and parcel of globalisation, the combination of distance-shrinking technology and market-opening government policy that is bringing the world closer together.

This is most obvious in the case of skilled professionals – people like investment bankers, management consultants and computer specialists – who increasingly operate in a global labour market. In some cases, such as the City of London and Hollywood, they cluster together in one place to serve the world market. Thus Goldman Sachs, an American investment bank, employs people from around the world in its London offices to trade in global financial markets. Warner Brothers assembles actors from different countries in southern California to produce films for a global audience. Arsenal scours the world for the best football players to spar against its London rivals Chelsea on television screens everywhere.

At the same time, multinational companies span the globe by

deploying skilled professionals around the world to serve separate national and regional markets. Thus Unilever, an Anglo-Dutch giant that produces everything from soap powder to margarine, sends out foreign managers to run its operations in far-flung countries. Governments do something similar, posting ambassadors to look after their interests abroad. And many businesspeople spend their year jetting around the globe, forever on the move, as medieval kings once were.

In the increasingly global market in higher education – where top-end universities like the London School of Economics, as well as less prestigious colleges like Luton University, increasingly draw students from around the world – people move to consume services rather than to produce them, although many universities are also busy setting up foreign franchises to educate students in their home country, or even allowing students in remote locations to complete their degree courses online. And while globalisation stimulates increased international migration, foreign migrants also create new cross-border trading links. In Silicon Valley, for instance, many Chinese and Indian entrepreneurs, who typically came to the US to study, have started new companies that trade with Asia. Others return home after working for a few years in the Valley and set up companies that trade with the US. Likewise, Americans who came to London to work for Goldman Sachs or J. P. Morgan in the City cross town to set up hedge funds, private equity funds and other global investment vehicles in St James's.

What is true for skilled professionals is increasingly true more generally – or at least it would be if rich-country governments weren't desperately trying to prevent it. While governments broadly accept, or are even actively encouraging, the creation of a global labour market for skilled professionals, they steadfastly refuse to allow most other people, especially those from poor countries, to cross borders in search of work. Although the US admitted 946,000 legal immigrants in the fiscal year 2004, most of them were allowed in because they already had family in America. Only 155,000 were admitted on work visas, and only 5,000 of those were for unskilled foreigners seeking year-round work. In effect, the door is closed to people like Inmer from Honduras. As Tamar Jacoby of the Manhattan Institute explained in her deposition to the US Senate in July 2005, 'A Mexican without family in the US who wants to do something other than farm work has virtually no legal way to enter the country. And even a man with family here must wait from six to 22 years for a visa.'[16]

Likewise, it is almost impossible for people from poor countries who do not have family in Europe to migrate legally to work in the European Union, as Lasso from Côte d'Ivoire can testify. And although Canada and Australia admit large numbers of foreign workers each year, you don't stand a chance of getting in unless you have certain skills or professional qualifications that politicians and bureaucrats deem necessary. No wonder illegal immigration is on the rise: most would-be migrants who want to move in search of a better life have no other option.

While governments are making it easier for goods and capital to circulate around the globe, they are seeking to erect ever-higher national barriers to the free movement of people. The US Border Patrol builds walls, puts up razor-wire fences, installs night-vision cameras, places heat and movement sensors, and deploys cars, trucks, helicopters and planes to try to keep out Mexicans and other poor people. Spain has built a double ring of walls around its colonial outposts in North Africa, Ceuta and Melilla, while its coastguard patrols the narrow stretch of water between Morocco and Spain for *pateras*, the flimsy rafts that desperate Africans use to cross. Australia's navy prevents boats that might be carrying refugees or migrants from entering its domestic waters.

Although most governments wouldn't dream of trying to ban cross-border trade in goods and services – only North

Korea aspires to autarky these days – outlawing the movement across borders of people who make goods and provide services is considered perfectly normal and reasonable. Yet the global economic forces driving poor people to cross the world in search of work are pretty similar – and seemingly just as beneficial – as those that lure foreign bankers to Tokyo, scatter Coca-Cola executives around the world or, indeed, cause us to import computers from China and beef from Brazil. Thanks to satellite television, cheap phone calls and the internet, people in developing countries are more aware than ever of job opportunities in rich countries; and thanks to the falling cost of international travel, they can more readily afford to try to get there. Would-be migrants have a huge incentive to relocate: even allowing for the higher cost of living in rich countries, wages for equivalent jobs are typically five times higher than in poor ones.[17] According to a survey of recent immigrants to the US by Rand, a Californian think-tank, the average immigrant ends up $20,000 a year better off.[18] The disparity in wages between rich and poor countries is so huge that university graduates from poor countries are often better off financially driving cabs in rich countries than doing graduate work in their country of origin.

So, They need Us. But, as this book will argue, We also need Them. Some migrants come to do the jobs that people in rich countries no longer want to do, like cleaning, waiting tables and picking fruit. Others come to do the jobs that not enough people in rich countries can do: filling a shortage of nurses in Britain's National Health Service, for instance. Many come to service the clusters of global professionals – and other residents – in places like London and Silicon Valley: preparing their lunchtime sandwiches, chauffeuring them around by cab, coaching them at the gym, looking after their children, cleaning their houses by day and their offices by night, cooking and serving them ethnic cuisine, decorating their houses and repairing their cars, and so on. And increasingly, as our societies age, they are caring for our old people. In effect, most of these migrants are service-providers who ply their trade in foreign countries, just as American investment bankers and European insurance brokers do. And just as it is often cheaper and mutually beneficial for us to buy computers made in China or use call centres in India, it often makes sense for us to import services that have to be delivered on the spot – such as nannying or personal training – from foreigners.

Over the next twenty years, the supply of potential migrants in poor countries is likely to continue rising. While rich countries' baby-boom generation are nearing retirement age, poor countries' much younger baby-boomers are just starting to enter the labour market. Many of these young people will be tempted by the prospect of a better life in North America, Europe or Australia, especially since moving to a foreign land seems less daunting now that there are established immigrant communities in most rich countries. At the same time, the demand for migrants in rich countries is set to rise, as ageing populations and shrinking workforces put a strain on businesses, economies and government finances. With more old people around, the demand for services such as nursing care will soar. With more rich people around, the demand for services such as cleaning and restaurant work will also grow fast. Since people in rich countries increasingly turn their noses up at such jobs, the demand for immigrants to fill them will inevitably rise. Demand for skilled immigrants is also likely to increase, as companies, cities and countries compete for an advantage in the global marketplace by trying to hire the most talented people, most of whom will increasingly come from poor countries, where the number of university graduates is rising fast. But whether this increased potential for migration translates into higher immigration in practice depends on what border controls rich-country governments maintain and how effective they are at enforcing them. Ultimately, then, it depends on Us.

An economic boon

Few people now bat an eyelid at the movement across borders of skilled professionals, in particular those from rich countries. It is considered normal, and perfectly acceptable, for an American management consultant – even one of Indian origin – to ply his trade in London, or for a German banker to be based in New York. Within the EU, this freedom extends to all workers, whatever their qualifications – albeit with temporary restrictions on the movement of labour from the eight relatively poor ex-communist countries that joined the EU in 2004 to most of the richer members. Yet most people baulk at the thought of people from poor countries coming to work in rich ones.

Why? Why can computers be imported from China duty-free but Chinese people not freely come to make computers here? Why is it a good thing for French insurance salespeople to hawk policies in Poland but a bad thing for Polish plumbers to offer to fix French pipes? Why is the door open for American managers to run factories in Honduras but the door slammed shut for Hondurans who want to work in American factories? Why, in short, is free trade and the free movement of Western elites a wonderful thing but the free movement of everybody else unthinkable? And why is it a good thing for workers to move within a country to where the jobs are, but a bad thing for people to move between countries for the same reason?

Until recently, Communist China strictly curtailed its people's movement. Unless you were a privileged party official, you needed a special permit to move – or even travel – from your home town to another part of the country. It sounds like a totalitarian nightmare, yet it is not too far removed from the situation that those on the other side of the global migration apartheid find themselves in.

China has now relaxed its constraints on internal migration and has witnessed the biggest movement of people in history as peasants flock to the cities to make a better life for themselves working in factories, fuelling the country's explosive economic growth. So would relaxing rich countries' controls on immigration from poor countries provide similarly spectacular economic gains?

Most likely, yes. Sober-minded economists reckon that the potential gains from freer global migration are huge, and greatly exceed the benefits from freer world trade. As I explained in my first book, *Open World: The Truth about Globalisation*, the freeing up of global trade in manufactured goods in the second half of the twentieth century led to a quintupling of the world economy and an unprecedented rise in living standards in both rich countries and poor. So just think how opening our borders to migrants could transform our world for the better in the twenty-first century.

Historical experience certainly suggests it would do a lot of good: the United States' stunning economic growth between 1870 and 1920 coincided with the migration of tens of millions of Europeans to America. A study of fifteen European countries finds that a 1 per cent increase in the population through migration is associated with a boost to the economy of between 1.25 per cent and 1.5 per cent.[19] The World Bank reckons that if rich countries allowed their workforce to swell by a mere 3 per cent by letting in an extra 14 million workers from developing countries between 2001 and 2025, the world would be $356 billion a year better off, with the new migrants themselves gaining $162 billion a year, people who remain in poor countries $143 billion, and natives in rich countries $139 billion.[20] And those figures grossly underestimate the likely economic gains from the added diversity and dynamism that immigrants bring. Foreigners don't just slot in to vacancies left by local people; they bring different skills, varied views, diverse experiences and a zeal for self-improvement that combine with the talents of local people to boost innovation, productivity and economic growth. Would the US be as dynamic and successful without all its immigrants trying to get ahead?

If you are sceptical about the merits of globalisation, you may not be swayed by the argument that the case for freer migration follows on logically from the case for freer trade – although you might be, since I am essentially arguing that rich countries should open their borders to service-providers from poor countries, which is not a million miles away from arguing that rich countries should open up their markets to farm produce from poor countries. But another way of looking at the case for freer international migration is this: if you want to help people in poor countries, freer migration is one of the most effective ways of doing so.

Campaigners for global justice quite rightly argue that rich-country governments should increase their aid to poor countries. Currently, aid is pitifully low, at a mere $79 billion or so a year, the equivalent to each of us in rich countries donating a miserly $1.60 a week (86p) to those in poor countries.[21] Worse, a lot of this aid fails to benefit needy people: it is spent on fat fees and five-star hotel bills for Western consultants, ends up in the Swiss bank accounts of African dictators, or is simply wasted. In short, poor countries need not only more aid, but better-targeted aid – which is exactly what migrants provide.

According to official figures, people from poor countries working in rich ones send home some $160 billion a year. Informally, they are reckoned to send home a further $320 billion a year. That makes $480 billion, or six times official government aid.[22] It is also nearly three times the $166 billion in foreign direct investment that developing countries received in 2004.[23] Mexico received $18.1 billion in official remittances from Mexicans working abroad in 2004 – and possibly a further $36 billion through informal channels. That could add up to nearly 8 per cent of Mexico's economy, a significant proportion by any standards.[24] Better still, it ends up directly in the pockets of needy Mexican people, who can choose how to spend it as they see fit. In the case of the Philippines, which received $11.6 billion officially and perhaps twice that unofficially, remittances from Filipinos abroad could conceivably account for some 40 per cent of the country's economy. So just think how much people in poor countries would benefit if rich countries allowed in more immigrants. Or, to put it another way, if you believe that the world is an unequal place and that the rich should do more to help the poor, then freer international migration should be the next front in the battle for global economic justice.

1

War on Our Borders

The hidden costs of immigration controls

The slaughter of some and the disablement of others is not an act of nature, such as an earthquake, a typhoon or a flood. It is not the result of wars or civil disorder. It is a regime constructed and maintained by the deliberate action of governments, by the calm, sensible and apparently liberal – even kindly – men and women who constitute civil authority. They do not intend the disasters. They probably regret them. Some of them no doubt espouse moral codes that forbid them to kill, that affirm the sanctity of life, that propose compassion for those in need. Yet the laws they have put in place turn all this to hypocrisy.

Nigel Harris, *Thinking the Unthinkable*[1]

The question should not be: 'How can we be cruel enough to enforce the law on the border?' The question should really be: 'How can we be cruel enough not to

> enforce it?' . . . Any parent confronted with a two-year-old at bedtime is familiar with the human truth: 'There are times when you have to be cruel to be kind.'
>
> Peter Brimelow, *Alien Nation*[2]

Lasso Kourouma's bloodshot eyes still burn with indignation. 'I thought Europe was the promised land, but I have been treated like a dog. I had to eat Europeans' rubbish to stay alive. I almost drowned trying to get here. I was put in prison for forty days and then dumped in the street with nothing to eat and nowhere to live. It's not right.'

Lasso earned a decent living as a car salesman in Côte d'Ivoire, but when civil war broke out in 2002 he fled the violence to seek refuge in Spain. He made his way north to Morocco, to the border with Ceuta, a tiny Spanish enclave perched on the northernmost tip of Africa, a mere eight miles from the European mainland across the Strait of Gibraltar. Now that Spain and fourteen other European countries that have signed up to the Schengen agreement have abolished border controls with each other, Ceuta (along with Melilla, another Spanish footprint on African soil) is in effect the southern gateway to Europe.

Dominated by a military fort on Monte Hacho, a hill that some claim is one of the Pillars of Hercules of Greek legend, Ceuta is a beautiful colonial town of windswept palm trees and gorgeous sunsets over the sea that nestles behind vast medieval walls. But beyond the city walls in Morocco the scene is rather less picturesque. Thousands of Africans live rough in makeshift refugee camps in the hilly woodlands, preparing their desperate nightly assault on Ceuta's border defences.

Only a lucky few succeed in breaching them. At a cost of some £200 million, the Spanish government has erected two six-metre-high barbed-wire fences punctuated by watchtowers and fitted with noise and movement sensors, spotlights and video cameras. The two walls are separated by a road along which armed border police patrol frequently. Each night, the police fend off would-be immigrants with truncheons, tear gas and rubber bullets.

'I tried to climb over the fence. I tried cutting through it. But every time I got through, I got caught by the Spanish police,' Lasso recalls. 'I must have been caught and thrown out fifteen or twenty times.' He spent six months living rough outside Ceuta. 'I survived by eating the rubbish that Europeans throw away. Eventually the Moroccan army chased us away.' The Moroccan authorities co-operate with the Spaniards to keep migrants out, but only sporadically, pointing out that if Spain returned Ceuta and Melilla to Morocco, they would no longer need such elaborate defences.

After Lasso was forced to leave the outskirts of Ceuta, he made his way to the nearby Moroccan city of Tangiers, and from there to the capital, Rabat, and finally to Layoun, in the Western Sahara on the west coast of Africa. There, with money sent to him by his brother, who emigrated to Italy many years ago, he paid €1,500 (around £1,000) for a place on a boat to smuggle him across the notoriously treacherous waters of the eastern Atlantic to Fuerteventura, the Spanish Canary Island nearest the African coast. 'It was a small boat, big enough for only ten people, but there were twenty-five of us on it. We sailed for two or three days. The sea was very rough,' he says. 'Then the boat sank. I thought I was going to drown. Most people did. But I was rescued by the Spanish coastguard. They took me to Fuerteventura and threw me in prison.'

Lasso is lucky to be alive, but there is something perverse about forcing migrants to risk their lives, then rescuing them, before finally arresting them. Spain's border police return most unwanted migrants to their country of origin, but Lasso did not have a passport or any other identification on him, and in any case Côte d'Ivoire does not have an agreement with Spain to take back its unwanted migrants. So he was locked up in a detention centre instead. 'I spent forty days locked up in a cell, and then I was dumped in the street in Malaga in the middle of the night,' he recalls. 'I had no money, nowhere to stay, nothing to eat. I had no papers so I couldn't work. Nobody would give me black-market work. I slept rough for two years. I got called "*negro de mierda*" [black shit] in the street. The police often asked me for my papers, and then arrested me for not having any, but after a day or two they would release me again.'

Lasso reached breaking point: 'I was so tired that I didn't want to know anything any more.' But then his luck turned: 'Finally, I got a break. Friends got me a job as a security guard at a disco in Torremolinos. Now I work in several nightclubs and I can afford to rent a flat.'

Lasso earns €800 (£533) a month; hardly a fortune, but enough to live decently. He is now married to Maria, who is also from Côte d'Ivoire and works as a cleaner. 'When I met her, she was a fifteen-year-old girl,' says Lasso. 'She had nobody to look after her. If I hadn't met her, she might have had to become a whore.' They have a lovely daughter, Sara, who was ten months old when I met them. Because she was born in Spain, she will become a Spanish citizen when she reaches her first birthday.

Although Lasso's life has finally taken a big turn for the better, he has suffered more than most of us in the West could possibly imagine. He has every right to be angry. 'Look how dangerous the sea is. People die every day,' he fumes. 'They rescued me but then they threw me in prison. And then they threw me out on the streets. They refused to let me work. They wouldn't even give me somewhere to sleep.'

Death on Europe's borders

Lasso's story is far from unique. Look around you in any big city: no doubt many of the anonymous people whose existence you barely acknowledge – those who clean the streets and offices, or who stand guard outside bars or inside shops – have similar tales to tell. We just never bother to ask.

But despite their often-terrible suffering, the migrants who make it to rich countries are comparatively lucky. Many are caught and turned back; others are injured trying; some die. Europe's border policy is in crisis. A continent that prides itself on being compassionate and civilised seeks to repel in increasingly inhumane ways people whose only crime is aspiring to a European way of life.

Violence against migrants trying to cross from Morocco to Spain is escalating, according to a report published in September 2005 by Médecins Sans Frontières, the international humanitarian-aid organisation. MSF doctors treated 2,544 migrants for violent injuries – such as gunshot wounds, beatings and attacks by dogs when trying to escape Moroccan security forces – between April 2003 and August 2005. According to MSF, this increasing violence, along with illnesses related to poor living conditions, are the biggest risks to migrants' health. 'MSF is concerned that these findings reveal systematic violence and degrading treatment which only serve to increase the suffering and marginalisation of people who are already exposed to extremely precarious and often inhumane conditions,' the charity said.[3]

In late September and early October 2005, at least fourteen people were killed and hundreds injured during violent clashes between Africans trying to force their way into Ceuta and Melilla and Spanish police determined not to let them pass. The Moroccan government said that the violence of the attacks forced its security forces to shoot migrants in self-defence. Amnesty International has accused both Spain and Morocco of violating migrants' rights. Several hundred migrants made it onto Spanish territory, where they plan to seek refugee status, but more than a thousand were flown back to Senegal and Mali. 'We go in a group and all jump at once. We know that some will get through, that others will be injured and others may die, but we have to get through, whatever the cost,' one African refugee said.[4] Official figures put the number of foreigners who died trying to reach Spain in 2004 at 141, but the Association for Human Rights in Andalucia claimed the death toll was 289, up from 236 in 2003.[5] Most recorded deaths occur when boats carrying immigrants are intercepted or challenged by Guardia Civil patrol boats, but many more occur because migrants now take longer, more dangerous routes in a bid to avoid the patrols.

Although we scarcely notice it, death is becoming commonplace on Europe's borders. Over the few months when I was writing this book, here are just a few of the other tragedies that occurred. In September 2005, the bodies of eleven African migrants were found on the coast of Sicily, while a fishing boat carrying thirty-nine migrants sank off the coast of northern Cyprus, leaving one person dead and thirty-three others missing. In October, six corpses were discovered floating off the coast of Malta, while nineteen African migrants died after their rickety boat capsized twenty-six miles off the south-eastern coast of Fuerteventura – just as Lasso's had. In November, the bodies of nine migrants were recovered near Ragusa, on the southern coast of Sicily, after their boat ran aground in stormy weather, while twelve people drowned and a further eighteen were missing after a boat carrying migrants to Greece capsized off the resort town of Cesme on the Turkish coast.[6]

Most of the deaths occur in the Mediterranean, but British readers may remember the horrific case of the fifty-eight Chinese people discovered dead by customs officers in the back of an articulated container lorry in Dover in June 2000. On one of Europe's hottest summer days, the truck's cooling system was turned off, leaving its human cargo to be slowly asphyxiated. According to the two survivors, the victims shouted and clawed at the sides of the container as they suffocated on their macabre ferry journey from the Belgian port of Zeebrugge.[7] The ill-fated

Chinese had travelled for four months from Fujian province, via Moscow and the Czech mountains. They were heading for restaurants in London's Chinatown, where there is a shortage of workers because the British-born children of Chinese immigrants prefer to go to university.[8] But although those fifty-eight died, many more keep coming.

United, a European non-governmental-organisation network, has documented over seven thousand deaths caused by Europe's border policies between 1993 and May 2006.[9] Most of the migrants died trying to cross the Mediterranean from North Africa in rickety boats on the way to Italy, Spain, Greece and, more recently, Malta, which joined the EU in 2004. *The Economist* reckons that around two thousand people a year drown in the Mediterranean on their way from Africa to Europe.[10] These are shockingly high numbers, but the true death toll is probably much higher: most of those who drown in the Mediterranean Sea are never found.

Failing to hold the line on the Mexican border

It's a hot sunny day in October and the Rio Grande looks pretty small from where I'm sitting. The 'Big River' that separates the US from Mexico is actually a thirty-metre-wide concrete gulley overgrown with shrubs and vegetation. On one side is El Paso, Texas, an urban sprawl of 750,000 mostly Mexican Americans. On the other is Ciudad Juárez, where the Hollywood blockbuster *Traffic* was filmed, a much bigger and poorer urban sprawl of nearly 1.5 million Mexicans. The twin cities live cheek by jowl – and yet unnaturally separated.

I'm safely ensconced in a patrol van on the American side with Michelle LeBoeuf, a charming third-generation American from Louisiana and a field agent for the US Border Patrol. 'Once you've done this job, you don't want to do any other,' she exclaims. 'You get all the excitement of law enforcement and you get to help people. If you find people who are dying of thirst in the desert, you take them to the hospital and save their lives.' She points to the canal that runs along the Rio Grande on the American side. 'That's the most dangerous place when it's full of water. It's twelve feet deep with slippery walls. The current runs at thirty miles per hour. See that metal rescue box: in there we have ropes we can throw to save anyone who is drowning. We are all trained at swift-water rescue.'

She points to nearby Juárez. 'It's a completely different world over there. I don't know how we can be so close and yet so different,' she remarks, again without noticeable irony. 'I thought it was kinda sad first time I saw it.' As we drive along the border, we pass big white vans with green stripes on them every quarter-mile or so: Michelle's colleagues, who lie in wait to pounce on any Mexicans foolish enough to try crossing in the midday sun. None are, so the Border Patrol sit there looking vaguely bored, their vans lurking menacingly.

Driving along the border is something of an anticlimax. As you head west out of El Paso along a gravel road into New Mexico, the natural border disappears altogether. All that separates the richest country on earth from its much poorer southern neighbour are a few rocks, a scrabble of broken bricks and the odd signpost. But the continuity of the brown dirt and infinity of the desert sky are deceptive: man has drawn an invisible line here – and the Border Patrol are desperately trying to hold it. As well as the vans, they have planes and helicopters at their disposal; noise and movement sensors, nightvision equipment, surveillance cameras and floodlights; dogs, batons and guns. Twenty-five miles in from the border, they man permanent checkpoints on every major highway, with the power to search every vehicle. Their budget has soared in the past ten years as America has sought to clamp down on illegal immigration – and dramatically so since 9/11 made securing the country's borders a priority. In the El Paso sector alone, over three hundred new Border Patrol agents have been recruited in the past year, swelling their ranks to over 1,250, with more reinforcements expected this year and next. 'Most of our agents are Hispanics,' Michelle remarks.

The El Paso sector was the birthplace, back in 1993, of Operation Hold the Line, the Border Patrol's strategy of concentrating their efforts on preventing people crossing in built-up areas. Within the El Paso city limits, seven miles of reinforced chain-link fencing now runs along the US side of the border. 'We used to be overrun,' says Doug Mosier, the spokesman for the El Paso sector. 'Once they get into downtown, you don't know who's who.' Quite deliberately, Operation Hold the Line drives migrants away from the safer crossing points in metropolitan areas, in effect forcing them to take more dangerous routes through mountain and desert areas, where they risk drowning or freezing to death in winter and dying from thirst or heat exposure in summer. As a result, the number of deaths on the borders has soared. The Border Patrol recorded thirty migrant deaths in the El Paso sector alone in fiscal 2005, and rescued nearly fifty people in distress.

The Border Patrol's top priority, Doug says, is preventing terrorism. Curbing illegal migration comes next, followed by combating drug-smuggling. I ask him if the Border Patrol had apprehended any terrorists in the El Paso sector. 'I'm not aware of that,' he replies, although they have caught some people from 'terrorist-watch' countries – the likes of Iran and Syria that are suspected of fomenting terrorism against the US. Some might call people escaping such awful places political refugees.

The Border Patrol may not catch any terrorists, but they do catch some migrants: over 122,000 in 2005 in the El Paso sector alone, up a sixth on the previous year. Those apprehended were nearly all Mexican – and most were repeat offenders. The majority were simply photographed, fingerprinted, added to the

Border Patrol computer database and returned to Mexico within a couple of hours. The only impediment to trying again is the $1,500 to $2,000 a head that smugglers, known as '*polleros*' or 'coyotes', charge. Migrants who have a criminal record, are not from Mexico or refuse to leave voluntarily are detained until a judge determines what to do with them. But many of those who post bail never show up to the hearing. 'You can't detain 122,000 people a year,' says Doug. 'You have to be practical. We're trying to make the best of a very challenging situation. Is our job difficult? Yes. It's all about manageability and control.' Inevitably, many migrants eventually make it. 'I have no estimate of how many people get through,' he says. 'Different studies come up with different figures.' Indeed, they do: estimates range from as 'few' as 300,000 to as many as a million each year.

On the Mexican side, they compare the Border Patrol to the SS, Hitler's stormtroopers. Unsurprisingly, the Border Patrol sees itself rather differently. 'We are the guardians of our nation's borders,' says its mission statement. 'We are America's frontline. We steadfastly enforce the laws of the United States while fostering our nation's economic security through lawful international trade and travel.' Doug Mosier describes Ciudad Juárez as 'our sister city', saying that 'We recognise that we are linked economically, but we are obligated to perform our mission of homeland security.' Michelle LeBeoef answers critics more directly: 'People forget that they are US citizens. They have the right to vote. We only enforce the laws they have voted for.' Quite.

America's war

What I witnessed in El Paso is just a snapshot of a much greater American tragedy. Every day Cubans and Haitians drown in the shark-infested waters off Florida when their flimsy craft sink. They usually travel in small makeshift boats to avoid detection, but occasionally smugglers use larger vessels. In November 2001, twenty-nine Cubans died when one of these larger boats sank. In August 2002, a boat designed to hold no more than eight people but believed to be carrying between twenty and twenty-five Cubans disappeared.[11]

In May 2000, Border Patrol agents found forty-one immigrants – eight Chinese, five Central Americans and the rest, including a baby, Mexicans – lying dead in an abandoned trailer truck in El Paso. On a boiling-hot day in May 2003, the driver of a truck headed for Houston opened the back door of his freight trailer at a petrol station near Victoria, Texas, to find seventeen people – including a five-year-old Mexican boy – had died from heatstroke and dehydration. Two more later died in hospital.[12]

Many more migrants die further west in the Arizona desert. Just as Operation Hold the Line diverts migrants from crossing near El Paso to the New Mexico desert, Operation Gatekeeper redirects them from San Diego, California, to the Arizona desert. Many migrants who attempt to walk for five days in Arizona's baking temperatures die of thirst. As Border Patrol agents point out, it is physically impossible to carry enough water, and the smugglers who guide the groups are all too willing to leave the weak to die. In May 2001, fourteen Mexican immigrants were found dead of exposure – and two more reported missing, presumed dead – in a remote part of south-western Arizona that Border Patrol agents call the 'Devil's Path'. Temperatures there regularly top fifty degrees Celsius and there are no human settlements within a 150-mile radius. 'They looked like they'd been in the desert for a month – shrivelled up,' declared emergency physician David Haynes of the Yuma Regional Medical Center. 'Have you ever seen a mummy from ancient Egypt? Well, that gives you an idea.' One of the survivors described how, overcome by thirst, he survived by sucking juice from cactus and drinking his own urine.[13]

It takes particularly gruesome incidents such as these to even fleetingly capture Americans' attention. Yet people die on the US border every day. How many? Nobody really knows and hardly anyone seems to care. According to the Border Patrol, a record 464 people, 260 of them in the Arizona desert alone, perished trying to cross from Mexico into the US in the twelve months to September 2005 (up from 330 the previous year). More than ten times as many migrants are recorded as having died on the US border with Mexico over the past ten years than were killed trying to cross the Berlin Wall during its twenty-eight-year existence – and many people think the true number of deaths on the US–Mexican border is much higher than the official figures.[14]

Fewer people associate Australia with the fortress-like policies of Europe or the United States, but it too is causing death and suffering as it seeks to deter asylum seekers and unwanted immigrants arriving by boat. Unauthorised immigrants and refugees, including women and children, are deported or locked up in offshore detention centres, notably in Nauru and Papua New Guinea, in isolated locations with poor facilities. The government has been widely accused of violating immigrants', and in particular children's, human rights. One first-hand observer, who wished to remain anonymous, told me that the conditions in detention centres were 'atrocious and appalling . . . I believe that animals are treated better'. There were many old people and unaccompanied children under ten: 'a seven-year-old Afghan child has no place in a detention centre. They could have been placed with the Afghan community. And eighty-year-olds don't spend $10,000 to come to Australia to destroy us.'

Perhaps the biggest loss of life has occurred in the waters between Indonesia and Australia. In April 2000, up to 350 asylum seekers were feared drowned off northern Australia. In December of that year, two boats carrying a reported 163 people sank in bad weather en route to Australia's Ashmore Island. In October 2001, 350 or more people, mostly Iraqis but also

Afghans, Palestinians and Algerians, drowned when a wooden boat carrying immigrants to Australia sank off the Indonesian coast. One survivor said it was 'just like the film *Titanic*', with the boat sinking very quickly.[15]

War dead

America, Europe and Australia are in effect waging a largely unreported war on migrants that claims several thousand lives every year. But while our border controls are cruel, they are also ineffective. Some 500,000 migrants are reckoned to slip through America's defences each year, and a further 800,000 or so make it into 'fortress' Europe. Some enter clandestinely through porous borders; others use forged documents; still others overstay their visa, or work illegally on student or tourist visas. There may be twelve million 'illegal aliens' in the United States alone.[16] The Home Office reckons there may be half a million in Britain, although others think the true figure may be as high as a million. When Spain decided in 2005 to allow illegal immigrants to regularise their situation, some 690,000 applied for temporary work permits. The EU as a whole may have seven or eight million illegal immigrants. Our border controls actually foster this illegality. By raising the costs and risks of migration, diverting migrants from legal channels to illegal ones, they create a growing market for criminals, leaving migrants vulnerable to exploitation and encouraging the growth of a black economy where taxes are not paid and labour laws are broken. Far from protecting society from the perceived threat of immigration, our border controls help undermine the fabric of law and order.

British readers will remember the tragedy of the twenty-three Chinese cockle pickers who died as the tide rose at Morecambe Bay in February 2004, their deaths as emblematic of the human cost of our fatally flawed immigration controls as those of their fifty-eight countrymen found asphyxiated in Dover four years earlier. The cockle pickers got past our border controls, but within our borders they enjoyed no legal protection.

Many of the people I interviewed for this book were once irregular migrants. Without work permits, they are forced to take black-market jobs that pay a pittance and can be dangerous. We are all wittingly or unwittingly complicit in this exploitation. Eat in a restaurant in a big American or European city and there is a good chance that the waiters or kitchen staff are working illegally.

Stephan from Ukraine came to London on a student visa that did not allow him to work. He got a black-market job in a kebab shop opposite Camden Town tube station. 'I worked five or six days a week, starting at six p.m. and working till four or five a.m. I made £120 a week, around £2 an hour,' he says. 'They knew I was illegal and they took advantage of me. I started in the kitchen but when my English improved I started dealing with customers. One day they said I made a mistake and they sacked me. I had no rights, I couldn't say anything.'

Alex from Brazil also came to London on a student visa. 'My friend was working in an Italian restaurant in Oxford Street and I went to work there as well,' he says. 'I was washing up. They didn't ask for my papers. They paid me like £2.50 per hour. One week I earned like £65 and I had to pay £70 rent. I don't know how I survived. The work was very hard and the place was disgusting. I burned one hand the first week and the next week I burned the other one. And all the time my hand was in the water as well. Because I didn't have papers to work, I could not complain, could not say anything to them. I needed to eat somehow. Eventually, two other Brazilian guys told me to go to this place in Marble Arch where you can find work doing escorting, and so I went there.'

Yemisrach is an Ethiopian journalist who applied for asylum in the United States. 'I used to work for an immigration lawyer from Nigeria in Jersey City. She exploited me as I had no papers. She paid me $150 a week, working nine a.m. till six p.m. five days a week. I spent six months commuting from Staten Island by ferry and bus. When her assistant quit, she wanted me to stay working until midnight. I said I couldn't, so she fired me.'

Illegality can make immigrants so afraid of being noticed that they put their lives at risk. 'When a big building burned down here in Malaga, many immigrants were afraid to come out,' explains Elena Muñoz, who runs Málaga Acoge, a group that helps immigrants in the southern Spanish town. 'Many of them suffered eighty-per-cent burns.'

The AFL-CIO, the US's biggest trade-union federation, has sought to highlight the plight of irregular immigrants. Hong Kong-born Agnes Wong, who has worked in New York City's garment industry for twenty-eight years and is now a union shop steward, says: 'More and more sweatshops are popping up and employers are taking advantage of immigrant workers without papers, working them like slaves. If people complain, the bosses tell them, "Take it or leave."' Jaime Contrera, who fled the civil war in El Salvador in 1988 and worked as a janitor in the Washington, DC, area before he received his 'green card' granting him permanent residency, says: 'We faced many abuses. There would be hours missing from our paychecks and if we said something, they would say, "We don't know anything about that. You can always go home."'[17]

Cynics might think that our immigration controls are designed to have this effect. First we select the strongest, smartest and most determined immigrants by making it hard for even them to get in. Then we exploit them mercilessly, keeping them in their place with the threat of expulsion if they complain. Companies get cheap labour while politicians can claim to be tough on unwanted foreigners. But even those who don't give a damn about what happens to migrants should worry about the corrosive impact on society of driving immigration underground.

As governments make it harder for people to cross borders, they push ever more immigrants into the hands of people-smugglers. Some smugglers are well meaning, but others are criminal gangs. Tougher border controls also push up the prices smugglers can charge, forcing more migrants who cannot afford to pay upfront to mortgage their futures instead. So these immigrants are not just illegal, they are also beholden to criminal gangs. As with America's failed experiment with banning alcohol in the Prohibition era, our callous but leaky immigration controls undermine the rule of law, bolster criminality and promote an untaxed and unregulated black economy.

Immigration authorities estimate that people smuggling in the Americas generates $20 billion (£11 billion) a year, a criminal activity second only to drugs trafficking.[18] Smugglers rake in around €4 billion (£2.7 billion) a year from the EU, reckons Michael Jandl, of the International Centre for Migration Policy Development, an intergovernmental think-tank based in Vienna. They charge €3,000–€8,000 to convey people from Pakistan to Europe, will fix a British marriage for £5,000 and falsify an Italian residence permit for €4,500. Some gangs even offer warranties (if the first attempt to cross the border fails, the second one is free) and money-back guarantees.[19]

It is clear that our border controls aren't working. In the case of the United States, Wayne Cornelius of the University of San Diego, one of the world's leading experts on migration, says:

> The consequences of the current US strategy of border enforcement, after nearly ten years of implementation, can be summarized as follows: Illegal entries have been redistributed along the Southwest border; the financial cost of illegal entry has more than quadrupled; undocumented migrants are staying longer in the United States and more of them are settling permanently; migrant deaths have risen sharply; and there has been an

> alarming increase in anti-immigrant vigilante activity. The following consequences have not yet materialized: That unauthorized migration is being deterred in Mexican places of origin; that would-be illegal entrants are being discouraged at the border after multiple apprehensions by the Border Patrol and returning home; that their employment prospects in the US have been curtailed; and that the resident population of undocumented immigrants is shrinking. All of the latter outcomes were predicted by proponents of the post-1993 strategy of border enforcement.[20]

Legalise and regulate

It is surely time to ask why we are fighting to keep out migrants in a war that causes untold deaths and suffering, foments criminality in our own countries, and doesn't even fulfil its main goal. The forces pushing migrants to leave their countries – the desire for a better life for themselves and their children, and the fear of hardship, persecution and death – are not about to disappear. Nor is the force pulling them towards rich countries – the huge demand for workers to fill the low-end jobs that our ageing and increasingly wealthy societies rely on but that our increasingly well-educated and comfortable citizens are unwilling to take. The workers of the world are happy to do the jobs we don't want to do, but we won't allow them in legally, so they come illegally. Surely it would be better if we legalised and regulated migration instead?

Or perhaps we could put a stop to illegal immigration with even tougher border controls? In November 2005, President George Bush argued that a combination of extra cash and improved technology could help seal the US border with Mexico. Michael Nicely, the Border Patrol chief for the Tucson sector, agreed: 'Don't let anyone tell you we can't control our borders,' he said. 'We just need more resources.'[21] In May 2006, Bush said he would raise the size of the Border Patrol to 18,000 agents by the end of 2008 and sent 6,000 National Guard to the border in the meantime. But the US Congress has quintupled spending on border security since 1993, to $3.8 billion in financial year 2004, and tripled the size of the Border Patrol without noticeably staunching the flow of illegal immigrants.[22] When the potential rewards of migrating are so great, can more money and tougher rules really put a stop to it? A senior Spanish policeman doubts it: 'It can't be controlled. Despite the Berlin Wall, people still came,' he says.

What would tougher border controls actually entail? For a start, people from poor countries would be denied student and tourist visas. No more Indians studying at US universities, no more Chinese tourists shopping in Paris, no more Africans studying English in London, no more Mexicans visiting their relatives in California. The impact on rich-country economies would be enormous, not to mention the damage it would do to relations with poor countries. Likewise, business visas would have to be reserved for the rich, so small traders could no longer slip across the border. Every car, truck, boat and container entering the US and Europe would have to be thoroughly searched, a Herculean task that would impose huge costs and delays on tourists and business, and which has proved ineffective in preventing the trade in illegal drugs. Governments would also somehow have to prevent passports, identity cards, birth certificates and marriage certificates being forged, something they have singularly failed to do until now.

What's more, as Peter Brimelow advocates in *Alien Nation*, America's border with Mexico would have to be sealed with 'a fence, a ditch and whatever other contrivances that old Yankee ingenuity finds appropriate'.[23] Illegal immigration could easily be controlled, he says. 'What is missing is not the way. It is the will.'[24] Although it would cost tens of billions of dollars, the US certainly has the means to build a wall along its border with Mexico, complete with all the modern electronic gadgetry that gives us eyes and ears everywhere, day and night. But Spain's experience in Ceuta and Melilla, whose borders are a tiny fraction of the 2,000-mile US–Mexican border, is that even that isn't enough, because desperate migrants will find ways to breach the barriers. Wayne Cornelius points out that 'the record of the past decade is that fixed fortifications do not stop unauthorized migrants, any more than they stop mechanized armies; they simply rechannel them and create more opportunities for professional smugglers to cash in on the traffic'.[25]

So, for good measure, the US could run an electric fence along the top of the wall with a current so high that it would fry any migrant who tried to pass. The Border Patrol, or the US army, could have the power – or why not orders? – to shoot to kill any unwanted foreigners who tried to pass. As *The Economist* sardonically remarked when the US House of Representatives voted in January 2006 to erect a 700-mile (1,125 km) fence along the border with Mexico:

> If Congress wants its anti-Mexican fence to be as effective, it should take some leaves out of the East German book. First, forget about lights and cameras; that's Hollywood stuff. Choose instead bunkers, anti-vehicle trenches, lots of concrete and even more barbed wire. Round all that off with minefields, booby-traps, tripwires and machine-gun posts. East Germany was virtually enclosed, so think big: the border barrier will have to be coast-to-coast, 3,200km long, and in the end a fence will not do. It will have to be a wall, as the East Germans discovered.'[26]

Europe could do the same: build a new wall between East and West a bit further east than the old Cold War dividing line.

Europe's navies and air forces could patrol the Mediterranean – the EU has already proposed a common EU coastguard to fend off immigrants' boats, and Britain's Tony Blair has proposed using the navy to keep out immigrants – with orders to sink any foreign craft that venture into Europe's territorial waters.

All of this would be extremely costly, of course. It would require a battery of people and expensive technology to enforce. It would put a big dampener on trade. It would provoke international outrage. It would leave rich countries desperately short of low-skilled workers. It probably wouldn't work. And some people might object that it is inhumane.

But then so is our current immigration system. Forcing people fleeing terror or seeking work to risk their lives crossing our borders is inhumane. That we rescue some of them, like Lasso, hardly changes that. (As Katherine Rodriguez, an organiser for Derechos Humanos, an Arizona-based immigrant-rights group, puts it: 'It's like throwing a baby into a pool, jumping in with a lifesaver and claiming to be a hero.') Is our war on migration humane because most of its victims are only indirectly our responsibility? Our border police may rarely kill migrants, but they do force them to risk death trying to evade them. In fact, all our immigration controls have is a veneer of decency, which conveniently allows us to turn a blind eye to their terrible consequences.

After all, we reason, the migrants who die were breaking the law, they knew the risks and they chose to come anyway; and in any case, we are not responsible for their deaths, the callous people-smugglers are. But poor people try to come to rich countries because there are jobs for them here. If there weren't, they would soon stop coming. The people-smugglers exist only because we prevent poor people crossing borders legally to fill those jobs. And why do the governments we elect enact and enforce immigration controls? Because we are afraid of being swamped with foreigners. You may think that these controls are justified, but you cannot deny that they result in people dying.

We do not mean for these people to die, of course. We would rather they didn't. But implicitly we consider it a price worth paying for protecting our borders. That sounds shocking – and it is. But how else can we explain public indifference to the deaths that our immigration controls cause? Why is there not an outcry each time a migrant dies? Why is the official response always that we must remain tough rather than questioning whether our immigration system makes any sense? If one is to justify these deaths in any rational way, one has to argue that somehow the benefits of border controls outweigh their costs, including the deaths they cause. But if our border controls are both cruel *and* ineffective, how can they possibly be justified? If they end up fostering criminality and undermining the rule of law, are they really protecting our society from harm? And if migration is going to happen anyway, surely it would be better if it was legal and regulated? After all, immigrants are not an invading army: they come in search of a better life. They are no different to someone who moves from Manchester to London, or Oklahoma to California, because that is where the jobs are. Except that a border lies in the way.

2

Border Crossing

How migrants got to where they are now

> The entrance into our political, social and industrial life of such vast masses of peasantry is a matter which no intelligent patriot can look upon without the greatest apprehension and alarm . . . They are beaten men from beaten races, representing the worst failures in the struggles for existence.
>
> Francis Walker, president of the Massachusetts Institute of Technology, 1896[1]

Imagine how their jaws must have dropped in awe as they sailed into New York harbour a century or so ago. After a hellish two weeks crammed into the dark, putrid and pestilent lower decks of one of the vast steamships that carried people and cargo across the Atlantic, peasants plucked from the rural backwardness of Ireland, Italy or Greece are suddenly confronted with the modern might of the city's magnificent skyscrapers. Blinking, they catch sight of the Statue of Liberty, a beacon of hope welcoming them to America. But then their attention is irresistibly drawn to the intimidating sternness of the red-brick buildings of Ellis Island. First they must pass through there to be vetted for official permission to enter the United States.

Over one hundred million Americans can trace their ancestry to a man, woman or child who passed through the world's most famous immigrant processing centre. In its heyday between 1892 and 1924, Ellis Island processed some five thousand immigrants a day: more than twelve million in total before its closure in 1954. As you follow in their footsteps and climb the steep stairs to its famous Registry Room, it is hard not to shudder. Just imagine their trepidation as they shuffled and jostled into the cavernous hall, disoriented, far from home, knowing that their fate would be decided there. Doctors scrutinise you for signs of disease or disability, weeding out the ill and infirm. Inspectors fire questions at you in a bid to eliminate those 'liable to become a public charge'. At the end of this gruelling ordeal, you are either granted a ticket to a new life in America – or sent back to Europe.[2]

People have been on the move since time immemorial; border controls are a rather more recent concept. At Ellis Island and elsewhere, the US pioneered the modern bureaucracy of reception centres, passport control and immigration criteria in the late nineteenth century.[3] At first, these were primarily designed to administer, rather than curtail, migrant flows: the US operated an 'open-door' immigration policy and only one in fifty migrants arriving at Ellis Island was denied entry. It was only after the First World War, when America slammed the door shut to immigrants, that the controls were used to curb the movement of people across borders in the way that countries routinely do today. (Britain first restricted immigration through the Aliens Act of 1905, which ostensibly sought to keep out 'undesirable' foreigners from outside the British Empire (including paupers, lunatics, vagrants and prostitutes), but was actually intended to limit Jewish immigration.)[4]

From Old World to New

Mass international migration had taken off in the early nineteenth century, made possible by a revolution in transport technology and stimulated by the huge demand for labour in the New World. As shoddy roads and slow sailboats gave way to steamships and railways, long-distance travel suddenly became much faster and much cheaper than ever before. A whole new world opened up – and in the century after 1820, around 60 million Europeans crossed the Atlantic to settle it.

They came from the British Isles and north-western Europe, and later from southern and eastern Europe. Three-fifths of them went to the United States, the rest to Canada and Latin America (mainly Brazil, Argentina and Uruguay). Most stayed, but around a third eventually went home. Over 100,000 Chinese moved to California between 1849 and 1876 after gold was discovered. Others, mostly Britons, crossed the world to settle in Australia and New Zealand. People were also on the move within Europe. In the 1890s, more Italians emigrated to France and Germany than to America. Some migrated seasonally: Italian farmhands crossed the seas to pick the harvest in Argentina while Irish labourers went to build American railways before returning home.

The Americas and Australia were rich in natural resources but short of labour, so wages were much higher than in Europe. Workers were needed to farm the land, mine the minerals, build the railways and, increasingly, man the factories. But the young nation states of the New World did not just need workers; they also needed citizens, to entrench their control over their vast empty expanses of land and bolster national power more generally. In the first decade of the twentieth century alone, nearly 9 million immigrants arrived in the United States, nearly 2.5 million in Argentina and Brazil, more than 1.5 million in Australia and New Zealand and over 1 million in Canada.[5] By 1910, one in seven people in the US was foreign-born.[6]

The First World War slowed migration to a trickle, but most people expected the disruption to be temporary. They had long lived in an open world and they considered it 'normal'. Yet the global economy that had emerged before 1914 fell apart over the next thirty years. The Great Depression that followed the Wall Street Crash of 1929 finally killed it off. Mass migration came to a halt as governments systematically sought to limit it and the economy soured. In the first fifteen years of the twentieth century, around 15 million immigrants entered the United States; in the next fifteen, only 5.5 million did; in the 1930s, fewer than 750,000 were allowed to stay. Migration from Spain and Portugal, mostly to Latin America, dropped from 1.75 million in the 1910s to less than 250,000 in the 1930s. This despite the huge flood of refugees displaced by war and revolution.[7] One country that bucked the trend was France, which recruited nearly 2 million foreigners in the 1920s – mostly Italians, Poles, Spaniards and Belgians – to replace its war-dead, with the newcomers accounting for around three-quarters of France's population growth in the 1920s.[8]

From Third World to First

Whereas international migration before the First World War was primarily from the Old World to the New, since the Second World War it has mainly been from the Third World to the First. Europe has switched from being a continent of emigration to one of immigration, and so both the Old World (Europe) and the

New (the US, Canada, Australia and New Zealand) have drawn immigrants from the rest of the world. Even today, the pattern of migration is still heavily influenced by history (such as former colonial links) and geographical proximity, but over time it has become less so: witness the emergence of big global cities such as London, New York and Sydney that play host to nearly every nationality on earth. And once two countries have established links through migration, the dynamic tends to be self-reinforcing: the first migrants bring over their relatives; the existence of an established migrant community abroad makes it easier for others from the same country to come and settle in a foreign land; new trade and investment ties are created that stimulate further migration. The current pattern of migration is thus the result of a complex mixture of economic incentives, government policy, political events, history, geography and family ties.

The Second World War displaced millions of refugees from war-torn Europe, but soon after, the continent began to draw in fresh blood from overseas. From the 1950s until the oil crisis in 1973, European countries imported foreign workers from poorer countries on the continent's periphery, as well as from their former colonies in the Caribbean, Africa and Asia. By 1970, France had 5.2 million immigrants (many of whom were descendants of French settlers in former colonies, such as Algeria, that had since become independent), Britain 2.9 million, West Germany 2.6 million and Switzerland 1.1 million.[9]

As their economies boomed in the 1950s, Germany, France, Belgium and Switzerland attracted workers first from southern Europe and then from Turkey and North Africa, while Sweden also tapped Finland and Britain mined Ireland. Many of these migrants came as 'guest workers' to man the factories and do the jobs that the increasingly prosperous locals spurned. They were not expected to settle permanently, but many did. As the Swiss writer Max Frisch remarked: 'We imported workers and got men instead.'

At the same time, Britain, France and the Netherlands imported workers from their former colonies on a more permanent basis. People from the Caribbean were shipped over to work on London's buses and in other menial public-sector jobs, while Pakistanis were brought to Yorkshire to work in textile mills and do other unpleasant manufacturing jobs. By 1961, Britain had admitted over half a million migrants from the so-called 'New Commonwealth' – the non-white Commonwealth, that is. Although economic migration was severely restricted from 1962 on, immigrants were still allowed to bring over their family members until this too was restricted in 1971. Even so, the number of migrants from the New Commonwealth continued to rise, from 1.2 million in 1971 to 1.5 million in 1981.

Migrants to France came mainly from North Africa, but also from West Africa and France's overseas territories such as Guadeloupe, Martinique and Réunion. By 1970, there were over 600,000 Algerians, 140,000 Moroccans and 90,000 Tunisians in the country, along with some 250,000 people from France's overseas territories. The Netherlands let in some 300,000 people from its former colony of Indonesia and a further 160,000 from Surinam.

After 1973, when soaring oil prices plunged western Europe into recession, European countries sought to put an end to this influx: guest-worker programmes were axed and immigration rules tightened. The newly rich, oil-producing Gulf states took over from western Europe as the main importers of migrant labour from poor countries, primarily North Africa, South Asia and then South-east Asia, with their immigrant population rising from 1 million in 1970 to 9.6 million in 2000, over half of them in Saudi Arabia. But European countries continued to admit some foreigners in the 1970s and 1980s: those who already had family living there, as well as small numbers of refugees. The German government had hoped that its foreign guest-workers would leave – and made sporadic attempts to expel them – but

German courts forced the government not only to allow those who stayed put to settle but also to allow their relatives to join them. The few refugees had fled the wars in Vietnam and Afghanistan, and the revolution in Iran, with Sweden admitting many Chileans fleeing the dictatorship of Augusto Pinochet.

Since the 1980s, and even more so since the 1990s, the previously poor countries on Europe's periphery that used to export workers have not only enticed some of their citizens back but have attracted large numbers of immigrants themselves. As its economy has grown by leaps and bounds in recent years, Ireland has suddenly become a country that people flock to. The number of foreign residents in Italy quadrupled in the 1980s and 1990s, with many more immigrants arriving illegally. While over 2.5 million Spaniards still live abroad, Spain's foreign population trebled in the 1990s to 800,000. Even though 4 million Portuguese citizens still reside abroad, its foreign population nearly doubled in the same decade to over 200,000, primarily from eastern Europe, Brazil and its former colonies in Africa. Immigration to Greece has also soared, so that foreigners, mainly from the Balkans, now make up 8 per cent of the population. A lot of the immigration to these Mediterranean countries has been illegal, prompting successive amnesties.

Migration to western Europe took off again in the late 1980s. The end of communism in eastern Europe and the break-up of the Soviet Union produced a big wave of migrants, notably ethnic Germans, mostly to Germany and Austria. Germany admitted over 4.5 million migrants from the former Eastern Bloc in the late 1980s and the 1990s. The wars in the former Yugoslavia in the 1990s generated the largest number of displaced people in Europe since the Second World War. Two million political refugees fled, primarily to Germany, but also to Britain, France, Sweden and other countries. Economic migration from countries in central and eastern Europe has also increased, especially since eight of them joined the European

Union in 2004. And the creation in 1992 of the EU's Single Market, which allows citizens of any member state to live and work freely in any other (albeit with temporary restrictions on flows from the former communist countries), has stimulated new migrant flows within Europe: British and German pensioners retiring in Spain, French and Italian students working in London, Poles doing construction work in Britain and Germany.

America, Canada and Australia

Whereas most of the immigration to Europe has come in two big bursts – in the 1950s and 1960s, and since the 1990s – immigration to the US has taken off only since the 1970s (although many Mexican farmworkers were allowed to come work on a temporary basis in the 1950s and early 1960s). While the US admitted only 2.5 million permanent immigrants in the 1950s and 3.3 million in the 1960s, it allowed in 4.5 million in the 1970s, 7.3 million in the 1980s and 9.1 million in the 1990s. Most of these immigrants live in just six states (California, New York, Florida, Texas, Illinois and New Jersey), but they are starting to spread out across the country.

The watershed year was 1965, when US immigration rules were reformed as part of the broader push for civil rights. The national quotas designed to keep out Latin Americans and Asians were abolished and preference given instead to the relatives of US citizens and residents. The reform was not designed to encourage immigration or alter its composition: it was reasoned that giving preference to reuniting families would skew the system in favour of existing immigrant groups. But in practice, it led to an upsurge in immigration, first from Europe and then from Asia and Latin America. The million or so refugees who had arrived from Vietnam, Cambodia and Laos, along with the existing Filipino and Korean communities, were much keener to sponsor the arrival of family members: Asians brought in four times as many relatives per initial immigrant than did Europeans or Latin Americans.[10]

At the same time, illegal migration, mostly from Mexico, has soared, with twelve million undocumented residents believed to be in the country. A limited amnesty after 1986 produced three million applications, over two-thirds of them from Mexicans, while new sanctions were imposed on employers of illegal workers. But with documents easy to falsify, the employer sanctions proved ineffective, prompting a change of strategy in the 1990s towards tougher border controls and the denial of welfare benefits to illegal residents.

In 1990 US immigration rules were reformed again to increase the number of immigrants admitted on the basis of their skills rather than their family connections or refugee status. A worldwide lottery was also established, granting 55,000 entry visas a year at random to citizens of countries other than the eleven that have sent the most legal migrants to the US. Applicants simply have to post their names and photographs along with those of their spouse and children to a processing centre. In 2000, Congress tripled the number of temporary work visas available for skilled workers to 195,000 a year, although this fell back to 65,000 again in 2004.

Canada has encouraged immigration throughout the post-war period. At first, only Europeans were admitted, mainly Britons and then Germans, Italians and Dutch; after the introduction in 1976 of a points system for selecting immigrants that did not discriminate on the basis of nationality, non-Europeans were allowed in too. The number of immigrants let in each year has risen sharply, with an emphasis on attracting skilled workers, selected since 2001 using broader criteria such as their level of education, language ability and possession of flexible and transferable skills rather than specifically on the basis of their occupation.

Australia was even more pro-active in attracting immigrants in the post-war period. Under the slogan 'Populate or Perish', the government sought to lure migrants and their families to settle in Australia. At first, pride of place was given to Britons, but when not enough could be attracted, white Europeans were also admitted, first from eastern and northern Europe, but then also from southern Europe. In the 1950s, most migrants came from Italy and Greece. But by the late 1960s, migration from increasingly prosperous southern Europe had slowed to a trickle, prompting the government to widen the net to Yugoslavia and Latin America, and to make family reunion even easier.

After the repeal of the 'White Australia' policy in the late 1960s and early 1970s, and the adoption of its own non-racially based points system for grading prospective migrants, Australia attracted increasing numbers of economic migrants from Asia, rising to half of the immigrant intake in the early 1990s. But the long-standing pro-immigration stance was reversed in 1996, limiting family reunion, excluding asylum seekers and putting a greater emphasis on skilled migration.

The current face of migration

Despite these many waves of international migration, there are surprisingly few migrants worldwide. Admittedly, measuring migration is tricky – who do you count and how do you count them? – and the statistics are often patchy, flawed and inconsistent. But the United Nations' official estimate, using census figures, was that in 2000, 175 million people had been living for over a year outside the country where they were born – just one in thirty-five of the world's population.[11] By extrapolating past trends, the UN reckoned that by 2006 the number of migrants had reached 200 million. (The true figure is probably higher, though, because some illegal migrants doubtless go uncounted.)

The number of international migrants more than doubled between 1970 and 2000, from 82 million to 175 million, but since the world's population rose from 3.7 billion to 6 billion over the same period, the migrant share of the world's population only edged up, from 2.2 per cent to 2.9 per cent – and a large part of that increase was due to borders moving, not people: the break-up of the Soviet Union, Czechoslovakia and Yugoslavia in the 1990s left many people living on one side or the other of international borders that had not previously existed.[12]

Why all the fuss, then? Less than 3 per cent does not seem a big enough figure to get worked up about. It is only when you look at the pattern of international migration that you realise why it is so controversial. Migrants, mostly from poor countries, are flocking to a handful of rich countries with low birth rates, where they account for a large and rising share of the population and an even larger share of the population increase. If your mental image of globalisation is of a Nike factory in China – rich countries putting their stamp on poor countries – then in the case of migration, the shoe is on the other foot: people from poor countries are making their mark on rich countries. And therein lies the rub.

While there are plenty of migrants in poor countries, their overall numbers are not rising.[13] But the number of immigrants in rich countries more than doubled between 1970 and 2000, from 35 million to 81 million. What's more, the migrant share of the population nearly doubled, from 4.3 per cent to 8.3 per cent. In rich countries, one in twelve people – and rising – is now an immigrant.[14] And while net migration accounted for less than an eighth of developed countries' population growth in the early 1970s, it made up nearly two-thirds of it in the late 1990s.[15] Without immigration, Europe's population would actually have fallen in recent years.

A fifth of the world's migrants live in a single country: the

United States. Another two-fifths live in a further twelve countries: Russia, Germany, Ukraine, France, India, Canada, Saudi Arabia, Australia, Pakistan, Britain, Kazakhstan and Hong Kong.[16] Immigrants now account for over three-fifths of the population in seven (mostly tiny) countries: Andorra, Macao, Guam, the Holy See, Monaco, Qatar and the United Arab Emirates. Among larger countries, those with more than ten million inhabitants, they account for over 10 per cent of the population in seven rich countries – Australia, Canada, France, Germany, the Netherlands, Saudi Arabia and the US – plus Côte d'Ivoire (due to a temporary influx of refugees), and three former Soviet states: Belarus, Kazakhstan and Ukraine.[17]

The foreign-born population of the US has soared from 10 million in 1970 (4.7 per cent of the total) to 37.6 million (12.8 per cent) in 2004 – not far short of the 15-per-cent peak reached in the heyday of Ellis Island in 1910.[18] In the 1950s, over half of US immigrants were European, with four in ten from the Americas and fewer than one in ten from Asia. But today over half are from Latin America or the Caribbean, a quarter from Asia and fewer than one in seven from Europe. Of these, 10.2 million were born in Mexico (up from only 750,000 in 1970), 1.5 million in the Philippines, just over a million in each of India, China, Germany, El Salvador and Cuba, and just under a million in each of Vietnam and Korea.[19] Among the million or so people who arrived legally each year from 2000 to 2002, over eight in ten were from developing countries, and a further one in ten was from an ex-communist country. Four in ten were from Latin America and the Caribbean and three in ten from Asia.[20]

Canada's foreign-born population has risen from 3.3 million in 1970 to 5.8 million (18 per cent of the total) in 2004. Some 600,000 are from Britain, around the same number from China and Hong Kong, and a further 300,000 or so from each of Italy and India. Among the 236,000 who arrived on average each year from 2000 to 2002, eight in ten were from developing countries (up from four in ten in the early 1970s) and a further one in ten from ex-communist countries.[21] Over half were from Asia, with China, India and Pakistan topping the list, followed by the Philippines, Iran and Korea.

In Australia, the foreign-born population has risen from 2.5 million in 1970 to 4.8 million (23.6 per cent of the total) in 2004. Half are from Europe, a quarter from Asia and a quarter from the rest of the world.[22] Of the 92,000 a year who arrived between 2000 and 2002, over half were from developing countries (up from one in five in the early 1970s) and one in twenty from ex-communist countries.[23] Four in ten were from Asia – mainly China, India, the Philippines and Indonesia – and just a quarter were from Britain and New Zealand. A fifth of New Zealand's 3.8 million people were born overseas. Of the 53,000 immigrants granted residency in 2002, over half were from Asia, with Chinese topping the list, followed by Indians, Britons and South Africans.[24]

Europe's foreign-born population has risen from 10 million in 1970 to 31.6 million (9.7 per cent of the total) in 2000.[25] But some countries in Europe have many more immigrants than others: they are 3.2 per cent of the population in Finland, 6.8 per cent in Spain, 9.3 per cent in Britain, 10 per cent in France, 10.6 per cent in the Netherlands, 11 per cent in Ireland, 12.2 per cent in Sweden, 13 per cent in Germany and 23.5 per cent in Switzerland.[26] For most of these countries – France is a notable exception – these are record-high figures.

There has been a big shift in the pattern of immigration since 1990. It has risen sharply in countries such as Spain, Finland, Portugal, Ireland and Italy, which had been previously countries of emigration; it has also risen significantly in Britain; but it has tailed off in France and the Netherlands.[27] Of the 2.8 million or so immigrants who arrived in the EU legally in 2004, Spain admitted 646,000, Germany 602,000, Britain 494,000, Italy

319,000, France 140,000 and the Netherlands 65,000.[28] At the same time, many foreigners left – 547,000 from Germany, 152,000 from Britain and 24,000 from the Netherlands, for instance – although emigrants are counted much less accurately than immigrants; indeed, many countries fail to count them at all.[29]

The national origin of immigrants varies widely among European countries. In Switzerland, they are mostly European, primarily from the former Yugoslavia, Italy and Portugal. In France, they are mainly from Portugal, Morocco and Algeria, and more recently Turkey and Tunisia. In Germany, they are largely from Turkey, and more recently Poland and other central and east European countries. In the Netherlands, they are mostly from Turkey, Surinam, Morocco and Indonesia, and more recently from Germany and Britain. In Italy, they come from Morocco, Albania and Romania. In Spain, they are from Morocco, Ecuador, Britain, Colombia and Germany – the Brits and Germans being primarily pensioners who have retired on the Costa del Sol. Migrants from any one country tend to cluster in a few destinations: nearly all Algerian migrants are in France, while most Greeks, Poles and Turks are in Germany; over half of all Portuguese migrants and nearly half of all Moroccans are in France; and over 40 per cent of Italian migrants and those who have left the former Yugoslavia are in Germany. In the EU as a whole, there are three million Turks and two million Moroccans.

The pattern of immigration in Britain is particularly interesting. The perception among many Britons is that the country is being overrun by immigrants from poor countries. In fact, most of the new arrivals in 2002 were from rich countries: Americans and Australians top the list, followed by Indians, South Africans, Filipinos and New Zealanders.[30] But since 2004, there has been a big rise in immigration from new EU countries in central and eastern Europe, such as Poland and the Czech Republic, whose citizens can now work freely in Britain.

Until the early 1980s, Japan largely shunned immigration. But as the Japanese have become richer and started to turn their noses up at certain low-paying jobs, the country has begun to admit some foreigners. Between 1975 and 2004, the number of legally resident foreigners in Japan more than doubled from 750,000 to almost two million, and the country admitted 372,000 immigrants in 2004 alone. Many of them were foreigners of Japanese descent, mostly from Brazil and Peru, but people from other Asian countries were also admitted as trainees or foreign students who are allowed to work part time. By 2002 there were also at least 220,000 foreigners in Japan illegally. Even so, only 1.5 per cent of the population was born abroad.[31]

International migration is not a one-way street. Although few countries compile accurate records of people who have emigrated, one can piece together an idea of the number of emigrants from the number of immigrants registered in other countries. Thus, even the United States is estimated to lose 200,000 emigrants a year – some of them immigrants returning home, others Americans going overseas – and there are significant populations of American expatriates in a number of European countries and elsewhere. Likewise, many Britons continue to emigrate, notably to Australia, Canada, New Zealand and Spain.

Classifying the unclassifiable

Broadly speaking, most migrants move in search of a better life. Why else would they leave home? But immigration systems tend to split migrants into three main categories: political refugees, who are fleeing violence in their home countries; family members, who are moving to be reunited with their relatives in rich countries; and economic migrants, who come to work. In practice, of course, refugees may choose the country where they wish to seek asylum for economic reasons, and family-reunion visas provide an opportunity for those lucky enough to have relatives in rich countries to find work there themselves. In short, nearly all migrants move at least partly for economic reasons. The same is true, of course, for illegal immigrants.

Contrary to popular perception, only a few of the new arrivals are refugees. Although the UN counted 16.6 million people in 2000 who had fled their country in fear of their lives, only 3.2 million of them ended up in rich countries. Despite the many wars in the 1990s, notably in the Balkans, the number of refugees in rich countries rose by only 1.2 million, almost all of them in Europe.[32] In 2001, with the notable exceptions of Denmark (where they accounted for a quarter of new arrivals) and Sweden (where they accounted for a third), refugees accounted for less than one in eight immigrants arriving in most rich countries.[33]

The panic about asylum seekers that has swept many European countries in recent years is therefore out of all proportion to the numbers involved. Yes, the number of asylum applications rose dramatically during the wars in the Balkans; and yes, they remained higher than previously even after the conflicts had subsided. No doubt some economic migrants were masquerading as asylum seekers in order to gain entry to rich countries. But, as Michael Dummett of Oxford University rightly points out, 'It needs only a moment's thought to realise that flight for economic reasons may be as justified and as worthy of sympathy and help as flight from political persecution.'[34] And in any case, even at their peak in 1999, asylum applications to west European countries reached only 453,000. Germany received 95,000 of these applications, Britain 91,000, Switzerland 46,000, the Netherlands 43,000 and Belgium, Italy and France around 30,000 each. These were applications, remember, not those actually granted asylum. In Australia, which was also swept by scare stories about hordes of invading refugees, asylum applications peaked at just 13,000 in 2000. By 2005, the numbers applying for asylum in Europe had fallen to 243,000, with Britain receiving only 30,500 applications, France 50,000, Germany 28,900, Austria 22,500, Sweden 17,500 and Switzerland 10,100. Australia received a mere 3,200.[35] Among the 49,000 asylum seekers Britain actually admitted in 2003, the main countries of origin were Somalia, Iraq, Zimbabwe, China, Iran and Afghanistan – all pretty repressive places. Even if, as some claim, a large proportion of the asylum seekers are in fact economic migrants, the numbers involved are so small that they scarcely warrant all the populist scaremongering. And in any case, despite the increasingly unpleasant methods used to deter economic migrants from pretending to be political refugees, there is no easy way of distinguishing them. We would not need to try, of course, if we let in immigrants more freely.

Most of those who migrate legally do so on visas that enable relatives to be reunited with their families. Some countries are stricter than others in deciding which relatives are allowed to come, but all make provision for family reunification. In 2004, around two-thirds of new arrivals in the US and France came in this way. In Canada and Australia, though, only a quarter of new arrivals made use of family-reunification visas. In Britain, less than a fifth did.

Those three are among very few countries that admit most of their immigrants on work visas: around 55 per cent of the total in 2004 in Britain and Australia, and 62 per cent in Canada (including their accompanying family). In the US the figure is just a sixth; in France a ninth. However, nearly all of these work visas are for highly skilled workers. So what are low-skilled workers meant to do?

3

Why We Need the Huddled Masses

The case for low-skilled migration

Give me your tired, your poor,
Your huddled masses yearning to breathe free,
The wretched refuse of your teeming shore.
Send these, the homeless, tempest-tost to me,
I lift my lamp beside the golden door!

Emily Lazarus, poem inscribed
on the Statue of Liberty

The real gains from trade come from exploiting differences. It is the flow of less skilled workers from developing to developed countries that promises the larger returns . . . The less skilled are relatively scarcer in the industrial world (and growing more so), more abundant in the developing world, and much more likely to be from, or connected to, poor families.

Alan Winters, University of Sussex[1]

Inmer Omar Rivera is a model of what many think an American citizen should be: God-fearing, hard-working and devoted to his family. Dressed in jeans, a baseball cap and a blue hooded top, he would not look out of place in a US city. But unfortunately, the United States won't let him in – because he is poor, from Honduras and has no family in the US. So Inmer is camped up in a hostel for migrants in Ciudad Juárez, Mexico, just across the border from El Paso, Texas, pondering what to do next.

That Inmer is exceptionally enterprising – another much-prized virtue in America – is not in doubt. He has spent twenty days and travelled two thousand kilometres by train across Guatemala and Mexico to reach the US border. 'There were around two thousand of us on the train initially. Only twenty of us made it this far,' he says. 'Getting here is a triumph.' He had to rely on the kindness of strangers for food. 'Of the twenty days, we ate on eight and didn't on twelve. Lots of people are good. They would help us and feed us. I didn't want to ask for a taco. I was too ashamed to beg,' he explains. But the biggest challenge for Inmer and his fellow-illegal migrants was dodging the Mexican military, risking their lives as they leapt on and off moving trains. 'Whenever the train approached a military checkpoint, we had to decide whether to jump off the train or stay on and hide. When we got off, we would go round the checkpoint and wait for the next train. I was lucky: sometimes I got off the train and the soldiers got on; other times I stayed on the train and the people who jumped off got caught. Some people got cut in two as they tried to get on a train. Others fell under the train as they jumped off and got cut in half.'

Back in Honduras, Inmer worked as an electrician in a factory making car parts for a US company called Empire Electronics. 'They treated me well,' he says, but he earned only 658 lempiras ($33) a week. It was a struggle for him and his wife Patricia to provide for their twenty-month-old son, Derek. So, aged only twenty-five, he decided to take his chances and try to reach the US to work. 'It was a very tough decision – I miss my family a lot – but it's a sacrifice I have to make so my kid can go to school and not have to suffer like me.' We interrupt the interview while he goes to call his mother to let her know he is OK.

Migrating to the US legally was not an option. 'To get a US visa you need to be rich: you need to own a big business, have an expensive house and a bank account with lots of money in it. If I had any of that, I wouldn't need to go to the US.' He doesn't have the $2,000 needed to pay a *pollero* to smuggle him in, so he is taking his chances on his own, but he is worried all his efforts will be in vain. 'I'm afraid I'll get caught and be deported back to Honduras. I'll have wasted twenty days' suffering. But if God wants it, I'll find a way,' he says, his voice straining between hope and dread.

I asked Inmer whether he thought the US was right to control its border so strictly. 'I think the United States should give an opportunity to those who need it. Because life is hard. The US is one of the most developed countries. I know that some people come with bad intentions but I don't have any vices. The US should give us permits to come work from Honduras. We come to work hard, not to destroy.'

Should we let him in?

We take it for granted that restrictions on the movement of people should exist. In particular, we assume that it is normal and desirable (for people in rich countries) that people in poor countries should be confined within their national borders, just as medieval serfs were once tied to the land. We never stop to think that perhaps we would all be better off if the latter-day serfs were set free, because they would be vastly more productive if they were not confined to their poor native lands.

Just as feudal lords never questioned whether their system made sense because they were comfortably at the top of the pile, people in rich countries tend to assume that immigration controls benefit them because they protect them from the poor in the rest of the world. In a way, of course, the controls *do* protect them – but at what cost? Might we have as much to gain from setting free people in poor countries as we did from shifting from feudalism to capitalism?

There is good reason to believe that the potential gains from freer migration could be huge. Rich countries have much more capital – machinery, buildings, infrastructure and so on – and far better technology than poor ones. This makes workers in rich countries far more productive than their equivalents in poor countries. But when workers from poor countries move to rich ones, they too can make use of rich countries' superior capital and technology, so they become much more productive. This makes them – and the world as a whole – much better off.

For example, a poor farmer in Africa might till his land by hand. If he goes to work in Europe, he can use a tractor. He produces more food each year, which means he earns a higher wage, and global food production also increases. Likewise, if a Mexican factory worker goes to work in the US, he can produce many more cars, boosting his wage packet as well as the world's output of cars. Given that the gap in productivity between rich countries and poor ones is huge, so are the potential gains from people in poor countries coming to work in rich ones.

Starting from that simple insight, Bob Hamilton and John Whalley, two economists at the University of Western Ontario, made a stab at calculating the potential gains from free migration back in 1984.[2] Their results were astonishing. They found that removing immigration controls could more than double the size of the world economy. Of course, these are little more than back-of-the-envelope calculations, but they give a rough idea of what is at stake – and it is massive.

In 2004, two other academics – Jonathon Moses, an American political economist, and Bjørn Letnes, a Norwegian economist, both at the Norwegian University of Science and Technology in Trondheim – explored the issue further. They found that the potential gains from free migration were even greater than they had been twenty years earlier, because the wage gap between rich countries and poor ones has grown. 'Using 1998 data, we find that the estimated gains from free migration may be as high as US$55.04 trillion . . . Even when several adjustments are made to make the analysis more realistic, the potential gains remain enormous,' they conclude.[3] Significantly, they find that even a small relaxation of immigration controls would yield disproportionately big gains.

Freer international migration would bring huge economic benefits to the world as a whole, because it would redeploy workers to where they are more productive. Even critics of immigration admit as much: 'the principles of free trade . . . suggest that the world would be much richer if there were no national borders to interfere with the free movement of goods and people. By prohibiting the immigration of many persons, the United States inevitably shrinks the size of the world economic pie, reducing the economic opportunities that could be available to many persons in the source countries,' writes George Borjas of Harvard University, the leading economic critic of immigration in the US.[4]

It is self-evident that migrants like Inmer would gain by moving to the US, because they would earn much higher wages. If for some reason they did not, they could always go home. It is also generally true that migrants' countries of origin will gain from their moving, as I shall explain in greater detail in Chapter 8. But the big question for the US, Britain and other rich countries is not whether immigrants, poor countries or the world as a whole would gain from freer migration, but how much rich countries themselves would gain economically from allowing in more immigrants – and whether any of their citizens would lose out.

The benefits of low-skilled migration

Economic fears about immigration rest mainly on three common misconceptions: that there are only so many jobs to go round, so that every job an immigrant takes is one less for locals to do; that immigrants and locals are competing for the same jobs; and, somewhat contradictorily, that immigrants often come not to work but to live like parasites off the host country. In short, immigrants are damned if they work and damned if they don't.

Over the past fifty years, the US population has risen sharply. If the number of jobs in the economy were fixed, surely there would now be mass unemployment? Clearly, there isn't – and yet the belief that there is only a limited number of jobs to go round remains pervasive, leading critics to assume that any job filled by an immigrant would otherwise be done by a native-born person. In fact, each person creates work for others, so the more people there are, the more work needs doing. People don't just take jobs; they make them too. While the number of jobs in an economy rises and falls, as do unemployment rates, this is mostly due not to immigration but to the economic cycle of boom and bust, along with structural changes, such as the rise of some industries and the decline of others. 'The problem for immigrants is that while the jobs they take are visible, the jobs they create for everyone else are largely invisible,' says Peter Stalker, an expert on migration[5] – and he is dead right. Through their willingness to do unskilled work at lower wages than native people would accept, immigrants fill jobs that would otherwise not exist: when nannies cost £5 an hour, there will be far more nannying jobs than when they cost £10 an hour. What's more, when immigrants spend their wages, they increase the overall demand for goods and services, which in turn boosts the demand for workers, some of them highly skilled, to produce them. Thus, far from taking local people's jobs, immigrants generally create new jobs for the existing population.

Critics of immigration think that immigrants compete for the same jobs as locals while at the same time believing that immigrants are different – read: inferior – to locals. This makes no sense: a semi-literate Mexican peasant with a poor command of English is no competition in the job market for an American who has finished high school. Only if immigrants were more or less identical to us would they compete directly for the same jobs as locals.

If immigrants were identical to us, the benefits of migration would be pretty small. The new arrivals would bring nothing new to the party: they would simply replicate the skills and characteristics of existing workers. At least initially, they would drive down the wages or reduce the employment opportunities of native workers, since they would compete directly with them in the labour market. Employers would benefit from lower wage bills and consumers from cheaper goods and services, but these gains would scarcely exceed the costs to workers of lower wages. Once the economy had adjusted to the influx of immigrants, with increased investment restoring to its previous level the amount of capital available for each worker to work with, it would look much like it did before the newcomers arrived, only bigger. A larger domestic market would have benefits for some firms, since they could spread their fixed costs over a larger number of consumers, for instance, but there might also be an increase in congestion, with more people crammed into the same area of land. In short, if immigrants were the same as us, we would have little to gain – or lose – from letting them in.

But when immigrants are different to us, the economic benefits of migration can be much greater. Immigrants with different skills and abilities allow us to consume goods and services that were not previously available or consume existing goods and services at much lower prices. Thus some Vietnamese immigrants have introduced us to the delights of their cuisine, while others have boosted the supply of nannies, making childcare more widely available and affordable. Immigrants whose skills complement those of native workers will also make them more productive. A Vietnamese childminder may not only relieve the burden on a hard-pressed mother, she may also allow her to return to work at her high-flying job in investment banking. Filipino nurses boost the level of care that British and American hospitals can deliver to their patients as well as increasing the number of patients they can treat. By sparking off each other, Russian-born Sergey Brin, who emigrated to the US in 1979 to escape the persecution of Jews in the Soviet Union, and US-born Larry Page were inspired to set up Google. Since it is clear that immigrants are very different to us in many respects, there is good reason to believe that we could benefit greatly from migration. I shall look at the case for letting in skilled migrants in Chapter 4 and the broader economic benefits of diversity in Chapter 5. In Chapters 6 and 7, I shall examine the potential costs of immigration to jobs and the welfare state. But in the rest of this chapter, I shall consider the benefits of the most controversial and widely resisted kind of migration: that of low-skilled workers like Inmer or Lasso.

When they are not blaming them for stealing our jobs, critics often portray immigrants as lazy welfare scroungers. If people from poor countries can claim more in welfare benefits in rich countries than they can earn working in poor countries, it is certainly conceivable that this could spur some of them to migrate. But there is no evidence for this, as even critics of immigration such as George Borjas admit: 'there exists the possibility that welfare attracts persons who otherwise would not have migrated to the United States. Although this is the magnetic effect that comes up most often in the immigration debate, it is also the one for which there is no empirical support.'[6] It should be clear that if migration is costly and risky, it does not pay to move to a rich country to try to claim comparatively low welfare benefits when you could earn much more by working instead. Would Inmer really leave behind his family and risk his life in order to go on welfare in the US? In any case, migrants are typically not entitled to most welfare benefits in rich countries. And last but not least, even if rich countries were to make it much easier for people in poor countries to come work, and there were signs that this was attracting migrants who were coming simply to claim welfare benefits, governments could restrict the availability of those benefits to citizens or long-term residents. That is precisely what the British government did when it opened the doors to east Europeans from the new EU member states in 2004. As a result, Poles are not entitled to claim £56.20 a week in jobseeker's allowance, so they must make do with earning at least £200 a week doing a minimum-wage job and most likely much more than that.

Immigrants all have different skills and characteristics, so any claim about them is by definition a generalisation. But even so, I shall make a bold one: immigrants tend to be younger, fitter, more hard-working and more enterprising than local people. Why? Not because foreigners in general are more industrious and adventurous, but because migrants are a self-selected minority. Young people have their whole lives ahead of them and so most to gain from migrating, while the old and the sick are generally not able to do so. While over half of the foreigners in the US – and nearly three-fifths of the immigrants who have arrived since 2000 – are in their twenties or thirties, only a quarter of natives are. Over four-fifths of the East Europeans who have applied to work in Britain since 2004 are aged 18–34.[7] And just as people who are willing to incur the costs and risks of starting their own business tend to be more hard-working and enterprising than most, so too are those who are willing to incur the costs and risks of upping sticks in search of better job prospects abroad. Hard-working people have more to gain from migrating than lazy people, while enterprising people are more willing to take the risk.

Inmer could have stayed in Honduras: he had a job there, as did his wife. They earned enough to survive. But he wanted more: a better standard of living and enough to put his son Derek through school so that he would enjoy a better future. Nearly everyone in Honduras would be better off if they went to work in the US, yet only a small minority try. Inmer is prepared to risk his life to secure a better life for his son: you can't get much more enterprising than that.

Moreover, once immigrants arrive in a rich country, they have a very strong incentive to make the most of the greater opportunities available to them. They start at the bottom of the pile, economically and socially. They have to pay off the cost of migrating. They have to provide for themselves and save for their families. The alternative is not the relative comfort enjoyed by a Western citizen with full welfare entitlements and potentially assets to inherit; it is penury.

Typically, then, immigrants tend to be more hard-working and enterprising than native people. For any given wage, in any given job, they are likely to be more industrious. Faced with a set of economic opportunities, they are more likely to opt for the more rewarding ones, even if they are risky and demand a lot of effort. So immigrants directly make an economy more productive – to the benefit of employers and local people who consume the goods and services they produce. And if they spur local people to work harder too, the benefits are even greater.

Small (and sometimes large) business

It is the drive to get ahead – as well as their exclusion from mainstream society – that helps explain why so many immigrants set up their own businesses. Think of Korean grocery stores in California or Pakistani newsagents in Britain. Immigrants have little to lose from striking out on their own, since they typically arrive with little or nothing – and sometimes they hit the big time.

Gulam Noon is one of the few people who can justifiably claim to have helped change a country's national dish. Sir Gulam, as he has been since 2002, arrived in London from India with hardly any money in his pocket. 'My circumstances meant I had to start work early but I wish I'd had the opportunity to go to university,' he says. Having developed a passion for food in his mother's kitchen back in Mumbai, he eventually founded Noon Products, which specialises in frozen and chilled Indian ready meals. 'My inspiration for Noon Products came from seeing Indian restaurants opening everywhere,' he explains. 'I knew the food would hit supermarket shelves with a vengeance. You could get Indian food in London supermarkets but it was badly packaged and nowhere near authentic.' If you have eaten an Indian ready meal from a British supermarket, chances are you have eaten some of Noon's food: he supplies Sainsbury's, Waitrose, Somerfield and Morrison's, as well as Birds Eye. 'I love the challenges involved in running your own business,' says Sir Gulam, who is now worth £50 million.[8] 'And the satisfaction of not just creating wealth for the company but for the country. I like the fact that we give jobs to so many people.' Noon Products employs around nine hundred people. What's more, 'we've changed the palates of the nation – chicken tikka massala is now the national dish'.[9]

Doing the jobs others won't do

The benefits of hard work and enterprise are significant, but the main reason why rich countries should let in people like Inmer is that there is a growing shortage of workers to do the jobs that almost anyone can do but Americans and Europeans no longer want to do.

Critics of immigration tend to think that unskilled immigrants and natives compete for jobs. But this is increasingly untrue, because even natives with no qualifications refuse to do certain dirty, difficult and dangerous jobs, while the increasing numbers that are highly qualified aspire to better careers. Yet someone has to clean toilets, collect rubbish and do casual labour. If we do not let in immigrants to perform these tasks, Americans and Europeans will have to be paid over the odds to induce them to do jobs they do not want to do when they could be doing more pleasant and highly skilled work instead.

A gap is opening between the skills and aspirations of most North Americans, Europeans and Australians and the jobs on offer in advanced economies. Ever more educated and ambitious workers want to do higher-skilled jobs that offer higher pay and increased social status. Politicians share their ambition: every rich-country government is committed to raising the education and skill levels of all its citizens. Yet even as rich-country economies create new skilled jobs, they continue to rely on low-skilled jobs too. In previous decades, the demand for low-skilled workers has slumped as new technology has allowed farms and factories to produce more with fewer workers and international trade has allowed us to import many labour-intensive goods and services more cheaply from abroad. But many low-skilled services cannot readily be mechanised or imported – old people cannot be cared for by a robot or from abroad – and demand for them is rising fast as our society gets older and richer. If governments want to maximise the welfare of their citizens, they will want as many of them as possible to be doing higher-skilled, higher-paid, higher-status jobs. But if the job market is entirely national, there is a limit to how many citizens can do such higher-end jobs. If the job market is opened up to foreigners, however, then all Americans and Europeans could conceivably be employed in higher-end jobs. Or, to put it another way, without immigrants, not all of us will have the opportunity to realise our aspirations.

Contrary to the prevailing pessimism, there has been a remarkable rise in education levels in rich countries, and this is likely to continue. Fewer and fewer Americans and Europeans leave school without a qualification, while ever more go on to complete university or further-education courses. As recently as 1960, over half of American workers over twenty-five were high-school dropouts, while only one in ten was a college graduate.[10] Now, out of every ten over-twenty-fives in the US labour force, only one has failed to finish high school, while three have only a high-school diploma, slightly fewer than two are college dropouts and over four have one or more degrees.[11]

Britain has witnessed an equally dramatic transformation. Whereas a fifth of working-age men and 28 per cent of working-age women over fifty have no qualifications, only 7 per cent of men and 8 per cent of women in their twenties do.[12] A similar pattern is evident in other rich countries. Over half of French people and Australians and nearly a third of Canadians aged between 55 and 64 have not completed secondary education, but only a fifth of the French, a quarter of Australians and one in ten Canadians aged between 25 and 34 have failed to do so.[13]

Not only are Americans and Europeans better qualified than ever before, they also have higher aspirations. Whereas young people from working-class backgrounds might once have been content with low-end jobs, nearly everyone now thinks they deserve better. While many might once have taken pride in manual work, people now increasingly shun it. Certain jobs in particular carry stigma: young people no longer want to harvest fruit in summer, for instance. Likewise, people prefer to work in offices and shops rather than in the street or in unskilled service jobs, such as cleaning, which they view as demeaning. In short, people expect to earn higher wages commensurate with their improved qualifications and perceived increase in status, and shun unpleasant jobs that they perceive as menial. As older unskilled workers retire, existing workers obtain new training and qualifications, and young people become better educated and more demanding, the number of Americans and Europeans willing to do low-skilled jobs will continue to drop over the next twenty years.

But even modern advanced economies do not consist solely of high-skilled jobs. Every hotel requires a few managers and marketing people but also many more receptionists, bellboys, chambermaids, cleaners, porters, waiters and kitchen staff. Likewise, every hospital requires not just doctors and nurses but also many more cleaners, cooks, laundry workers and security staff. And all of those workers in hotels and hospitals rely on people to build, repair and clean the roads, to drive taxis, buses and ambulances, to fix leaky roofs and unblock drains. So even as advanced economies create more high-skilled jobs, they inevitably create many more low-skilled jobs too.

What's more, as our society becomes older and richer, our demand for relatively low-skilled, labour-intensive services is rising fast. As the number of old people increases, the demand for nursing care soars, for instance. And as people get richer, their demand for personal services rises disproportionately. As more mothers go back to work, demand for childcare and cleaners grows. Rather than preparing their own meals, people increasingly buy sandwiches at lunchtime, have dinner delivered to their homes or eat out in restaurants. They pay someone to paint their house, mow their lawn and wash their car rather than spending their precious weekend time doing so. In other words, as people get richer, they increasingly pay others to do time-consuming and arduous tasks that they once did themselves, freeing up more time that they can devote either to more productive work or to more enjoyable leisure. All of this boosts the demand for unskilled labour.

Only a third of the US workforce works in management, professional and other high-end occupations to which, by and large, highly skilled natives aspire.[14] A further 38.1 per cent work in the jobs to which, in broad terms, less skilled natives aspire: sales and administration (26.7 per cent), manufacturing production (8.5 per cent), the emergency services (2 per cent) and as supervisors in construction, mining and transport (0.9 per cent). That leaves 28.3 per cent of jobs that most less-skilled natives would rather not do at all: the 12.9 per cent of jobs in relatively low-end services, such as healthcare support, preparing and serving food, cleaning and maintaining buildings and grounds, and personal care and service; the 8.7 per cent in non-supervisory roles in construction and mining as well as installation, maintenance and repair jobs; the 5.9 per cent in non-supervisory transport jobs; and the 0.7 per cent in farming, fishing and forestry. In states where there are many immigrants, few natives are employed in such jobs – and as the number of low-skilled natives shrinks, the shortage of people to do such work will grow.

Admittedly, this is only the crudest of categorisations, and I would not claim that it is wholly accurate. But it gives a broad idea of the number of low-skilled jobs remaining in the most advanced economy in the world. What's more, a study prepared for the US Congress forecast that around half the jobs on offer in 2050 – in personal services, cleaning, construction, security, retail sales and so on – would require only a high-school diploma or less.[15]

A glance at Britain's workforce shows a broadly similar picture. In 2002, four in ten workers were employed in management, professional and other higher-end occupations. Another one in three workers do less skilled work, with 21.1 per cent working in administration, clerical and secretarial roles, or sales and customer services, and 11.4 per cent classified as skilled tradespeople. The remaining 27.3 per cent of jobs are largely low-skilled work: personal services, transport and machine operatives, and other unskilled labour.[16] The fastest-growing occupations between 1992 and 2002 were customer services and caring personal services.[17]

Forecasts by the Institute for Employment Research at Warwick University give an idea of what Britain's job market might look like in 2012. The share of jobs in higher-end occupations is predicted to rise to 45.1 per cent. The share working in administration and sales is set to remain broadly stable at 20.4 per cent, with a rise in sales and customer-service jobs compensating for a fall in admin and secretarial jobs, while the share of skilled tradespeople will shrink to 9 per cent. The share of people working as transport and machine operatives and other low-skilled labour will shrink from 20 per cent to 16.1 per cent, but employment in personal services is set to rise sharply, from 7.3 per cent to 9.4 per cent. All of those new jobs will be in the care sector, where employment is set to rise from 5.3 per cent of the workforce to 7.4 per cent. Even in 2012, then, low-skilled jobs are forecast to account for over a quarter of employment in Britain.

At the level of individual businesses, an excellent study by the RSA Migration Commission gives an indication of the shortage of unskilled workers that already exists in certain industries in Britain.[18] Take the hospitality sector, which covers tourism, catering, restaurants, hotels and so on. This provides over two million jobs, most of them low-skilled, and generates over a ninth of Britain's economic output. Many of the workers are women or students. The RSA study reports that the labour shortages are greatest for cooks, waiters, bar staff and other food and beverage work, as well as for housekeeping jobs, such as chambermaids and cleaners. These are precisely the jobs in which migrants predominate, with documented ones most likely to work supplying food and drinks or in front-of-house tasks such as reception, while undocumented ones tend to have back-of-house roles, such as security and moving stock, as well as housekeeping. Migrants also do most of the seasonal work, since native workers tend to prefer permanent jobs. Earnings within the sector as a whole are generally below the national average. An estimated 70 per cent of catering jobs in London are carried out by migrants, and four in ten London-based employers in this sector say they have difficulty recruiting sufficient workers. According to the RSA, 'Industry experts believe that the addition of recent East European migrants has benefited the sector tremendously by raising skills standards and service levels and easing skills shortages in the process.' But it warns that undocumented workers tend to face exploitation at the hands of unscrupulous labour agencies and subcontractors, as a report by the Trades Union Congress conclusively documents.

Richard Lyon, the general manager of the Marriott Hotel in London's Chancery Court, needs no convincing of the benefits of immigration. 'Immigrants make a massive contribution. We have three hundred full-time staff and fifty-two different nationalities represented. Less than a quarter of our employees are from Britain. Most of them are from Brazil or eastern Europe,' he says. 'If I had to rely purely on a British workforce I'd be in serious trouble.' What's more, he claims, the multinational workforce 'creates a really good atmosphere. People from lots of different nationalities working together with a common goal, bringing with them all sorts of different skills.'

This mismatch between the education levels and expectations of native workers and the jobs available can only grow. So who is going to do this low-skilled work? To some extent, machines can replace low-skilled workers: we can buy a can of Coke from a vending machine rather than a person. In Japan, where one in four people will be over sixty-five in 2015 but which steadfastly refuses to admit foreign nurses, companies are developing gadgets that can keep an eye on – albeit not care for – old people remotely. One company makes a sensor that can be placed on the fridge door; every time the door is opened, a message is sent via the internet connection to a company database, and from there health workers or family members can be alerted if there is no fridge-opening activity. Another company has developed an electric kettle, the iPot, that keeps water hot all day for tea or miso soup and transmits a message to a computer server when the water-dispensing button is pressed. Twice daily, the usage record is sent to the designated mobile phone or email address of a family member or friend.[19] In other cases, new technologies may make it feasible and economic to import services that previously could be delivered only face to face: security guards could be replaced by CCTV cameras, and the feeds could conceivably be monitored from abroad.

Even so, many services in rich countries will continue to be provided by people. London's streets, hotels, hospitals and homes can only be cleaned on the spot. New York cabs and buses can be driven by people who live in New Jersey but not by those in New Delhi. The kids of Silicon Valley entrepreneurs can only be looked after by nannies who live in the Bay Area. Tables in Toronto restaurants can only be waited on locally, and sending the dishes to be washed overseas would hardly be economic. Streetlamps in Sydney can only be repaired by someone on a ladder under the lamp. Old people in Munich cannot be helped to cook and wash over the internet. Building materials can be imported, but houses must be built where they will stand. Parking tickets must still be given on the spot. Lawns cannot be mowed remotely. To some extent, teenagers and students can help with these tasks, although since Americans and Europeans are having fewer children, the number of young people in rich countries is set to fall too. In short, if North Americans,

Europeans and Australians are to specialise in higher-skilled jobs, these lower-skilled jobs must primarily be filled by immigrants.

For a rich-country government that is concerned solely with maximising the welfare of its own citizens, the economic benefits of immigration are analogous to those of international trade. In effect, immigration allows rich countries to import low-cost, low-skill, labour-intensive services from poor countries. By doing so, we reduce the cost of such services, which allows more people to benefit from them, while freeing up Americans and Europeans to pursue better-paid and more productive careers.

Consider how America, Europe and Australia benefit from international trade. Increasingly, we import goods and services from developing countries such as Brazil, China and India. We do so because it is relatively cheaper to produce beef in Brazil, computers in China and IT services in India than to try to produce everything ourselves. This makes us richer in three ways. First, it gives us a wider choice of cheaper products to consume, which means our wages stretch further, allowing us to buy more with the same income. Second, it frees up workers, capital and land for more productive uses. If we buy beef from Brazil, we need fewer farmers and less farmland. Our ex-farmers might open guesthouses instead, while their children will be free to move to the city to do whatever they please. Farmland might be turned over to retirement cottages, golf courses or nature reserves. If we buy computers from China, we need fewer factory workers and fewer factories. Factory workers might find a job in higher-skilled precision engineering or retrain to do something else. The money that was tied up in factories and ailing manufacturing companies can be reinvested in the industries of the future, like biotechnology and software. If we buy IT services from India, we need fewer back-office staff and fewer offices. Back-office staff might find secretarial or other administrative roles or they might retrain to work in marketing or customer services. The money that was tied up in back-office functions can be redeployed to the core elements of a business: researching and developing new products, for instance, or devising a clever new promotional campaign.

This continual redeployment of people and resources from less productive to more productive uses, whether within a country or between countries, creates economic growth, allowing our living standards to rise each year. The increased competition from abroad also brings with it new ideas and technologies, and spurs companies to continue innovating and raising their game, boosting economic growth year in year out. In a nutshell, international trade allows countries to specialise in what they do best and buy the rest for less from abroad, while competition forces companies to continually improve their performance – and thus our living standards. Thanks to the explosion in international trade since the Second World War, living standards in rich countries have more than trebled over that period.

When services can only be provided locally, immigration can deliver similar benefits to international trade. Americans and Europeans need not do them; Brazilians, Chinese and Indians can do them for less. For a Mexican arriving in the US with no qualifications, or an African arriving in the EU, a minimum-wage cleaning job is an attractive proposition. Even allowing for the higher cost of living in rich countries, a cleaning job pays much more than they could earn back in Mexico or Africa. Moreover, immigrants are less likely to find such work demeaning, since their expectations are lower than those of Americans and Europeans: their point of comparison is other immigrants or people back home. If they are earning enough to send money home to their family back in Mexico or Africa, they are more likely to feel proud of their new job than ashamed.

Because immigrants and natives have different sets of opportunities and expectations, both can benefit from immigration. Immigrants are happy to do the jobs that natives don't want to do at lower cost, allowing natives to concentrate on better-paid and more attractive jobs. Immigrants don't cost natives their jobs; they allow them to specialise in different ones. Because immigrants are willing to work at lower wages, many more unskilled jobs that would not otherwise exist are created. Remember that skilled jobs and unskilled jobs are complementary: more childminders enable more young parents to work in finance; hotel managers require more cleaners in order to manage their establishments efficiently; and immigrants spend money as well as earning it, thereby boosting domestic demand for goods and services and creating new jobs too.

Imagine for a moment that there were no immigrants at all in your country: none. No Filipino nannies, no Mexican kitchen staff, no Latvian waiters, no Ghanaian street-sweepers, no Turkish shop assistants. How much would you, or your children, need to be paid to convince you to take a job sweeping streets or cleaning toilets? Even if you were unemployed, you would be loath to take a job that you did not want to do, and for which you were overqualified. You would rather wait until a better job came along, surviving until then on welfare benefits, savings or with the help of your family. Vacancies for cleaning jobs coexist with unemployment in every rich country. At some price, though, you would probably agree to swallow your pride and sweep the streets. But you would hate it, and the cost of providing the service would be much higher. That would factor through into higher prices, or higher taxes, in the case of government-financed services. This would lower people's spending power, and in particular the demand for these more expensive, labour-intensive services. The streets might be cleaned just once a week rather than twice. People would eat out less and restaurants would make do with fewer waiters, lowering the quality of service. Only mothers with the highest earning prospects could opt to go back to work; or, in countries where the state subsidises childcare, its availability would doubtless be rationed. The upshot is that society as a whole would be much worse off, because the cost of labour-intensive services would be much higher, so we could afford fewer of them, and some people who could be doing more skilled jobs would be cleaning dishes, or forced to stay at home looking after their kids or parents.

The case of agriculture is different. If the cost of picking fruit by hand in California, Kent or Andalucia rose dramatically, much of the work could doubtless be mechanised, as it is in Australia. In any case, if the higher cost of picking fruit pushed up its price, we would doubtless import more of it from the developing world instead. So in this case, the choice is not between allowing in immigrants and doing the unpleasant jobs ourselves; it is between allowing in immigrants and importing fruit. Ironically, nationalists who might be keenest to keep out foreign labour may also be particularly reluctant to eat foreign fruit, while more liberal voices who might look more kindly on immigration would thereby help sustain domestic agriculture, even though they would have no problem with eating imported food.

How do the Japanese, who are viscerally opposed to immigration, cope? In part, they simply do without: no foreign nannies, for instance. They also pay a much higher price for services that are relatively cheap in America and Europe, such as eating out. Since their cost of living is much higher because of this, their standard of living is correspondingly lower. But increasingly, while the official policy of resisting immigration remains unchanged, Japan cheats: it brings in foreigners to do unskilled work through a variety of means.

Through the front door, it allows in the descendants of Japanese emigrants who moved to Brazil and Peru a century ago. It also admits 'entertainers', fragrant young ladies mainly from the Philippines and Thailand. Through the side door, it allows in 'trainees' and 'technical interns', young people mostly from China who earn a pittance working as unskilled labourers for up to three years. 'The idea of the trainee and technical intern system is the transfer of technology to developing countries, but the reality of many cases is a kind of rotation system for inviting cheap unskilled foreign workers,' says Atsushi Kondo of Kyushu Sangyo University.[20] Students in Japanese-language schools are also allowed to work on the side. Through the back door, many immigrants enter Japan legally as tourists, then work illegally and overstay. The government estimates there are only 220,000 illegal immigrants in the country, but experts think there are many more. Already the construction industry makes widespread use of immigrants, mostly from other Asian countries, to fill the most dangerous and low-paying jobs. 'We have already reached the point where the Japanese economy cannot function without foreign workers,' says Mioko Honda, a leader of the two-year-old Union of Migrant Workers. 'The construction companies use Thais and Filipinos by day, because they are inconspicuous, and Africans and others are used at night or in factory work.'[21] As Japan's population shrinks and continues to age over the next twenty years, the pressure to allow in more foreign workers openly or illicitly will only grow.

Skills bias

While rich countries remain set against low-skilled immigration, they are increasingly competing to attract highly skilled migrants, as I shall discuss further in the next chapter. But their lopsided immigration policies, in particular Australia's and Canada's skills obsession, actually exacerbate the shortage of unskilled workers. If governments allow in only highly skilled foreigners, then either local people will have to do the menial jobs or, more likely, the highly skilled foreigners will waste their talents on menial work. Predictably, in both Canada and Australia, highly skilled newcomers often have great difficulty finding jobs commensurate with their education and experience. Jane Cullingworth, the British-born executive director of Skills for Change, a Toronto-based organisation that helps skilled immigrants adapt to the local job market, points to the example of a Pakistani-born professor who could find work in Canada only as a security guard. 'When he was in Pakistan, the professor had his own security guard,' she says. 'But people make sacrifices for their kids.' Uzma Shakir, a fiery activist who runs CASSA, a support group for South Asian immigrants in Greater Toronto, rages that 'in Toronto we have the most educated and highly qualified cab-driving force. Every second one has a Ph.D. or a medical degree.' Mark Webster, of immigration agency Acacia Immigration, points to a similar problem in Sydney: 'Taxi drivers are mostly first-generation immigrants. They are people like Indian IT professionals who met the entry requirements but couldn't find jobs.'

Of course, Indian doctors may be better off financially driving cabs in Toronto or Sydney than practising medicine in Mumbai. Moreover, their kids may have much better prospects growing up in Canada or Australia than in India. But the immigrants may pay a heavy psychological price if they end up permanently stuck in jobs that do not match their abilities. At a wider level, it makes little economic sense for rich countries to spend a fortune trying to keep out people like Inmer who would be more than happy to do such low-skilled jobs while scouring the globe to recruit highly-skilled workers who end up having to do menial jobs instead.

In part, governments may simply not have thought through their policies properly. 'The Canadian government thinks: we don't want plumbers and carpenters,' says Uzma. 'Statistics Canada says we are shifting to being a knowledge-based economy. Workers need to be skilled even to be a cashier. Now that we are trying to attract highly skilled labour from Africa, Asia and South Asia, we think that only a Ph.D. can perform a technician's role. Middle-class people are prepared to work hard, but they don't want to be permanently declassed.' Glenn Withers of the Australian National University, an economist who used to advise the Australian government on immigration, is adamant that 'Australia needs balanced migration: at least fifty per cent skilled, but we also need to bring in unskilled workers through the humanitarian and family programmes, including to care for old people. Perhaps more guest-workers too, from diverse sources if society is welcoming.'

But government policies may also be deliberately designed to reassure voters who are wary about immigration. Letting in foreign graduates may seem less threatening than opening the door to the huddled masses. Better-educated immigrants may be expected to adapt better to rich-country societies. Thus rich-country governments may purposefully be seeking out highly-skilled immigrants to do the unskilled work that natives no longer want to do. Stepan Kerkyasharian, who runs the Sydney-based Community Relations Council for New South Wales, says that Australia needs a high level of immigration and, 'to make it marketable, we have a very strict skills requirement – for instance, only letting in people with a masters from a university with a good reputation'. Such a policy may benefit rich countries, but it is not so good for the immigrants themselves or for their countries of origin. It would be better if rich countries let in more low-skilled foreigners, but at the very least, the current policy ought to be made more explicit, so that highly-skilled immigrants who move to rich countries do so with their eyes open. They may still come, not least for their children's sakes, even if they know their own talents are going to be wasted.

Low-tech jobs in a high-tech world

We are forever being told that we live in an increasingly high-skilled, knowledge-based economy – and there is an element of truth to this. But the prosaic reality is that we have not eliminated drudgery and are unlikely ever to do so. The paradox of our high-tech world is that although technology permits us to travel in space, decipher the human genome and communicate globally and almost for free, it cannot perform some of the tasks that almost any human can do. But we can substitute foreign labour for our own, and thereby make everyone better off.

But isn't it demeaning to bring in immigrants to do the dirty, dangerous and ill-paid jobs that natives refuse to consider? Nigel Harris, the author of *Thinking the Unthinkable*, has an eloquent response to this: 'To insist on protecting someone's welfare by not allowing them to work when they are willing to, the work needs to be done and people gain both in the country where the immigrant works and where he or she is from, is perverse . . . One might as well argue that native workers should be less educated so that they would be willing to do the lousy jobs.'[22]

You may object that when immigrants move to rich countries, their aspirations change. The longer they stay, the less they will tolerate doing low-paid jobs for richer native-born people. And, of course, you would be right. When immigrants settle in a rich country, over time their earning power and expectations tend to rise. They master the local language, gain experience of local working practices and improve their skills more generally. Eventually, they may no longer wish to do menial work. And their kids certainly will not. After all, they will be native-born, and if they are forced to perform society's lowest tasks, they may end up as a resentful underclass.

But most people in poor countries aspire to work in rich countries only temporarily. They want to earn enough money to boost their standard of living back home, where the money they earn in America or Europe stretches much further. They may want to make enough to pay for their children's education, or to provide for their own old age. Or they may want to spend six months a year working in America or Europe and then go back home for the rest of the year to see their families. That is certainly what Inmer wants to do. But our immigration controls make this almost impossible. Since crossing the border is expensive and dangerous, once migrants have made it into America or the EU, they are reluctant to leave, because they know it will be equally hard to come back. So they end up staying longer than they originally intended and start to put down roots. Their thoughts turn to bringing their families over, rather than returning home. And thus they become permanent settlers, rather than temporary migrants, and they aspire to more in their new country than just work: they want a life there too.

This is perverse. I happen to think that having lots of foreign-born people in a country makes it more interesting and culturally rich. But many people do not. They would rather fewer foreigners settle in their homeland. And most migrants would rather not settle in a new country either, because they love their own: it is economic necessity, not a desire to uproot themselves, that typically drives them to migrate. But by voting for immigration controls that raise the costs and risks of migration but do not prevent it, voters end up making permanent settlers out of temporary migrants. If we made it almost impossible for commuters who lived in the suburbs to travel into the city to work each day, most would settle in the city centre – not because they wanted to, but because they had to in order to work.

Look at it another way. Big American and European companies regularly deploy their staff around the world. An American investment banker may spend a couple of years in Singapore, then three in London, then a year in Tokyo. Rarely will the American decide to settle permanently where he is posted. A Filipino cleaning company could do the same: send cleaners for a two-year stint cleaning offices in London, then a couple of years in Dubai and a few more in Hong Kong. A Mexican agricultural company could contract its staff to work for six months a year picking fruit in California, then bring them home. A

Russian building company could deploy its builders and decorators to work on contracts around Europe. Under such contracts, most temporary migrants would remain just that. They would be lower-skilled equivalents of American management consultants in London or Australian mining executives in Africa. Under such contracts, most of the political, social and cultural problems that many people attribute to migration would disappear: since few of the contract workers would settle, the local balance of the population would not change. Making this possible is relatively easy: it is a key demand of developing countries in the World Trade Organization's services negotiations. If we cannot countenance opening our borders to allow all but criminals and other undesirables to travel freely, then we should instead permit such temporary work schemes, which can provide many of the benefits of migration with less friction. But while rich countries press for developing countries to open their services markets to Western companies – to allow Wal-Mart to open supermarkets in India, for instance – they steadfastly refuse to allow Indian computer companies to deploy their staff in the US. Such protectionism is misguided.

Even if some migrants settle permanently, as they inevitably will, they will probably be happy to do unskilled jobs for many years, to the benefit of all. But, of course, the longer They stay, the more They start to become like Us. The challenge both for Them and for Us is to make this adjustment happen more smoothly, so that both parties feel comfortable with the change. Getting integration right is difficult, as I shall discuss in Chapter 14, but the added diversity that immigrants bring can be a boon rather than a burden.

4

The Global Talent Contest

The pros and cons of high-skilled migration

Harinder Takhar is the kind of person whom rich countries are increasingly competing to attract: highly educated, highly motivated – and from India. But when he arrived in Canada back in 1974, aged twenty-three and with hardly any money in his pocket, he found many doors slammed in his face. Employers were unimpressed with his masters degree in economics and political science from Punjab University. 'I came to Canada looking for a better future,' he says. 'But I didn't realise the challenges I would face.'

'After a while I felt lonely. I saw no future and I had no money. I wanted to go back to India. But, as I said, I had no money. I struggled. I took a job paying minimum wage filling in for a woman on maternity leave.' His Indian qualifications were not recognised in Canada, so he started working in a factory. ' "I'm going to succeed in this country," I said to myself. "I'll do whatever it takes,"' he recalls. 'I realised I needed Canadian qualifications and good Canadian experience.' So he studied for a professional qualification as a management accountant: 'For five years, I worked during the day and studied at night.' After he finished his studies, he juggled two jobs for many years, including driving taxis and teaching accountancy.

In 1982, he joined Timex Canada, where he rose to become the chief financial officer. Then he secured ever more senior positions in a succession of companies. In 1993, he became an entrepreneur, buying and turning around an ailing firm that had previously employed him, Chalmers Suspensions, which makes truck and trailer suspension systems and whose clients include Mercedes-Benz and Volvo. 'I was the company's first controller back in 1978,' he said, 'but I'd moved on to other things. Then I ran into one of my former colleagues at the grocery store several years later, and he told me that Chalmers wasn't doing very well. I was a little surprised, because I knew the potential of the technology they had.'[1] Soon he had bought four other companies, two of them in the United States. When he and his team took it over in 1993, Chalmers had twenty-three employees and sales of just C$2.7 million. By 2001 total employment for the Chalmers Group had risen to around 180 and sales had surpassed C$50 million. Exports had risen from less than half to more than three-quarters of sales. 'We export to the US, Mexico, Australia, New Zealand, India and several countries in Asia,' he says. 'As an immigrant, I thought beyond North America. We had a big project where the engineers said: "You can only do it this way." We brought in some engineers from abroad and our productivity went up 25 per cent in one month.'[2]

But Harinder Takhar is not just a successful entrepreneur and businessman. He is also the chairman and main fundraiser of a community-based provider of health and social services, as well as the chairman of a local hospital board. His community work has led him into politics, where in 2003 he won a seat in Ontario's provincial parliament representing Mississauga, a wealthy suburb of Toronto. He was immediately made minister of transport in the province's Liberal government and is therefore no longer directly involved with the Chalmers Group.

Unsurprisingly, he is a passionate advocate of skilled migration. 'It gives us access to a pool of talent not otherwise available,' he says. 'Half our engineers are foreign. They went to the very best schools. Thanks to them, productivity and quality are improved. It's a question of drive and sheer hard work. The construction industry in British Columbia is now owned by visible [non-white] immigrants. All taxi drivers and independent truck drivers are immigrants. I couldn't even get an interview in a bank when I arrived but now immigrants are very near the top.' His kids, though, are like many other Canadian-born kids: 'They don't have the same drive. They have a different outlook. They are more interested in quality of life, in material comforts.'

Immigrants come equipped with more than just their technical skills. They also bring with them their culture, their knowledge, their language, their experience of how business is done in their country – all valuable assets in a globalising world. 'Canadians don't travel much. They go to the US, maybe Mexico, maybe Europe,' Harinder remarks. 'Diversity is our window to the world.'

The global competition for skilled migration

Canada now actively seeks to recruit skilled workers from abroad. Immigrants must be highly educated and have flexible skills, with preference given to those who speak English or French. Investors, entrepreneurs and self-employed workers are also sought after. Canada let in 59,300 highly-skilled workers and businesspeople in 2004.[3] This compares with a US quota of H-1B visas, the main gateway for skilled migrants, of only

65,000 in 2004, which the US Senate voted to increase to 95,000 a year in November 2005.

Along with Canada, Australia is at the forefront of the global competition to attract highly skilled foreign workers. It holds recruitment fairs around the world, and workers can also apply directly. Prospective migrants are selected through a points system that rewards youth (over-forty-fives need not apply), knowledge of English, recognised skills (make sure Australia recognises your diploma) and work experience (not too much, though, or you'll be too old) in a painstakingly detailed list of skilled occupations. Over 66,000 workers were granted entry through the country's skilled-migrant programme in 2003, and some 47,000 came in on temporary visas that allow skilled workers to stay for up to four years, after which they can apply for permanent residency.[4]

Whereas Canada tries to attract foreigners with broad-based skills, the Australian government goes to absurd lengths to try to select the specific immigrants it thinks the economy needs. Its fiendishly complicated system is a bureaucrat's dream, and a boon for the army of immigration agents who help prospective applicants. Mark Webster, the genial head of Acacia Immigration, showed me the Australian Standard Classification of Occupations, a 700-page, 5-kilo volume that specifies the 986 occupations bureaucrats have identified in Australia. Only 399 of these potentially qualify you for a skilled migrant visa, if you can accumulate enough points on the other criteria. No luck? Then check the list of sixty-one occupations deemed to be in short supply nationally and the four separate lists of occupations deemed to be in demand in specific Australian states. If an employer is sponsoring your application, then consult the list of 515 occupations if you are applying for temporary residence, or a separate list of 478 if you are seeking permanent residence. 'Nobody knows why the lists should be different,' says Mark. If your relatives in Sydney are sponsoring your application, make sure you work in one of 102 privileged occupations. And if you are applying for a skilled independent regional visa, check out the many lists of local occupations in demand that are used by various regional sponsors. Confused? You should be. Perhaps mastering this labyrinthine immigration system is a skills test in itself.

Europe too is stirring. In 2005, the British government published a five-year plan that envisages creating a system modelled on Australian lines.[5] Points will be allocated according to qualifications, work experience, income and other factors deemed relevant. This will replace work permits – 89,000 of which were issued on a temporary but renewable basis in 2002,[6] mostly to skilled professionals and managers – as well as the 'highly skilled migrant programme', launched as recently as 2002 to attract workers with special skills and experience. Under the new plan, a top tier of highly skilled workers, such as doctors, engineers, finance experts and IT specialists, will be able to enter Britain without a job offer. They will be assessed on the basis of their degrees, work experience and current salaries, with additional points for those with skills in short supply. A second tier of skilled workers, such as nurses, teachers and administrators, will be able to come if they have a job offer in a shortage area, and where an employer cannot find the skills they require within Britain or the EU. Finally, there is a highly restricted third tier of low-skilled workers, although most of Britain's demand for these workers is expected to be met from central and eastern Europe for now. The plan says, 'Where additional needs are identified in future, we will introduce small tightly managed quota-based schemes for specific shortage areas and for fixed periods only, with guarantees that migrants will leave at the end of their stay.' Migrants may be required to post a financial bond that would be recoverable only when they left.

France has made it easier for graduates and other highly skilled people to enter the country, but few have come so far. In

2004, the Netherlands enacted a new law to let in 'knowledge migrants' for up to five years, albeit subject to tight restrictions. A successful applicant, along with their prospective Dutch employer, must prove that the job pays at least €45,000 (£30,000) per year (less if they are under thirty). By July 2005, only four hundred knowledge migrants had been granted entry. Even Germany, itself the target of recruitment campaigns by Australia, Canada and others as its economy has stagnated in recent years, is edging the door open for skilled migrants. A new law allows highly qualified workers from outside the EU, such as scientists or top-level managers, to obtain a residence permit of unlimited duration. But companies can only hire non-EU workers if there are no EU citizens available for the job. Entrepreneurs who invest at least a million euros in a new business that creates at least ten jobs will also be admitted.

At an EU-wide level, concern that skilled migrants prefer to move to the US, Canada and Australia has prompted the European Commission to propose a 'job-seeker's permit' that would allow highly skilled immigrants who receive the permit from any EU member state to work in any industry in all twenty-five EU countries. The plans – set out by Franco Frattini, the EU's justice commissioner, in November 2005 – would also make it easier for non-EU citizens working for European companies to travel between their employers' European offices. But although EU countries have agreed to move towards common policies on immigration, many member states believe that such laws should remain the prerogative of national governments.

Competition for foreign university students is also hotting up. The US has long been the destination of choice for foreign students, many of them from India and China, and until recently America welcomed them with open arms, conscious that most end up staying and making a big contribution to the US economy. But since the US tightened up its visa policy in the aftermath of 9/11, making it harder for students from some countries to enter, numbers enrolling in US universities have stagnated. Even so, in 2003, 586,000 foreigners studied in US universities.[7] Britain ranked second that year, with 255,000 foreign students keen to take advantage of tuition in English at a lower cost than in the US in 2003. The year before, Britain had made it easier for foreigners to come and study – science, mathematics and engineering, in particular – and then stay and work. Germany, which attracted 241,000 foreign students in 2003, is now allowing them to stay in the country for a year after finishing their studies to look for a job. In 1998, France eased its admission rules for foreign students, whose numbers have since nearly trebled to 222,000 by 2002, with most of the increase coming from Africa and China.[8] The number of foreign students in Australia soared to 188,000 in 2003 – nearly one in five of the total student population – after the government made it easier for them to stay and work after they graduate. Canada is also making it easier for foreign students enrolled in the country (69,000 of them in 2002) to work there after they finish their degree, while Japan (87,000) and Spain (54,000) are also attracting many more students from overseas.

So who is ahead in the global brain race? In terms of sheer numbers, the United States is streets ahead. By 2000, it had attracted 10,354,000 highly-skilled immigrants and lost only 431,000 US graduates overseas, giving a net brain gain of ten million.[9] But relative to the large population of working-age Americans, its net brain-gain rate of 5.4 per cent leaves it in third place.[10] In second place is its northern neighbour. Although 516,000 highly skilled Canadians have emigrated – many of them to the US – 2,742,000 foreign graduates have arrived, a net brain-gain rate of 10.7 per cent. In the lead so far is Australia. It has notched up a net gain of 1,423,000 talented workers – 1,540,000 immigrants less 117,000 emigrants – a net brain-gain rate of 11.4 per cent. The only other countries with significant net brain-gain rates are Switzerland (3.8 per cent), New Zealand

(2.9 per cent), and Sweden (2.3 per cent). The EU as a whole isn't in the race at all – with immigrants and emigrants almost evenly balanced – while Britain hasn't even reached the starting post. Although it has attracted 1,257,000 highly-skilled foreigners, 1,441,000 British graduates are currently working overseas, giving a net brain *loss* of 0.5 per cent.

Benefits of skilled migration

Skilled migration can bring three main benefits. First, foreigners may have different skills and qualities – or superior ones. According to an old joke, in heaven the cooks are French, the police are British, the mechanics are German, the lovers are Italian, and everything is organised by the Swiss; in hell the cooks are British, the police are German, the mechanics are French, the lovers are Swiss, and everything is organised by the Italians. If these national stereotypes were correct, and the French were particularly talented cooks, for instance, then it would make sense for France to specialise in training chefs and export some of them. But not all cooks are the same, and if Americans also like Asian cuisine, they might also want to import chefs from Asia. Moreover, a bubbling pot of immigrants from around the world may inspire innovative fusion cooking that blends the best of national cuisines in appetising new ways, like at the famous Asia de Cuba restaurants. Another useful skill that immigrants have is knowledge of their country of origin, which can be a big help for local companies who want to export there. And since, as Harinder Takhar puts it, 'immigrants bring a burning desire to succeed and make themselves', foreigners can boost productivity and economic growth – especially if the extra competition they bring spurs locals to up their game too.

Second, talented foreigners may boost innovation, the elixir of long-term economic growth in rich countries. US universities attract the world's top graduate students in science and engineering: in some leading engineering schools, foreigners account for nearly four-fifths of doctoral students. A recent study found that a 10 per cent rise in the share of foreign graduate students tends to increase total US patent applications by 4.8 per cent and patent grants earned by universities by 6 per cent. It also raises patent grants earned by others (mostly commercial firms) by 6.8 per cent, as foreign graduate students who stay on in the US add to the productivity of the wider economy. More generally, a 10 per cent rise in the number of skilled immigrants as a share of the US labour force tends to increase future patent applications by 0.8 per cent and university patent grants by 1.3 per cent.[11]

Third, in industries where companies tend to cluster together in a single location – think of the City of London or Silicon Valley – there are big benefits to drawing on as wide a pool of talent as possible. As technology and government policy help fuse previously national markets into a single global one, the pattern of production is changing. Some of it is dispersed around the world: computers that were once made entirely in the US from US components are now assembled in China from parts made in Taiwan, South Korea, Costa Rica and elsewhere. Some of it becomes increasingly concentrated in one location: French shares, German bonds and Japanese yen that were once traded primarily in Paris, Frankfurt and Tokyo, respectively, are now mainly traded in London; a merger between a Canadian and a French company may be planned and implemented by bankers and lawyers in New York; fashion houses congregate in Paris; filmmakers in Hollywood.

Clustering together

One of the paradoxes of globalisation is that it sometimes reinforces the importance of geography: although industries might now conceivably locate anywhere, they often cluster in particular places. Why? Because although it is costly for an individual company to set up shop somewhere – since it has to invest in training workers and developing a local network of suppliers, for instance – once this initial investment has been made, it is much cheaper for the business to expand in the same place, and for other companies to locate near by. These economies of scale encourage industry to locate in a single place through a virtuous circle: as the industry grows, costs fall, and falling costs encourage further growth. Geographical clusters soon benefit from some hefty advantages: a large pool of skilled workers for companies to choose from as well as a wide range of companies for workers to apply to; a broad network of suppliers and specialised services; and a healthy exchange of ideas and information, which stimulates technical progress. Globalisation can reinforce this clustering effect, because as transport costs and trade barriers fall, so do the impediments to serving not just a single country but a continent or even the whole world from one location.

Because money can now be moved freely around the world, London has become a global financial centre as well as a national and regional one. Yet London's global dominance also depends on its openness to foreigners. It thrives on the mix of talent drawn from around the globe, continuously rubbing shoulders with each other, sparking off each other and driving each other forward. If London-based companies had to rely solely on a British workforce, they would be at a disadvantage if firms locating elsewhere – in New York, for instance – could draw on a wider pool of talent. And as the number of graduates in developing countries rises, it is increasingly important for London to be able to attract talent from poor countries as well as rich ones. In short, London's global dominance in certain industries, notably finance, has come about because it has allowed the best in the business to congregate there; had it tried to exclude foreigners, or were it to try to do so in future, they would most likely eventually gather elsewhere. One reason why Tokyo has failed to rival London or New York is precisely because of its insularity. The cornerstone of London's success, and that of other dynamic cities of the future, is its continuing openness to foreigners. And because skilled migration exacerbates the shortage of low-skilled workers, London also depends on the immigration of low-skilled workers.

When I asked Jo Valentine, the chief executive of London First, a group that represents businesses based in the capital, how important to London's success immigrants are, she replied: '[They] are part of the fabric of London. Historically it was a world port, now it is a world airport. It is almost impossible to separate immigrants from normal life. I couldn't imagine London without immigrants. The city needs to be permanently challenged and reinventing itself.' A quarter of the people working in London – nearly two million people – were born overseas. Highly-skilled immigrants are 'essential to keep at the forefront of being globally competitive', she says.

The same is true of Hollywood. If the US film industry relied solely on American actors and directors, other clusters might arise to challenge its dominance. But it is precisely because Hollywood is not fussy about the national origins of its stars and filmmakers that its position is almost unassailable. The best and brightest from around the world are drawn to the bright lights of Hollywood instead of filmmaking being dispersed to different countries. Even Paris is bowing to the logic of globalisation, as – *quelle horreur!* – foreign designers, such as the American Marc Jacobs at Louis Vuitton and John Galliano, an Englishman, at Christian Dior, are drafted in to revitalise venerable old French fashion houses.

But perhaps the most interesting example of how globalisation and migration feed off each other is Silicon Valley.

The valley of opportunity

Most people think of Silicon Valley as the epitome of the US's high-tech superiority. But it is actually a global cluster that brings together the best of America – deep-pocketed investors prepared to take a punt on new ventures; top universities that encourage their students to put their research ideas into practice; and a favourable business and legal climate that fosters entrepreneurship – with the cream of the world's talent. Scan down the roll-call of Silicon Valley's success stories and most of them involve foreigners. I have already mentioned Google, whose co-founder is Russian-born. The co-founder of the internet portal Yahoo!, Jerry Yang, is a Taiwanese-American who moved to California when he was ten. Andy Grove, the co-founder of Intel, the world's leading computer chip-maker, is a Hungarian-American. The founder of eBay, Pierre Omidyar, was born in Paris to an Iranian father and a French mother. Hotmail, the leading web-based email service, was co-founded by Sabeer Bhatia, who came to the US from India in 1988 with $200 in his pocket; he sold Hotmail to Microsoft ten years later for $10 million. Likewise, Oracle, Solectron, Cirrus Logic and hundreds of other firms all have at least one foreign founder. Sun Microsystems, which makes UNIX computers and servers as well as the Java language which is the platform for so much of the internet, was co-founded by Andy (Andreas) von Bechtolsheim, who was born and studied in Germany, and Vinod Khosla, an Indian venture capitalist.

Khosla also helped found The Indus Entrepreneur (TiE), a global network of technology entrepreneurs and professionals that helps them start their own businesses by mobilising information, know-how, skill and capital through networking events, education and training, and mentoring. TiE, which was started in 1993, now has forty-two local chapters in nine countries and 10,000 members, 85 per cent of them South Asian.

'We have created jobs and whole industries,' boasts Seshan Rammohan, who runs the Silicon Valley chapter of TiE and himself studied first in India and then in the States. It is hard to argue when one learns that a TiE charter member wrote the $100,000 cheque that got Google started in another TiE member's garage.

I ask Seshan why immigrants have been so successful in the Valley. 'Indians and Chinese are entrepreneurial by nature,' he replies. 'The new ingredient is that Indian institutes of technology are churning out science and technology graduates. They have loads of energy and intelligence but the local economy in India couldn't absorb them: if they stayed in India they would be underemployed. So they do their graduate studies in the US and then stay and work for US companies. Then, when it became fashionable for technical people to start companies in the Valley, they were in a prime position to do so.' The combination of foreign drive and the entrepreneurial environment of the Valley has been crucial. 'The environment fostered it: they want to prove something, to do something better, they all believe in it,' says Seshan. 'But the immigrants also helped create that environment. HP is local and to a certain extent Apple is too, but almost every other firm isn't.' In short, Silicon Valley wouldn't be the hub of the global technology industry were it not for immigrants – who are also helping it develop trading and investment spokes across the Pacific.

AnnaLee Saxenian, a professor of city and regional planning at the University of California at Berkeley, has highlighted the importance of immigrants to Silicon Valley's success. By the end of the 1990s, Chinese and Indian engineers were running 29 per cent of the Valley's technology businesses. By 2000, these companies collectively accounted for more than $19.5 billion in sales and 73,000 jobs. Moreover, the pace of immigrant entrepreneurship has accelerated dramatically in the past decade. 'Far from simply replacing native workers, foreign-born engineers are starting new businesses and generating jobs and wealth at least as fast as their US counterparts,' she says.[12]

The Valley's high-tech immigrants have succeeded in part thanks to networks like TiE, the Silicon Valley Chinese Engineers Association and the Korean IT Forum, which provide contacts and resources for recently arrived immigrants. Foreign-born engineers and scientists see themselves as outsiders to the mainstream technology community, and such organisations help them overcome some of the hurdles they face. But although many immigrants socialise mainly within their own ethnic networks, they routinely work with US engineers and US-run businesses. 'Recognition is growing within these communities that although a start-up might be spawned with the support of the ethnic networks, it must become part of the mainstream to grow,' says Saxenian. 'The most successful immigrant entrepreneurs in Silicon Valley today appear to be those who have drawn on ethnic resources while simultaneously integrating into mainstream technology and business networks.'

But perhaps the most interesting and positive aspect of these new entrepreneurial networks is that they are fostering new trading links between the United States and Asia, and new businesses in immigrants' countries of origin. TiE not only brings together budding immigrant entrepreneurs in the US, but also connects them with businesspeople back home in India, providing local producers with the information and contacts they need to participate in the increasingly global economy. Seshan points out that US companies that once outsourced the manufacture of semiconductors to Taiwan and Korea now do so to India and mainland China, with TiE playing a vital role in putting together business partners.

'The dynamism of emerging regions in Asia and elsewhere now draws skilled immigrants homeward,' says Saxenian. 'Even when they choose not to return home, they are serving as middlemen linking businesses in the United States with those in distant regions.' Taiwanese engineers in Silicon Valley work closely with their counterparts back in Taiwan, while Indian engineers help US companies link up with low-cost software expertise in India. 'These cross-Pacific networks give skilled immigrants a big edge over mainstream competitors who often lack the language skills, cultural know-how and contacts to build business relationships in Asia,' she says.

Miin Wu came to the US from Taiwan in the early 1970s to study electrical engineering. After earning his doctorate from Stanford University, he decided to stay in America, where he could put his skills to better use. He worked his way up several semiconductor companies in Silicon Valley, including Intel, and co-founded a firm called VLSI Technology. In the late 1980s, when Taiwan's economy had developed dramatically, he decided to return home. In 1989 he set up one of the country's first semiconductor companies, Macronix, as well as becoming an active member of Silicon Valley's Monte Jade Science and Technology Association, which was building business links between the two technical communities in the Valley and Taiwan. In 1996 Macronix became the first Taiwanese company to list on Nasdaq, the US stock exchange for high-tech companies. It is now the world's ninth-biggest supplier of flash memory (used to store information on devices such as Apple's iPod Nano) and has nearly 4,000 employees. Although its manufacturing facilities and most of its workforce are in Taiwan, it has an advanced design and engineering centre in Silicon Valley, and a Macronix venture-capital fund invests in promising start-ups in both the Valley and Taiwan to develop technologies related to their core business. In short, Miin Wu's activities bridge and benefit the Taiwanese and Silicon Valley economies.

When we think about globalisation, we tend to think of colossal companies like Microsoft and Coca-Cola bestriding the earth. But increasingly, falling transport and communication costs are allowing small companies to operate internationally, too. To do this, though, they need to find reliable foreign partners and then manage complex business relationships across cultural and linguistic barriers – and immigrants can provide that vital missing link. Silicon Valley start-ups are often global companies from day one: many raise capital from Asian sources, subcontract manufacturing to Taiwan, rely on software development in India and sell their products in Asian markets. 'The challenge is keenest in high-tech industries whose products, markets, and technologies are continually being redefined – and whose product cycles are exceptionally short,' says Saxenian. 'For them, first-generation immigrants like the Chinese and Indian engineers of Silicon Valley, who have the language, cultural, and technical skills to thrive in both the United States and foreign markets, are invaluable. Their social structures enable even the smallest producers to locate and maintain collaborations across long distances and gain access to Asian capital, manufacturing capabilities, skills and markets.' These ties have measurable economic benefits. Saxenian calculates that for every 1 per cent increase in the number of first-generation immigrants from a given country, California's exports to that country rise by nearly 0.5 per cent. California exports nearly four times more to countries in the Asia-Pacific than to comparable countries elsewhere.

Silicon Valley can also bring together immigrants from different countries, allowing individual companies to take advantage of, for instance, India's software talent and Taiwan's manufacturing excellence. Along with other Indians, Mahesh Veerina started Ramp Networks in 1993. Their aim was to develop low-cost devices to speed internet access for small businesses. Short on money, they soon decided to hire programmers in India for a quarter of the Silicon Valley rate. By 1999 Ramp had sixty-five employees in Santa Clara and twenty-five in India. Having used his Indian background to link California with India, Veerina then met two principals of a Taiwanese investment fund, InveStar. In less than three months, he had set up partnerships with three Taiwanese manufacturers to ramp up production of Ramp's routers. (It took nine months to establish a similar partnership with a US manufacturer.) The Taiwanese price per unit was around half what Ramp was paying for manufacturing in the States, and Ramp increased its output a hundredfold because of relationships Veerina established with key customers in the Taiwanese computer industry. Ramp also opted to use the worldwide distribution channels of its Taiwanese partners, and when the firm designed a new model, the Taiwanese manufacturer was prepared to ship product in two weeks, rather than the six months it would have taken in the US. Veerina puts his success down to InveStar's partners and their network of contacts in Taiwan. In a business where product cycles are often shorter than nine months, the speed and cost savings that they provided were critical competitive advantages.

As Silicon Valley's skilled Chinese and Indian immigrants create social and economic links to their home countries, they also open up foreign markets and identify manufacturing options and technical skills in Asia for US business more generally. Ever more US companies now turn to India for software programming and development talent and Taiwan for manufacture of semiconductors and other components – and these distant resources are now just as accessible to start-ups like Ramp as to more established companies. These new international links are boosting the US economy while providing fresh opportunities for once-peripheral Pacific economies.

Silicon Valley's example highlights how the simplistic suspicion of critics of immigration – are foreigners poaching our jobs? – is increasingly outdated. In a globalising economy, trade and investment require people as well as products to move, and people moving in turn stimulates new trade and investment. Likewise, where immigrants foster innovation, either within existing organisations or by creating new ones, they benefit the economy more broadly. Our old-fashioned way of thinking conditions us to think of people as belonging to countries, so that one country's gain is another's loss. In fact, people can move around the world producing economic gains in several countries. Such benefits are in no way limited to Silicon Valley. Look at how Harinder Takhar has boosted Canadian exports. Consider how many foreigners have set up global hedge funds and private-equity groups in London's St James's. And see how Australia's Chinese community has created new trade links with East Asia.

Prompted in part by America's technology boom, the leaders of the European Union agreed at their Lisbon summit in 2000 a raft of reforms that aimed to make the EU the most dynamic and competitive economy in the world by 2010. Many of these reforms are sensible, although in many areas governments have so far failed to deliver on their ambitious targets. Noticeably absent from their plans, however, were reforms to encourage freer immigration, even though it is clearly an essential ingredient of America's remarkable high-tech success. Europe has only grudgingly made it easier for highly-skilled foreigners to come work; it has certainly not sought to welcome them. When in 2000 Germany's chancellor, Gerhard Schröder, proposed granting temporary work permits to Indian computer specialists, a leading opposition politician replied that Germany needed '*Kinder statt Inder*': more children instead of Indians. Funnily enough, Germany failed to fill even its meagre visa quota: Indian computer experts generally opted to go to the US instead.

A paper produced in 2000 for a meeting of ministers from the OECD, the Paris-based think-tank for rich-country governments, argued:

> While openness to immigration is therefore generally needed, highly skilled personnel, such as good scientists and entrepreneurs, are even more in demand. A country

> that can attract and retain such people may be at an advantage in an economy where innovation and new firms are necessary to success . . . There are indications that the United States was able to sustain rapid growth in the ICT [information and communication technology] sector, particularly in the software segment where human capital is the key input, by tapping into international sources of skilled workers. Immigration may therefore be one of the factors that have enabled the US boom to continue, as it filled some of the most urgent skill needs. The United States attracted skilled workers to the country, and US firms went overseas to access the required skills. A quarter of Microsoft's employees are foreign-born.[13]

Powerful stuff from a quasi-governmental body – yet such is the hostility to immigration in some quarters that the topic was quietly dropped from subsequent recommendations.

The Australian model?

Foreigners with different skills, new ideas and complementary talents may be a boon. But rich countries' skills-based immigration policies do not always make sense. As we saw in the previous chapter, if countries admit only highly-skilled workers, they will exacerbate the shortage of low-skilled workers. But more generally, are governments capable of correctly picking the people that an economy needs? In short, is a highly selective skills-focused immigration policy like Australia's really a good model for the world to adopt – as many people suggest – or is there a better way?

The man in charge of developing and implementing Australia's immigration policy, Abul Rizvi, is convinced that his country is on the right track. Rizvi has an interesting background: a Shia Muslim born in India, he came to Australia in 1966 aged seven as the country was taking the first steps to dismantling its infamously racist White Australia policy. 'That year Australia admitted twenty-eight non-European skilled migrants – and six of them were my parents and immediate family,' he says. 'My mother, who had grown up in rural India, felt isolated living in Australia, but I felt incredibly accepted, even though I was the only Asian in the whole school I went to in Canberra.'

The overarching aim of Australia's immigration policy, Rizvi explains, is to offset the decline of its native population. Like people in other rich countries, Australians are not having enough kids to replace the existing workforce. 'Within five to ten years the working-age population will start declining,' he says, 'so immigration will make up more than 100 per cent of the growth in the labour force.' But the benefits of immigration are economic as well as demographic. 'We need to recruit highly skilled young people to fill skills shortages,' he says. 'Immigrants also support the development of trade links. And cultural diversity helps Australian companies understand different markets and compete more effectively.' Letting in young, English-speaking, highly skilled immigrants will make Australia richer and boost its public finances, he argues, pointing to a study commissioned by his department which suggests that Australia's shift to a skills-focused immigration policy will boost GDP per person by 0.7 per cent (A$247 a year) between 2000–1 and 2007–8.[14]

Fair enough, but what about the absurdly complicated points system? Can government bureaucrats really know exactly which workers Australia needs? 'Points are only one dimension of policy,' Rizvi replies, adding that thanks to what he calls the 'refinement' of the points test, immigrants are now finding jobs with greater ease. But doesn't the country need low-skilled workers to do the jobs that Australians no longer want to do, such as looking after its swelling ranks of old people? 'We don't want to surrender in terms of unskilled workers,' he answers, unconsciously hinting at fears that the world's poor are an invading army. 'We have a very large offshore refugee intake who tend to do unskilled jobs and we also have working holidaymakers and students. There is pressure from industry for unskilled workers. Maybe in twenty years we'll need to bring them in.'

What Rizvi says is not quite true: Australia admits only 12,000 refugees a year, and many of them are skilled. As for working holidaymakers – such as young Britons spending a year visiting Australia and working to fund their travels – they are unlikely to want to tend to the old and the sick, sweep streets or clean toilets. Peter Costello, Australia's finance minister, hinted as much, when he suggested in October 2005 that the country should consider allowing in less skilled migrants too.[15]

Serendipity

If Leonid Dinevich had tried to migrate to Australia, his application would surely have been turned down. Red Army generals hardly rank high on its list of sought-after occupations, and his age, fifty, would in any case have disqualified him. But Israel welcomed him with open arms – and he has amply repaid his new country's faith.

Back in the Soviet Union, General Dinevich, a specialist in atmospheric physics, was in charge of the 'Militarised Service for Active Influence on Hydro-Meteorological Phenomena', a secretive project that focused on cloud seeding, a human attempt to play God with the weather. 'We tried to protect crops from bad weather, like hail, by using radar stations, rockets and aeroplanes,' he explains. 'We made it rain more, we reduced the cloud cover at airports, and so on.' It was a mammoth endeavour. 'I had several thousand people working for me and I reported directly to the deputy chairman of the Soviet Union's council of ministers.' Bursting with pride, he shows me a picture of himself in full army uniform.

But as the Soviet Union started to fall apart and nationalist fervour rekindled in Moldova, the small ex-Soviet state bordering Romania where the project was based, a resurgence of anti-Semitism made Leonid and other Jews feel unsafe. 'People started leaving for Israel in 1990,' he says. 'I could have just ignored the anti-Semitism. I was in a position of authority, after all. I was even a deputy of the city parliament in Kishinev [the capital of Moldova]. But I thought of my family and decided to leave.' So he gathered together over a hundred family members and together they left for Israel in 1991, leaving behind everything except for some clothes, furniture and a few books. I never thought I would empathise with the plight of a former Soviet general, but I found myself warming to Leonid. 'Even though we weren't forced to sink or swim, it was tough when we arrived in Israel,' he continues. 'Before I had felt needed – and suddenly I was no use to anyone. I had been the pillar supporting my family, yet here [in Israel] I couldn't help anyone.' The Israeli government provides all immigrants with Hebrew lessons and a basket of benefits for the first two years. With the money, Leonid and his family rented a flat in Jaffa, just south of Tel Aviv on the Mediterranean coast, and tried to start a new life. But what would he do for a living? 'The Israeli army had no need for someone like me,' he sighs.

But then Leonid's luck turned. Through a professor at Hebrew University who knew him from his Soviet days, he met Yossi Leshem, an ornithologist who had just finished his dissertation on the radar tracking of birds. The university and Yossi needed a radar station in order to track clouds and birds, and Leonid knew just where to find one at a knock-down price. 'There is an old Russian saying that it is better to have a hundred friends than a hundred roubles,' he says with a smile – especially when roubles were by then virtually worthless. Leonid managed to acquire a Soviet-era radar station for a fraction of its market price and brought it to Israel. But despite all Leonid's efforts, and to his great frustration, Yossi's project did not get off the ground for a further three years, as the birdwatcher struggled to raise enough money and find a suitable site. 'It was a bitter pill to swallow,' says Leonid. 'I was no longer receiving benefits from the government so I had barely enough money to live on.' Eventually, though, Yossi succeeded and Leonid now tracks birds for a living, selling the information on their flight paths and migration patterns to the Israeli defence ministry, so that military planes can avoid flying into them. Call it serendipity, but thanks to an ex-Soviet general, birds in Israel are now better protected than before – and Leonid has found a new purpose in life.

No bureaucrat could have guessed how Leonid's area of expertise was going to benefit his new country, but immigrants often benefit countries in unexpected ways: remember Gulam Noon and his Indian food. Consider too how the Jewish diaspora from Germany and central Europe enriched the countries they fled to before and after the Second World War, especially the United States. Would similar migrants be admitted nowadays? Or look at how the Hong Kong Chinese who were shunned by Britain have prospered in Canada. Mark Webster of Acacia Immigration points out that nearly all of the people on the *Business Review Weekly*'s list of the five hundred richest people in Australia are immigrants, notably refugees admitted after the Second World War. 'They wouldn't get in nowadays,' he says pointedly. 'They wouldn't fit the pattern for any skills we want.'

Reasons to doubt

Australia's skills-based immigration policy is particularly flawed. Governments simply do not have enough information to know exactly which workers the economy needs at any given time.

Moreover, the economy is forever changing, and with it the demand for specific skills. So any government assessment, however accurate, of what skills are required will almost immediately be out of date; nor can it know how migrants might eventually contribute. If governments are going to try to select skilled workers at all, it makes more sense to do it as Canada does, by admitting highly educated people with flexible skills, than by the Australian method of trying to identify exactly which slots need filling and then matching prospective migrants to those vacancies. Workers with broad and transferable skills can more readily adapt to the changing pattern of demand than workers with highly specific skills that might soon no longer be needed. 'It's better to go for broad-based labour-force enhancement than specific targets,' says Glenn Withers of the Australian National University. 'The government is not able to identify well the right people at the right time. Skills assessment was previously broad-based, but now the pressure to micro-manage is irresistible for governments and bureaucrats – and they are not good at it.'

But it's not just trying to pick and choose workers with specific skills that is misguided. Rich countries' focus on skilled immigration in general is also misplaced. As I argued in the previous chapter, its basic premise – high-skilled immigration good; low-skilled immigration bad – is incorrect: rich countries need low-skilled immigrants to do the jobs that locals are no longer prepared to do. Moreover, the notion that governments should try to select immigrants at all is highly questionable.

In the short term, it might make sense to import foreign workers to meet shortages of specific skills. Demand in the US for Arabic-speakers and Middle East specialists has soared since 9/11, for instance. Companies are also scrambling to hire internet-security specialists who can protect their computer systems against hackers and viruses. Britain's huge increase in healthcare spending since Labour took over in 1997 has created an even greater need for doctors and nurses. When there is some slack in the economy, part of this extra demand can be met nationally: existing workers can work longer hours, unemployed workers can be hired, and to some extent workers can shift between occupations after a little retraining. But often the extra demand cannot be wholly met by locals, so it makes sense to draft in foreigners to help out temporarily. Russian-speakers cannot suddenly become fluent in Arabic; their knowledge of Kremlin politics cannot be converted into instant expertise on Iraq; doctors' training takes years; and so on. Foreigners can help plug the gaps.

In the longer term, though, it is not always obvious that importing foreign specialists is preferable to training or retraining local ones. Yes, it will almost certainly be cheaper and easier to bring in Arabists from the Middle East than to teach enough Americans to be proficient in Arabic and the ins and outs of Palestinian politics. But it might make more sense to train internet-security specialists and doctors locally. In a genuinely global labour market, the market would match up workers and jobs – with a little help from governments where problems arise. But when labour markets are segmented along national lines, with quotas for some workers and enticements for others to migrate, governments are in effect trying to second-guess the market – and inevitably they do not have enough information to get it right.

Doctors are a good example of how the best remedy for a shortage of highly-skilled workers is not necessarily to encourage them to come from abroad. Many rich countries face a shortage of doctors and so seek to recruit them from poor ones. For developing countries, this raises tricky questions about the potentially harmful impact of this brain drain of skilled professionals, who are already desperately rare in the poorest countries (an issue I shall consider in Chapter 9). For rich countries, the issue is different. While it clearly makes sense to import foreign staff to meet a temporary shortage of doctors, allowing patients who would otherwise languish on a waiting list to be treated quickly, does it make sense to import foreign doctors on a permanent basis? For sure, if doctors are trained abroad, rich countries can economise on the vast costs of their education. But the quality of care that foreign doctors deliver may be inferior if they are not as well trained as Western ones. Local talent might also be going to waste. It depends on the alternative careers available to potential medics, and how productive they might be in them. If rich countries allowed in more low-skilled migrants, or more foreign professionals in occupations that potential medics might otherwise choose, perhaps more natives would opt to train as doctors.

It seems odd that rich countries are importing foreign doctors, since they would appear to have a comparative advantage in medicine: they have a bigger pool of skilled talent, medical colleges with better facilities, and the most advanced research labs. One might therefore expect them to be exporting medical services – as they do when rich foreigners seek treatment at American or European hospitals – rather than importing them.

The issue is further complicated by the level of government intervention, in European healthcare in particular. As the main medical employer in Britain, for instance, the government-funded and largely state-run National Health Service has used its market power to depress doctors' wages artificially, just as a monopoly producer can use its market dominance to push up prices. Britain's shortage of doctors therefore partly reflects the fact that the market is rigged: low wages have driven many British doctors to work abroad and deterred many potential medics from studying medicine.

The RSA study sheds some light on this complicated picture.[16] Around 40 per cent of vacancies in the healthcare sector are due to skills shortages. Britain has not been producing – or retaining – enough medical staff to meet its needs. Over half the newly registered doctors in 1992–2002 qualified outside Britain. Likewise, over two-fifths of newly registered nurses since 1999 have come from outside Britain. The proportion of doctors who qualified domestically has decreased from 76.3 per cent in 1993 to 70.6 per cent in 2003 – and in 2004 alone, the UK lost nearly ten thousand physicians to the US, Canada and Australia. Only a third of junior doctors who graduated from British medical schools in 1999 said that they definitely intended to practise medicine in Britain. Over 40,000 nursing staff left the NHS in 2004. Moreover, many South Asian doctors who immigrated in the 1960s and 1970s are now retired or approaching retirement age. They tend to work in deprived inner-city areas and in specialties such as geriatrics that most new doctors find unappealing and inferior. Medically qualified refugees and asylum seekers are currently an untapped resource: of the 1,000 or so in the country, only around 160 work in the NHS.

The NHS recently increased medical schools' intake by 1,000 places a year to 6,000, and has boosted the number of nurses entering training by 57% since 1997. The private sector has also recognised the need for more medical training. But the expansion and improvement of the NHS, combined with an ever richer and older population, will continue to boost demand for healthcare workers, while working-time regulations reduce the number of hours that junior doctors are required to work. Projections commissioned by the Home Office suggest that over the next twenty years Britain will need an extra 300,000 or so healthcare workers, including 62,000 more doctors, 108,000 more nurses, 45,000 more professionally qualified therapists and scientists, and 74,000 more healthcare assistants. Despite increased training and recruitment, shortages of 10,000 nurses and 25,000 doctors are anticipated for 2020. Some of this demand could be met by patients being treated abroad, but most will require an infusion of immigrants – or greater inducements to British people to train and remain working in the NHS.

So should Britain be importing foreign doctors? It is almost impossible to say. Perhaps Britons do not have a particular aptitude for medicine, or prefer to work in other fields. If so, it makes sense to bring in doctors from other countries. But who knows whether enough Britons would opt to train as doctors and remain in the NHS if doctors' wages rose to internationally competitive levels – as is slowly starting to happen – and if Britain's labour market were generally open to all comers?

The bigger point is that if workers could move freely around the world, the market would generally match people and jobs efficiently, but when governments intervene selectively, obstructing some workers from moving while actively encouraging others to do so, the market becomes distorted. Just imagine if governments tried to plan how workers were allocated within an economy, deciding which could move from Oklahoma to California and which could not, setting quotas for the number of software engineers that Oregon could import from Massachusetts, or mandating that fast-food employees could work only in the state where they were born. The Soviet Union tried to do that – and look what happened. Governments simply don't have enough information to make such judgements, especially since the labour market is continually changing, nor do they have the proper incentives to get it right. In the same way, governments' attempts to second-guess companies' and countries' foreign-labour needs will almost inevitably be wrong – and potentially very costly. If they are going to place restrictions on immigration at all, it would generally be better if they did not discriminate arbitrarily between different types of worker and if they used flexible taxes instead of fixed quotas, an issue I shall discuss in greater depth later.

5

Cosmopolitan and Rich

The economic benefits of diversity

> The mind is but a barren soil; a soil which is soon exhausted, and will produce no crop, or only one, unless it be continually fertilised and enriched with foreign matter.
>
> Joshua Reynolds[1]

> Strangers instinctively question things that natives take for granted. They stimulate new perspectives because, simply, many things strike them as odd or stupid. That's why it's great for any tribe to have a smart stranger injected into it.
>
> G. Pascal Zachary, *The Diversity Advantage*[2]

They congregate once a week for their special Sunday service, over a thousand devotees, sometimes more. They come from all walks of life and all over the world: gay and straight, young and old, British, Brazilian, Italian, Indian, Chinese, Canadian, music producers and management consultants, artists and writers, singers and doctors, hairdressers and hookers. The venue: Fabric nightclub in London's Clerkenwell. The occasion: DTPM, the best club night in town, and possibly the world.

Many things combine to make DTPM special: DJs like Mark Westhenry and Malcolm Duffy; an amazing sound and visual system; the friendly staff and fantastic venue; but above all, it's the unique mix of people sparking off each other that sets it apart. That's why DTPM has been going strong since 1993. 'Over the years, DTPM has attracted a big following of regulars,' explains promoter Lee Freeman. 'They come from all sorts of backgrounds but now they feel like a big family.'

There is a buzz about big global cities like London, New York and Sydney – and you can capture the essence of it in a place like DTPM. It's why people from all over the world flock to live in these cities – and the creativity that this diversity stimulates helps explain their economic vibrancy. So many people want to live – and work – in London and New York because they are exciting, cosmopolitan places. There is a huge variety of people – potential friends, partners or colleagues – and a vast choice of ethnic restaurants and cultural experiences. As well as contributing directly to a city's prosperity, immigrants may help it attract other talented people – and their diversity may enrich it in every sense.

In *The Rise of the Creative Class*, Richard Florida, a professor of public policy at George Mason University, argues:

> Regional economic growth is powered by creative people, who prefer places that are diverse, tolerant and open to new ideas. Diversity increases the odds that a place will attract different types of creative people with different skill sets and ideas. Places with diverse mixes of creative people are more likely to generate new combinations. Furthermore, diversity and concentration work together

> to speed the flow of knowledge. Greater and more diverse concentrations of creative capital in turn lead to higher rates of innovation, high-technology business formation, job generation and economic growth.[3]

Florida does more than just assert that diversity is good for economic growth: his analysis of fifty US metropolitan areas finds a solid link between diversity and economic success. His research shows that a large gay population is the leading indicator of a city's high-technology success, followed by a high concentration of what he calls 'bohemians': artists, writers, musicians, actors and so on. Finally, cities with many foreign-born residents also rank high as technology centres. Eight of the top ten metropolitan areas with the highest percentage of foreign-born residents – Los Angeles, New York, San Francisco, San Diego, Chicago, Houston, Boston, and Washington, DC – were also among the US's top fifteen high-technology regions.[4] In short, Florida finds that diverse cities tend to have a bigger and faster-growing technology sector, thus greater diversity leads to greater innovation.

Historically, most of the great cities were highly cosmopolitan: in part because they attracted talented people from afar, but also because their diversity sparked new ways of doing things. This was true of ancient Athens, medieval Florence, Elizabethan London, post-revolutionary Paris, *fin-de-siècle* Vienna and Weimar Berlin. In *Cities in Civilization*, Peter Hall notes that: 'The creative cities were nearly all cosmopolitan; they drew talent from the four corners of their worlds, and from the very start those worlds were often surprisingly far-flung. Probably, no city has ever been creative without continued renewal of the creative bloodstream.'[5]

Big global cities capture the whole world in one place. Among them, the seven million or so people who live in London speak over three hundred languages; three in ten are from so-called 'ethnic minorities'.[6] Nearly half of New Yorkers, who come from over 180 different countries, speak a language other than English at home. In the London Olympics of 2012, as in the Sydney Games of 2000, there will be a local community cheering for nearly every national team competing.

Guillermo Linares, the Dominican-American who runs the New York Mayor's Office of Immigrant Affairs, says, 'People who come to New York City are fortunate to be exposed to different cultures and languages. They come into contact with so many diverse perspectives. It's a source of strength from which the US benefits tremendously.' In a paper seeking to explain New York's continuing success, economist Edward Glaeser of Harvard University remarks that the 'concentration of immigrants tends to suggest a benefit from very particular groups of immigrants locating near one another'.[7]

How much is buzz worth?

Cultural diversity may be a good thing, but how do you put a price on it? (I will look at the broader cultural impact of immigration in Chapter 14.) People like George Borjas, the Cuban-born immigration sceptic at Harvard University, dismiss this potential benefit of immigration because one cannot readily measure its economic contribution: 'there is little to be gained – and a lot of potential mischief to be had – by basing important social policy decisions on "facts" that can never be measured objectively, far less verified'.[8] For sure, we should be cautious, but that is no reason to ignore it altogether. While the boost to creativity and innovation from greater diversity may not be easy to quantify, it is still incredibly important. Many things that cannot readily be measured have huge economic impacts: think of Max Weber's 'Protestant work ethic'; or consider the importance that values such as leadership and trust may have; or look in the mirror and ask yourself how much your productivity at work each day depends on your mood and self-confidence. It is hard to measure the value of diversity, yet John Stuart Mill was right when he said, 'It is hardly possible to overrate the value, for the improvement of human beings, of things which bring them into contact with persons dissimilar to themselves, and with modes of thought and action unlike those with which they are familiar.'[9]

In fact, there are good reasons to believe that the higher wages people earn and the higher rents they are willing to pay in cities like London and New York are directly related not merely to the fact that these cities are economic hubs, but also to their cultural diversity. Two Italian economists, Gianmarco Ottaviano and Giovanni Peri, have attempted to estimate the economic value of cultural diversity by examining wages and rents in US cities with varying proportions of foreign-born residents. 'Who can deny that Italian restaurants, French beauty shops, German breweries, Belgian chocolate stores, Russian ballets, Chinese markets, and Indian tea houses all constitute valuable consumption amenities that would be inaccessible to Americans were it not for their foreign-born residents?' they argue. Although all these services could in theory be provided by Americans, in practice the skills of a French chef and an American cook who has learned French cuisine are not interchangeable – and the appeal of a genuine French restaurant is not the same as that of an American restaurant serving French food. 'Similarly the skills and abilities of foreign-born workers and thinkers may complement those of native workers and thus boost problem solving and efficiency in the workplace,' they continue. That is crucial: diversity may boost creativity because people with different backgrounds, viewpoints and experience stimulate new ideas in each other. Admittedly, there could be a downside – 'natives may not enjoy living in a multicultural environment if they feel that their own cultural values are being endangered' – but if

Americans are free to live and work wherever they want in the US, then presumably those who like living in cosmopolitan cities, such as the creative class that Richard Florida mentions, will flock to them, while those who prefer to live in an ethnically homogeneous area will move elsewhere.

When Ottaviano and Peri looked at data from 160 US cities between 1970 and 1990, they found that the average wages earned by US-born people and the average rent they paid were much higher in cities that are more culturally diverse. The higher wages suggest that productivity is greater in culturally diverse cities, while the higher rents suggest that people are willing to pay more to live in cities that have plenty of foreign restaurants and other exotic cultural opportunities. Their findings stand up to a battery of statistical tests that assess whether the link might just be a spurious coincidence.

A bigger problem lies in establishing whether increased diversity leads to higher wages, or whether higher wages simply attract greater diversity. It is plausible that when cities boom, wages rise, and those higher wages attract immigrants, thus increasing diversity. But Ottaviano and Peri found that even allowing for the fact that higher wages tend to attract more immigrants, greater diversity does tend to boost the wages (and rents) of US-born workers. New York's diversity is not just a consequence of the higher wages on offer there; it is also one of the reasons *why* earnings are higher there. Ottaviano and Peri conclude that 'a more multicultural urban environment makes US-born citizens more productive'.[10]

The two economists expand on their findings in a more recent article. This time, instead of measuring diversity by country of origin, they use their mother tongue. Again they find that richer diversity is associated with higher wages for native people. The positive effect seems strongest for highly skilled workers, but holds for unskilled workers too. 'These results are compatible with the idea that different cultures provide different skills to production, beyond the formal schooling of their members,' they say. They also find that the benefits from immigrants who have been in the US for longer and speak English well are larger than those gained from new immigrants.[11] That makes sense: if people are to benefit from each other's perspectives, they need to be able to communicate with each other.

Edward Lazear, an economist at Stanford University, has looked in greater detail at how immigration could boost creativity. He argues that the gains from immigration are greatest when individuals have different knowledge: so migration from China to the US is more likely to be beneficial than migration from Canada to the States, since Canadians and Americans have much more in common. Second, the different knowledge that migrants bring has to be relevant. This relevance may not be immediately obvious: a Turkish professor's intimate knowledge of Ottoman history may at first appear to have little value in the US, but if it helps American policy-makers understand the Middle East and thus come up with a more effective foreign policy, it may be hugely valuable. Third, others need to be able to learn from immigrants at low cost – which is why everyone speaking a common language is so important. So, for immigration truly to boost creativity, immigrants should ideally come from a wide range of countries that all have different cultures but should still be able to speak the local language.[12] Both New York and London benefit from just this situation.

Increasing innovation

When asked why they think economics is important, people will often reply that it helps us find ways to make the economy grow faster, making us all richer and allowing us to spend more on improving healthcare, reducing poverty and cleaning up the environment. Unfortunately, though, economists are remarkably bad at explaining why economies grow. The standard model of economic growth says that it comes from increasing the size of the workforce and improving their skills, investing in more and better capital, and improving technology. Studies show that most economic growth in rich economies is the result of improvements in technology that enhance productivity. But what causes these improvements in technology? Understanding why some economies innovate faster than others, and why others are better at diffusing new technologies throughout the economy, is vital, and yet incredibly difficult to do. One can make some broad-brush statements: it helps if workers have a good education and a high level of skills, but they also need to be go-getting, adaptable and open to new ideas. Companies must be willing to invest, but they also need to invest wisely – and new companies have to be able to attract investment easily. Governments have to invest too: in education, infrastructure, healthcare and basic science. At a deeper level, since nobody knows which innovations will work best, economies grow through a mixture of competition and trial and error. The desire to steal a march on your competitors gives companies an incentive to try out new ways of doing things, and competition weeds out the good ideas from the bad. But the most basic question – what sparks new ideas? – remains largely unanswered.

Innovation could come from individual geniuses who apply themselves to a problem and come up with an ingenious new way of solving it. Historically, many of these people have been immigrants, perhaps because as outsiders they are less likely to conform to a society's conventional wisdom. But more often innovation comes from groups of talented people bouncing ideas off each other. By looking at a problem from a variety of perspectives, they are more likely to solve it. Although there is a great deal of variety within individual societies, most people in a society also tend to share a number of assumptions. Immigrants bring something different to the mix – and that could be the key to increasing innovation and growth. As Diane Coyle, who runs the consultancy Enlightenment Economics, remarks: 'It seems very plausible that in a knowledge-based economy the economic value of new ideas, different types of experience, diverse ways of thinking about problems, are all the more valuable.'[13]

A growing body of work on problem-solving and group decision-making suggests that the more diverse the group, the faster and more efficiently it will solve problems. At the forefront of this research is the Los Alamos National Laboratory in New Mexico, which is best known for its role in developing the atomic bomb during the Second World War. The leading expert in the new science of diversity is Norman Johnson.[14] 'Diversity is complex – as complex as it means to be human,' he points out. It encompasses all the dimensions of how we identify and connect with each other in visible ways, such as race, gender and ethnicity, and less visible ones, such as our approach to problem-solving, job level, sexual orientation and religion. 'Older schools of thought considered diversity to be a performance killer, not a performance booster,' he says:

> It was argued that diversity destabilised efficient groups. Darwin's 'survival of the fittest' proposed that the best way to develop new solutions and boost group performance was to let individuals or ideas compete, reproduce the most successful ones, and let everything else die away. This selective process reduces diversity in the name of achieving higher performance. In this viewpoint, introducing more diversity actually lowers group performance, until selection removes the 'low' performers.

The notion that diversity is harmful is still widespread. For instance, many people attribute Japan's astonishing economic success after the Second World War in part to its society's remarkable homogeneity (although the economy's more recent stagnation has silenced some of those voices). But new research suggests that diversity actually boosts group performance in complex situations.

To test how diversity affects problem-solving in complex environments, Johnson set up an experiment to study how people make their way through a maze. He asked volunteers to try to do so on their own, without the benefit of a global perspective or knowing where they were in the maze. All they could see was their next choice: turn or go straight. Each person tried to get through the maze as best they could, without any help from others. When Johnson added together each individual's experience of the maze to create a hypothetical 'collective person' who had their combined knowledge but no additional skills, the collective person outperformed the individual every time. By adding together several individuals' experience, the collective person found the shortest way through the maze – even though the individual or group could not 'see' or measure the optimal solutions, just as someone who is lost in Hampton Court's maze and manages to find their way out does not know whether the path they took was the shortest route or the longest.

When Johnson looked at why the collective person outperformed the individuals, he found that the diversity of each person's contribution was the key to higher group performance, even with groups that had a mix of high and low individual performance. 'In all cases, however you define diversity, the more the diversity, the better the performance and more robust the solution,' he says. 'The reason for increased performance in the maze was the ability of the diverse contributions to find shortcuts that could not be found by a single individual. This is especially true when individuals habitually solve a changing problem, one where new options arise, but old choices are selected.' When a problem becomes too complex for even an expert to understand, the diversity of the group is able to solve the previously unsolvable, even if each individual cannot understand how their contribution has been useful. This is why diverse groups (such as amateur investment clubs) can achieve better results when attempting to solve hard problems (such as beating the stock market) than so-called 'experts' (such as financial analysts).

'We all have different starting points, different goals, and different experiences in our lives,' says Johnson. 'But we often have common activities that allow us to find synergy – random interactions that help us solve problems. We might interact with diverse individuals in the office next door, at the water cooler, or in the gym, and *voila!* we unexpectedly find the solution to at least part of a problem we're solving.'

Johnson makes clear that problem-solving emerges from synergy rather than formal cooperation: people bouncing ideas off each other or gaining unexpected insights from what others say or do. Synergy can come about in different ways: from common goals, such as plotting a route through the maze; from a common identity, so that even if individuals have different goals and tasks, they have a common knowledge and concern for each other; or from a common world view, when people may have different preferences but agree on the options. Well-run companies provide at least the first two of these: common goals and a common identity. A network of independent computer programmers may still work towards a common goal of improving a piece of software. Groups – starting from couples and families, through neighbourhoods, cities and countries, and in some cases up to all of humanity – can have elements of a common identity, but Johnson warns that if a group does not share a common goal, world view or identity, diversity might lead to competition and conflict in the group. Clearly, if immigration causes ethnic conflict, it may harm economic performance. But if natives and immigrants have shared economic goals, they should both end up better off.

In some cases, though, synergy from diversity is not the best strategy. In problems that require a consistent, repeated solution – such as creating really efficient assembly lines – optimisation through rigid rules and regulations works better. This may explain why Japan excelled at improving its manufacturing productivity. Selection through survival of the fittest, though it wastes valuable resources, works well when a group is in its formative stages, trying to build solutions in new problem areas.

This may seem like a long digression into theoretical science, but it is extremely relevant to the question of how companies and economies innovate and thus grow richer. A mass of academic research about companies has found that more diverse groups take better-quality decisions and have the potential for increased productivity.[15]

Problem-solving teams

An increasing share of the economy comprises companies that solve problems: those that search for cures to diseases, write software and video games, provide management advice, design homes and bridges, handle legal cases, produce research, develop pollution-reducing technology, draw up welfare policies, make films, and so on. Whereas in traditional manufacturing companies workers were just cogs in a big machine, the employees of problem-solving firms perform non-standard tasks where ingenuity is crucial to their performance. Improving productivity doesn't come about from bashing out more widgets faster; it comes from thinking up new ideas, devising new ways of solving problems.

A study by Lu Hong of the University of Syracuse and Scott Page of the University of Iowa showed that employees with limited ability but different perspectives and different approaches to problem-solving can find the optimal solutions to very difficult conundrums. Moreover, in many cases a diverse group of people with limited abilities can outperform a like-minded group of high-ability problem-solvers, because an individual's likelihood of improving decisions depends more on their having a different perspective from other group members than on their own high expected score.[16] As Ivan Seidenberg, the then boss of Bell Atlantic, a US telecoms company, put it: 'If everybody in the room is the same, you'll have a lot fewer arguments and a lot worse answers.'[17]

Edward Lazear argues that the success of global firms, whose workforces are drawn from people from many different countries and cultures, suggests that there must be gains from diversity that offset the potential costs of different languages and cultural friction.[18] He claims that a global firm gains from having a diverse workforce when its employees from different countries and cultures have different skills and experience that are relevant and can be learned easily by their teammates. In a sense, he points out, cultural diversity is just like any other search for 'best practices'. Success comes to those who look not just outside their own firm or industry, but in those places where new and useful ideas can be found.

Football is a good example. The club I support, Arsenal, was once a solidly reliable team of overwhelmingly British players. We often won 1-0, prompting chants of 'Boring! Boring! Arsenal!' Now we chant it ironically. Under our French manager, the professorial Arsène Wenger, Arsenal has been transformed into a multiculturally talented team, which at its best plays the most beautiful football in the world (although obviously I'm biased). In goal is Germany's Jens Lehmann. In front of him is the unlikely pairing of Switzerland's Philippe Senderos and Kolo Touré of the Ivory Coast, combining well in central defence with France's Gael Clichy to their left and Cameroon's Lauren to their right. In midfield Brazilian Gilberto's defensive attributes complement Spanish prodigy Cesc Fabregas's exquisite passing and attacking flair, with Sweden's Freddie Ljungberg and the Czech Republic's Tomas Rosicky on the wings. Up front are the exceptional talents and outstanding ball skills of the world's best player, Thierry Henry, working hand in glove with Holland's Robin Van Persie. On the bench might be Belarus's battling Alexander Hleb, France's hard-working Mathieu Flamini and Brazil's bullish Julio Baptista, and a string of other talented foreign players. You can't get more diverse, and it works (usually). 'Each person brings from his own culture the positive side,' Wenger explains, 'which all comes together in the service of efficiency. That is the beauty. It is almost magical.'[19] Since Wenger's reign began in 1996, Arsenal have won the Premiership title three times, the FA Cup four times, and the double (both titles in the same year) twice. And in 2006 they reached the final of the Champions League for the first time.

Andrea Prat of the London School of Economics has looked in greater detail at whether teams of similar or different people perform better. He finds that in activities where a good fit between various units is of the utmost importance, a homogeneous workforce is better because it make coordination easier: think of a bureaucracy, for instance. But in activities that revolve around exploiting new opportunities, a more diverse workforce is preferable, because it maximises the chance of developing successful innovations.[20]

The diversity advantage

Alberto Alesina of Harvard University and Eliana La Ferrara of Bocconi University have taken a broader look at the way in which diversity interacts with economic performance.[21] They find that while ethnic diversity acts as a drag on economic growth in poor countries, it is beneficial at higher levels of development. This may be because only advanced economies are sophisticated enough to reap the productivity benefits of having workers with complementary skills and different insights, as well as having robust institutions that can cope with the potential for conflict that diversity may entail, and isolate or moderate its negative effects.

The value of diversity comes into its own in societies at the forefront of rapid change. When countries are technologically backward, they can make huge leaps forward simply by copying what more advanced economies are doing. They may benefit from being culturally uniform, since this makes it easier for everyone to move forward in unison. Likewise, in periods when economic change is slow, more homogeneous companies and countries may find it easier to organise themselves efficiently than more diverse and fissiparous ones. But in advanced economies in periods of rapid economic change (such as now), the value of diversity and the creativity it spurs come into their own.

In *The Diversity Advantage*, G. Pascal Zachary argues that 'the ability to apply knowledge to new situations is the most valued currency in today's economy. Creativity bestows more rewards than ever before . . . How creativity comes about is a great riddle, but a few things seem clear. Highly creative people don't necessarily excel in raw brainpower or test-taking. They are misfits on some level. They tend to question accepted views and consider contradictory ones.' This appreciation for paradox, Zachary argues, defines the cosmopolitan mentality and fosters it.[22]

American psychologist Howard Gardner finds the source of creativity in what he calls a 'lack of fit': highly creative people tend towards marginality for a variety of reasons, including their nationality and ethnicity. Zachary concludes from this that 'Divergent thinking is an essential ingredient of creativity. Diverse groups produce diverse thinking. Ergo, diversity promotes creativity.'[23]

The sociologist Alvin Gouldner argues that when a person can toggle between two or more lines of thought, they can forge new understandings. Psychological research bears this out. According to one respected survey, people from bicultural backgrounds may be mentally more flexible and 'find it easier to encode and access information in diverse ways'. They may have richer associations with a single concept than does a monocultural person, and they 'may have a greater tolerance for ambiguity because they are comfortable with situations in which one basic idea may have different nuances', depending on the community they inhabit at the time. 'Tolerance of ambiguity is considered a valuable trait for creativity because there is often a place in which incompatible, ill-defined elements co-exist during problem solving.'[24]

Thus, culturally diverse societies tend to be more productive than more uniform ones because they contain a wider variety of goods, services, skills and ideas available for consumption and production – as epitomised by cities like London and New York. Moreover, by bringing together complementary skills, different abilities and alternative approaches to problem-solving, diversity also boosts creativity, innovation and ultimately growth. That is one reason why problem-solving firms with diverse workforces prosper. But diversity can also lead to communication problems, conflict and racism. Reaping the full benefits of diversity therefore requires a degree of tolerance from local people and a willingness to integrate from immigrants, which I shall discuss further in Chapter 14.

6

Stealing Our Jobs?

Do immigrants displace local workers?

There is more than a touch of the mad scientist about Sonia Michaeli, the chief scientist at Israel's absorption ministry. With her bottle-blonde hair, overenthusiastic use of make-up and slightly demented cackle, one could easily imagine her nonchalantly mixing together combustible potions – and triggering a large explosion that blows up her laboratory along with herself. And yet Sonia's ministry, which is responsible for integrating immigrants into the Israeli economy and society, has overseen one of the most dramatic experiments in the history of immigration – and confounded fears that it would all go up in smoke.

Critics of immigration are forever claiming that immigrants cost home-grown workers their jobs and depress their wages. For instance, the leading anti-immigration lobby group in the United States, the Federation for American Immigration Reform (which rather inappropriately abbreviates to FAIR), claims that 'Mass immigration is displacing American workers by importing a constant flow of immigrants willing to work for substandard wages,' and that 'Large-scale immigration is flooding the labour market and driving down wages for everyone, immigrants and native-born workers alike.'[1] Such fears are so commonplace that they have become conventional wisdom: it is 'common sense' that immigrants are taking 'our' jobs and undercutting 'our' wages.

Imagine, then, what would happen if over 15 million foreigners were suddenly to arrive in the US over the next two years, rising to 29 million over eight years. Twenty-nine million people who don't speak English, don't have jobs to go to and don't even have any experience of working in a capitalist economy. Or likewise what would happen if three million such people arrived in Britain in two years and as many as six million over eight years. Mass unemployment? Riots in the streets? Perhaps even the collapse of society?

Fortunately for Israel, none of these calamities occurred when a mass exodus of Jews from the former Soviet Union of equivalent proportions arrived in the early 1990s. Jews everywhere have an automatic right to settle in Israel, which leaves the country open to mass inflows of immigrants, irrespective of the country's economic needs and circumstances. The economic viability of Israel's 'right of return' policy was sorely tested in the 1990s.

Between 1990 and 1997, over 710,000 Russians emigrated to Israel, increasing its working-age population by over 15 per cent. In the two peak years, 1990 – the year in which Sonia Michaeli herself arrived from Ukraine – and 1991 (when Leonid Dinevich, the cloud-seeding general, came from Moldova), over 330,000 Russian Jews arrived, raising Israel's working-age population by 8 per cent. Did Sonia, Leonid and the others take jobs away from native Israelis? No they did not. According to Sarit Cohen Goldner, an economic expert on the matter at Bar-Ilan University in Tel Aviv, 'natives hardly suffered at all'. Between 1989 and 1991, the unemployment rate among native Israeli men actually fell (although female unemployment rose slightly). Between 1989 and 1997, unemployment among both native Israeli men and women fell considerably. So much for natives losing their jobs. As for the ex-Soviets, they soon found jobs too: whereas most of them naturally started off unemployed or not even looking for a job, by 1997 their employment rate was comparable to that of natives. Miraculously, then, Israel's economy seems to have absorbed a vast number of new workers without a rise in unemployment.

How did it do this? Initially, the huge inflow of immigrants did cause the wages of native Israelis to fall – by around 5 per cent for men between 1989 and 1991. It also led to a sharp rise in interest rates, because it stimulated demand for investment, to build houses for the new arrivals and factories in which they could be employed. This led to an investment boom between 1990 and 1994, largely financed by borrowing from abroad. Higher investment in turn caused wages to recover after 1991 – because it made workers more productive – as well as causing interest rates to decline after 1994. By 1997, natives' wages had recovered to where they would have been without the mass immigration, and interest rates had fallen to their pre-immigration levels.[2] In short, Israel was able to absorb a huge and unexpected inflow of immigrants without a rise in unemployment, and with only a temporary fall in wages. It could have done even better if the inflow of immigrants had been anticipated. Then the investment boom would have preceded the immigrants: houses for them would have been built in advance and factory capacity expanded in preparation.

The upshot is clear: flexible advanced economies can absorb large numbers of immigrants without any cost to native workers if the inflows are reasonably predictable, and with only a short-term cost to them if they are unexpected.

Economies adjust

If Israel can absorb a huge influx of immigrants whose arrival was motivated by political crisis rather than economic need, then surely rich countries can cope with much smaller inflows of migrants whose labour is in demand. Study after study confirms this: immigrants do little or no harm to the wages or employment prospects of native workers.[3] And why should they? If it were true that increasing the size of a country's labour force led to a rise in unemployment, then presumably we could cure joblessness by banning women from working. Few politicians suggest this these days. The only reason why people are forever seeking to blame unemployment on immigrants is that foreigners make convenient scapegoats. Even when they do compete for jobs with native workers, they create many more jobs, because as consumers they boost the demand for local goods and services and the workers who supply them. And even if some native workers did lose out from immigration, rich countries would still gain overall, because their capital would be used more productively and because consumers would benefit from cheaper goods and services. The workers who lost out could be compensated for their losses and everyone else would still be better off. But what if workers in rich countries actually gained? If immigrants have different skills and characteristics that complement those of native workers, then immigration will benefit everyone. That is precisely what recent studies show: immigrants boost the wages of native workers and lower unemployment.

When critics of immigration argue that immigrants harm the job prospects of native workers, they implicitly assume that they compete directly with each other in the labour market – and that the economy never adapts to their arrival. If immigrants were identical to native workers and suddenly arrived in an economy with no vacancies, they would indeed have a negative impact on local workers in the short term. In a country with a flexible labour market, where wages adjust freely, the extra supply of immigrant labour would temporarily drive down the wages of local workers until employers had created extra jobs for the immigrants to fill. In a country with a rigid labour market, where wages are sticky, the immigrants would in the short term remain unemployed, although some might find jobs at local workers' expense. Soon, though, the economy would adapt to the increased labour supply and the increased demand for goods and services: companies would invest in extra capacity and all the workers – immigrants *and* natives – would find jobs at the previously prevailing wages.

But critics of immigration would be the first to argue that immigrants and native workers are not identical. The newcomers will almost certainly speak the local language less well, have fewer contacts and less knowledge of local practices, and typically they will have less education and fewer skills than local workers. At most, then, they are imperfect substitutes for local workers, which implies that they only indirectly compete with them in the labour market – thus limiting any short-term harm they might cause natives. But since 90 per cent of natives entering the US job market in 2004 had completed high school,[4] while the typical migrant from rural Mexico has six years of education and does not speak English,[5] is it really plausible that they are competing for the same jobs on any level? More likely, immigrants take jobs that local workers shun, such as street-cleaning and pizza-delivery, and thus do not compete with natives at all. So it is not surprising that studies fail to find any evidence to confirm the prejudiced view that immigrants harm the job prospects of local workers: immigrants are not taking jobs from native workers.

Most studies of the labour-market impact of immigration are based on evidence from the US. But the first weighty study of Britain, published in 2003 by Christian Dustmann and his colleagues at University College London, is equally sanguine. It finds that 'there is no strong evidence of large adverse effects of immigration on native employment or wages' and that 'Insofar as there is evidence of any effect on wages, it suggests that immigration enhances native wage growth.' The authors therefore conclude that 'on current evidence fear of large and negative employment and wage effects on the resident population are not easily justifiable grounds for restrictive immigration policy. The perception that immigrants take away jobs from natives, thus contributing to large increases in unemployment, or that immigrants depress wages of native workers, do not find confirmation in the analysis of data laid out in this report.'[6] In short, immigrants do our job prospects no harm at all.

Far from competing with native workers, immigrants often complement their efforts. An immigrant nanny may allow a hotel manager to return to work, where her productivity is enhanced by hard-working foreign chambermaids. A foreign computer scientist may contribute fresh ideas that boost local workers' productivity, or set up a new company that employs them. In such cases, one would expect to find immigrants having a positive impact on natives' wages in countries with flexible labour markets, and a positive impact on natives' employment prospects in countries with rigid labour markets. And that is precisely what many recent studies find. For instance, a study of Germany, which has witnessed a very large increase in immigration in the past twenty years, found that a 1 per cent increase in the share of foreign workers in the labour market raised blue-collar workers' wages by 0.2 per cent and white-collar workers' wages by 1.3 per cent, boosting natives' wages by 0.6 per cent overall.[7] Another study – entitled 'Three Million Foreigners, Three Million Unemployed? Immigration and the French Labour Market' – tackles head on the fallacy that immigrants cause unemployment.[8] Dominique Gross of the International Monetary Fund finds that while immigration may cause a very small short-term rise in unemployment, in the long term it reduces joblessness. More broadly, although countries such as the United States, Spain and Britain have admitted large numbers of immigrants in recent years, unemployment in each of these countries has fallen, not risen. There is no correlation between rich countries' unemployment rates and the share of immigrants in their populations.[9]

Critics of immigration wilfully ignore the other positive impacts that immigrants can have on jobs. New arrivals add to the demand for domestic goods and services, boosting the demand for native workers. Moreover, immigrants are likely to grease the wheels of the labour market, especially in Europe, where natives are particularly reluctant to move to where the jobs are. Since immigrants have already made the huge leap of leaving their home country to come to a new one, and since they are generally poorer and therefore more responsive to economic incentives, they are typically more willing than locals to move to particular areas and industries where demand is high. For instance, immigrants in the US have traditionally been concentrated in the six states where the demand for them is highest, but they are now spreading out across the country, to states where natives are reluctant to move. Immigrants therefore make the economy more flexible and thus allow it to grow faster without running into inflationary bottlenecks. They help the economy as a whole adapt faster to economic change, reduce the costs of doing so for native people, and allow a higher employment rate among native workers without triggering inflation. As Alan Greenspan, the head of America's Federal Reserve from 1987 to 2005, has pointed out, the sharp rise in immigration in the 1990s helped sustain the long boom without wages spiralling upwards.

Even in a recession, immigrants do not cost jobs. They are still consumers who create jobs for others, and they will still do work that others refuse to do. Australia's Bureau of Immigration Policy Research, for instance, looked at the impact of immigration during the country's recessions of 1974–5, 1982–3 and 1992–3 – long before Australia developed its current obsession with skills-based immigration. It found no relationship between immigration and unemployment. Moreover, those who benefited most from the new jobs were the Australian-born.[10]

One notable critic disagrees with this rosy picture: George Borjas claims that immigration does harm native workers. Looking at the impact of immigration in the US across different levels of skills and experience, he estimates that the 11 per cent rise in the labour supply of working men brought about by immigration between 1980 and 2000 reduced the wage of the average native worker by 3.2 per cent.[11] Borjas claims that nearly all native workers lost out, with high-school graduates' wages falling by 2.6 per cent, college graduates' by 4.9 per cent and high-school dropouts' by a whopping 8.9 per cent. But by his own admission, his analysis ignores the impact of immigration on capital investment and productivity growth. In essence, he assumes that although the US workforce grew, firms did not invest in extra capacity – and that Silicon Valley does not even exist. It is hardly surprising, then, that he comes to such a negative conclusion.

Borjas also assumes that immigrants are close substitutes for native workers with the same number of years of schooling and job experience, but that workers with different levels of work experience scarcely compete with each other in the labour market. So a Mexican high-school dropout with five years' job experience is a close substitute for a US-born high-school dropout with five years' job experience, but neither is a close substitute for a US-born high-school dropout with ten years' experience. By assuming that US and Mexican workers are similar while artificially segmenting the US job market by years of experience, Borjas's very questionable assumptions allow him to reach his desired conclusion. If one assumes that immigrants compete for the same jobs as natives but that the pool of alternative jobs available to natives is small, it is no wonder that natives lose out, especially since Borjas also assumes that the capital stock is fixed, so that any increase in labour supply tends to reduce wages.

You don't have to take my word for it. Through a combination of cogent thinking and statistical heavy-lifting, Gianmarco Ottaviano and Giovanni Peri have comprehensively demolished Borjas's claims.[12] They argue that foreign-born workers are not close substitutes for US-born workers, even when they have similar levels of education. In part, this is because they have different occupations. For instance, among high-school dropouts, immigrants are highly represented in occupations like tailoring (where 54 per cent were foreign-born in 2000) and plaster-stucco masonry (where 44 per cent were foreign-born in 2000), while US-born workers are highly represented among, for instance, crane operators and sewer-pipe cleaners (where, in both of which, less than 1 per cent were foreign-born in 2000). Foreign tailors are hardly competing for the same jobs as US crane operators. Likewise, among college graduates, foreign-born workers are highly represented in scientific and technological fields (45 per cent of medical scientists and 33 per cent of computer engineers are foreign-born) while US-born workers are highly represented among lawyers (less than 4 per cent are foreign-born) and museum curators and archivists (less than 3 per cent are foreign-born). Again, foreign computer engineers are scarcely a threat to US-born lawyers. What's more, even within the same profession, natives and immigrants often provide different services, and hence complement each other, regardless of education level. For instance, Chinese and American cooks do not produce similar meals; nor do Italian and American tailors provide identical types of clothes. A European-trained physicist (more inclined towards a theoretical approach) is not perfectly substitutable with a US-trained one (who would usually adopt an experimental approach), and a French architect will likely create a starkly different building to an American one.

The two Italian economists' arguments make sense, and they are borne out by the evidence. Ottaviano and Peri find that the average wage of US-born workers rose by between 2 per cent and 2.5 per cent in response to the inflow of foreign-born workers between 1990 and 2000 (which added 8 per cent to the US labour force in that decade). While immigrants lowered the wages of native workers without a high-school diploma by 1 per cent, they increased the wages of those with at least a high-school diploma by as much as 3–4 per cent. The workers who gain from immigration accounted for 92 per cent of the US-born labour force in 2000, while the losers – high-school dropouts, who lose only slightly – are a very small group whose numbers continue to shrink each year.

Ottaviano and Peri conclude that:

> For a flow of migrants that increases total employment by 10 per cent and a skill distribution that mirrors the one observed in the nineties, US-born workers experience a 3–4 percentage point increase in their wages. This results because US and foreign-born workers are not perfectly substitutable, even when they have similar observable skills. Workers born, raised and partly educated in foreign environments are not identical to workers born and raised in the US. This set of differences that we might label 'diversity' is the basis for the gains from immigration that accrue to US-born workers.

For a native worker earning $30,000 a year, that represents a gain of up to $1,200 a year, with correspondingly larger gains for better-paid natives. And remember that every American who owns shares, either directly or through a pension fund, also gains from immigration, because capital is used more productively when there are more immigrants.

Fears about immigrants taking jobs are ancient and deep-seated. They rest on the twin fallacies that there is only a fixed number of jobs available – so that one man's gain is necessarily another's loss – and that foreign workers are simply substitutes for native workers, when in fact they have different skills and characteristics that are often complementary. Even supposed experts on immigration make this basic mistake. Based on the false assumption that immigrants and natives are exact substitutes for each other, Peter Brimelow, who claims to be economically literate, tries to turn the absence of evidence of falling wages against supporters of immigration. He argues that:

> The formal economic logic of immigration is that only if wage rates are driven down – meaning that American owners of capital can hire workers more cheaply and make an increased profit for themselves – can the economy derive an overall benefit. That increased profit is the basic way in which native-born Americans are supposed to benefit from immigration. If it can't be shown to exist, then native-born Americans are just not benefiting.[13]

But this is utter nonsense, since the economy can also benefit if immigrants and natives have complementary skills, especially if the added diversity sparks faster productivity growth.

7

Snouts in Our Trough?

Are immigrants a burden on the welfare state?

> It's just obvious that you can't have free immigration and a welfare state.
>
> Milton Friedman[1]

> The United States is not a pile of wealth but a fragile system – a lifeboat. And lifeboats can get overcrowded and sink.
>
> Peter Brimelow[2]

'All you bleeding hearts want to invite the whole world in here to feed at our trough without a thought as to who's going to pay for it, as if the American taxpayer was like Jesus Christ with his loaves and fishes,' says a racist lawyer in *The Tortilla Curtain*, T. C. Boyle's book about illegal immigration in California.[3] The fear that immigrants are coming to 'feed at our trough' is almost as old as the fear that they are stealing our jobs. At Ellis Island, remember, inspectors attempted to weed out foreigners 'liable to become a public charge', while through the Aliens Act of 1905 Britain sought to exclude paupers and vagrants. More recently, critics of immigration have whipped up fears that immigrants come to sponge off our welfare system. It is an article of faith among opponents of immigration that foreigners are out to screw us for every penny they can get. But is there any evidence to support their prejudice?

If people from poor countries are better off on welfare in rich countries than working in their country of origin, this could conceivably motivate them to migrate. And if enough poor people did this, the welfare state could become economically and politically unsustainable. As George Borjas puts it:

> Welfare programs will probably attract people who qualify for subsidies and repel persons who have to pay for them. A strong magnetic effect, combined with an ineffective border control policy, can literally break the bank. In addition, immigration can easily fracture the political legitimacy of the social contract that created and sustains the welfare state. No group of native citizens – whether in the United States or in other immigrant-receiving countries – can reasonably be expected to pick up the tab for subsidising hundreds of millions of 'the huddled masses'.[4]

Note the exaggeration for effect: even a supposedly level-headed academic like Borjas cannot resist talking about subsidising 'hundreds of millions' of destitute foreigners – a ludicrous fear, since even with our current leaky borders immigration is nowhere near that level.

But having stoked up his readers' fears, Borjas cannot substantiate his arguments. He is forced to concede that although the attraction of welfare 'is the magnetic effect that comes up most often in the immigration debate, it is also the one for which there is no empirical support'.[5] His get-out clause is that this is the 'hardest to corroborate', since 'It is doubtful that many immigrants would willingly volunteer the information that they came to the United States to collect SSI benefits [welfare for the old and disabled poor] or Medicaid [public healthcare for the poor].'[6] Elsewhere in *Heaven's Door*, the leading economic critique of US immigration, Borjas is quick to dismiss any potential benefits of immigration that cannot readily be measured, but when it comes to counting the cost, he is not as scrupulous.

In truth, though, migrants are highly unlikely to move in search of welfare benefits. It simply does not pay to move to a rich country to try to claim comparatively low welfare benefits, especially if migration is costly and risky. Would an asylum seeker from Afghanistan really pay a smuggler £5,000 in order to come to Britain and claim £50 a week in unemployment benefits? Borjas argues that a poor immigrant household with two children in California that received food stamps and made full use of free public healthcare could claim benefits worth as much as $12,600 a year.[7] He says this compares favourably with the annual income per person (adjusted for differences in the cost of living) of $6,600 in Colombia and $3,500 in the Philippines. Really? If the average income per person is $3,500 a year in the Philippines, then the average income for a household of four is $14,000 a year, $1,400 *more* than the maximum benefits an immigrant household could claim in California. And in any case, most illegal immigrants do not bring their families with them, so they would not be able to claim all those benefits.

Now consider the choice that a potential illegal immigrant like Inmer from a desperately poor country like Honduras faces. He earned $33 a week in his home country, which is equivalent to earning $100 a week in the US, or $5,200 a year, allowing for the fact that the cost of living in the States is around three times higher than it is in Honduras (according to the World Bank). *Polleros* charge around $2,000 to smuggle migrants into the US. Given the risks involved – the possibility that Inmer might be caught, injured or even die – and given his reluctance to leave behind his wife, son and home in the first place, migrating makes economic sense only if the likely rewards from it are much greater than $2,000. It is scarcely conceivable that Inmer would end up better off on welfare in the US than he was working in Honduras, still less that he would actually migrate in order to go on welfare. It is even less plausible that Mexican immigrants might end up better off on US welfare. Average wages in Mexico are around $100 a week, the equivalent to earning $250 a week in the US, or $13,000 a year.

Even in cases where immigrants might be better off on welfare in rich countries than working in their country of origin, they would make more money if they worked in their new home. So for the fears of people like Borjas to be realised, immigrants would have to be enterprising enough to migrate in the first place but then suddenly lose all their drive once they arrive in a rich country, such that they prefer a lazy life on welfare to the much greater rewards of work. Again, this is highly improbable.

What's more, illegal migrants have scarcely any right to social benefits in any country. Though they might in theory be entitled to emergency healthcare, they will be reluctant to make any use of it, for fear that they might be caught and deported. Admittedly, a smuggler might provide them with forged documents that enabled them to claim benefits, but illegal migrants are much more likely to have to work to pay off their debts to their smugglers and make the move worthwhile. Even legal migrants' access to social benefits is increasingly restricted in most rich countries. In 1996, the US Congress passed the Personal Responsibility and Work Opportunity Reconciliation Act (PRWORA), commonly known as the Welfare Reform Act, which cut off immigrants' access to federal public benefits. Legal immigrants (except refugees and those granted asylum) are barred from all federal means-tested public benefits for five years after entering the country and denied Supplemental Security Income (assistance for needy old and disabled people) and food stamps until they gain citizenship. Illegal immigrants are barred from the following federal public benefits: grants, contracts, loans, licences, retirement, welfare, health, disability, public or assisted housing, post-secondary education, food assistance and unemployment benefits. States are barred from providing state or locally funded benefits to illegal immigrants unless a state law is enacted granting such authority. The only benefits available to immigrants include school lunch and breakfast programmes, immunisations, emergency medical services, disaster relief and other programmes that are necessary to protect life and safety as identified by the Attorney General.[8] Asylum seekers and temporary workers are denied access to nearly all social benefits. Although some of these provisions have subsequently been relaxed, immigrants' access to social benefits remains highly restricted.

In Britain, temporary migrants, non-EU labourers and those admitted on family reunification visas are not eligible for any social benefits, except housing assistance, for which eligibility varies locally. The Asylum and Immigration Act of 1999 barred immigrants seeking to remain permanently in Britain from non-contributory social programmes, such as income support, for five years. In order to qualify for indefinite leave to remain in Britain, foreigners must prove that they have sufficient income and adequate housing and that neither they nor any of their family have claimed benefits.[9] Asylum seekers are entitled to healthcare and housing assistance, while social assistance is at local authorities' discretion. Much of the fuss in Britain has been about asylum seekers allegedly sponging off taxpayers. But, in fact, the government bans them from working and provides them with vouchers that are below what it deems necessary for subsistence in Britain. If asylum seekers were allowed to work, doubtless most would prefer to.

In France and Germany, temporary workers and asylum seekers are denied most social benefits. Australia limits immigrants' access to social assistance, housing, healthcare and social security for the first two years. Canada severely restricts temporary workers' access to most social benefits. Those sponsoring a visa for a foreign relative have to sign a ten-year contract making them legally responsible for their food, clothing and shelter, and guaranteeing that the relative will not apply for social assistance. If sponsors do not stick to their side of the bargain, they can be taken to court for repayment and their ability to sponsor another relative is impaired.

Last but not least, even if rich countries were to make it much easier for people in poor countries to come and work, they could at the same time further restrict the availability of welfare benefits so that only citizens or long-term residents could claim them. Even though all citizens of EU countries are in principle allowed the same social benefits as national citizens in other member states, the British government barred East Europeans from the new EU member states from claiming social benefits for two years when it allowed them to come and work freely in Britain in 2004. Likewise, although New Zealanders are free to move to Australia, since 2001 they no longer have access to social benefits until they become permanent residents.

George Borjas and Milton Friedman are wrong. Free immigration is compatible with the welfare state, not only because few migrants are likely to move merely to claim social benefits when they could be earning much more by working, but because they can be – and are – denied benefits that are available to citizens and long-term residents.

Do migrants pay their way?

Immigrants might not move to rich countries in order to claim welfare benefits, but critics claim that they end up a drain on the public purse all the same – because they may be disproportionately poor and unemployed, for instance. At the other extreme, some enthusiasts argue that young immigrants' taxes could pay for the pensions that rich-country governments have promised their swelling ranks of old people. But one should not make a simplistic case for immigration on the basis that it boosts tax revenues – any more than one should oppose immigration on the simplistic basis that it increases welfare bills. The truth is that immigrants are unlikely to make a big difference to government finances either way – some will end up net contributors, others net beneficiaries – although if they help boost long-term economic growth, some of the proceeds will end up in government coffers.

Calculating the net impact of immigrants on public finances is fiendishly difficult. It depends on who immigrates – their skills, experience, education and the number of kids they have – and on what terms, such as which taxes they have to pay and which social benefits they have access to and when. Their age is crucial: if they arrive aged twenty, having completed their education abroad and with a full working life ahead of them, they will probably be net contributors; if they arrive in their sixties, they will probably be a net drain. The calculation depends heavily on which methodology is used, which time-frame is considered, which expenditures and revenues are included, how they are allocated, and whether individuals or households are considered. For instance, do immigrants add to the cost of building and maintaining roads, and if so, how much? Do they lower the cost of national defence for natives by spreading its cost over a wider population? Should the cost of educating an immigrant's daughter count as a net drain that offsets the taxes he pays, or should his daughter be considered separately, with the spending viewed as an investment that will be repaid many times over through the taxes she pays in later life? Nor is cutting benefits to immigrants necessarily a saving in the long run: free language classes and skills training will enhance their productivity and are thus likely to boost the future taxes they pay. Viewed over a lifetime, natives are broadly speaking a net burden on the state while they are in state-financed education; net contributors while they are working; and a burden again when they are unemployed, retired or if they require expensive medical services. The same is likely to be true for immigrants. Thus, for instance, those who are working might be net contributors now, but they may eventually be net beneficiaries over their lifetime if they have a costly medical condition, while their children may in turn be net contributors. Looked at over several generations, how do we value the benefit of the future taxes that immigrants' children and grandchildren might pay? Are governments with big debts likely to put their house in order in future, with immigrants footing part of the bill, or will they continue with their profligate ways? The permutations are endless and there is no right answer.

But, despite the complexity of the issue, one can make some broad-brush generalisations about the potential fiscal impact of future immigration. First, immigrants who come to work temporarily without their families and are not eligible for social benefits will clearly be net contributors to public finances, since they will pay taxes on their income and on their spending in the country without receiving any social benefits in return. Since we have seen that immigrants do not harm the job prospects of native workers, they will also not affect social spending on natives. And it is stretching credulity to claim that the extra spending on roads or parks that the arrival of immigrants might require would be greater than the taxes they pay, since such investment in infrastructure is only a small fraction of total government spending. A temporary-worker programme would therefore unambiguously swell the coffers of rich-country governments.

Second, if some temporary workers are allowed to become permanent residents with full social rights after a certain number of years, they are likely to remain net contributors over their lifetime, provided they remain in work. Why? Because the government has not had to fund their education – a huge saving – and because they will have been net contributors for the years they were temporary workers without social rights. If they remain in work, they will also be paying taxes and not claiming unemployment benefits. So they would have to be exceptionally low earners in a country with very generous social provision for the poor, or have a costly medical condition, to be a drain on the public purse over their lifetime.

Third, contrary to public prejudice, illegal immigrants are unlikely to be a burden on taxpayers. If they have fake documents, they may pay taxes and social-security contributions without accruing any entitlement to a pension or other contributory benefits. One study estimated that between 1990 and 1998 employers paid the US government up to $20 billion in welfare contributions for the irregular immigrant workers they employed, using fake social security cards that cannot be matched to legally recorded names and so do not give the immigrants the right to any benefits in return. If illegal immigrants work in the black economy, they will still pay value-added (or sales) tax on their spending, but they will draw almost nothing in return, not only because their illegal status makes them ineligible for nearly all social benefits, but because they will be wary of using even those to which they are entitled, such as emergency healthcare, for fear that they could be arrested and deported.

Studies that follow immigrants over time generally conclude that while they might receive a little more than they pay in, their descendants are significant net contributors.[10] The US National

Academy of Sciences found that the average foreign-born resident was a net recipient of $3,000 from government over their lifetime, while their kids were net contributors to the tune of $80,000 each.[11] Ronald Lee and Jonathan Miller, both at the University of California at Berkeley, conclude that 'the overall fiscal consequences of altering the volume of immigration would be quite small and should not be a major consideration for policy'.[12] They find that allowing in 100,000 more immigrants per year would initially raise taxes for natives, and later reduce them, in both cases by amounts less than 1 per cent of current tax levels.

Alan Auerbach and Philip Oreopoulos, also at the University of California at Berkeley, agree that immigration has little impact either way on the government's fiscal position. Even an outright ban on immigration would have only a small impact, so that 'more realistic changes in the level of immigration should be viewed neither as a major source of the existing imbalance, nor as a potential solution to it'.[13] If defence spending rises in line with the population, immigration worsens the fiscal situation; if it doesn't, immigration improves government finances. The US government is currently racking up huge debts, to pay for the war in Iraq and to fund President Bush's huge tax cuts, among other things. These will eventually have to be paid off. But because new immigrants and their offspring account for a rising share of the US population, shifting the burden of paying off the national debt onto future generations also shifts it, relatively, onto immigrants. So if the government puts its finances on a sound footing now, the benefits of immigration are less than if the government delays. Finally, attracting more skilled immigrants would improve the government's finances – since they tend to be higher earners and hence pay more tax.

In Australia, one study suggests that by 2010 the average immigrant will be a net contributor to the government's budget to the tune of A$5,800.[14] More broadly, Australia is likely to gain from immigration by spreading the huge cost of defending and providing infrastructure for its vast, continent-sized country over a larger population.

A study by Britain's Home Office estimated that the foreign-born population paid about 10 per cent more in tax than it received in spending, a gain of £2.5 billion in 1999–2000.[15] As a snapshot of one year, this figure is easy to pick holes in, not least because the government was running a budget surplus that year, so the native population also paid more in tax than it received in spending – albeit less so than immigrants. A more recent study by the Institute for Public Policy Research extended the framework of the Home Office report to see how the situation had changed over the following years.[16] It found that whereas in 1999–2000, immigrants accounted for 8.8 per cent of tax receipts (and 8.4 per cent of government spending), by 2003–4, they accounted for 10 per cent of tax receipts (and just 9.1 per cent of government spending). Total revenue from immigrants grew in inflation-adjusted terms from £33.8 billion in 1999–2000 to £41.2 billion in 2003–4, a 22 per cent increase, compared with only a 6 per cent increase for natives. In short, immigrants' contribution to Britain's public services is increasingly positive.

Although the net impact of immigrants on government finances over several generations is likely to be small, immigration could in principle help mitigate the looming pensions crisis in some countries. For instance, if Germany, where a shrinking workforce has to support a growing pensioner population, attracts millions of young, foreign-educated immigrants over the next few decades, this could deliver a one-off boost to public finances that eases the tax burden on natives, especially if the immigrants are primarily highly skilled high earners. Moreover, by increasing the number of future taxpayers, thereby spreading government debt over a wider base, immigrants automatically reduce the individual burden on native taxpayers. One study finds that immigrants who arrive in Germany between the ages of twelve and forty-five on average make a net contribution to public finances over their lifetimes (as much as $136,800 if they arrive aged thirty).[17] Since three-quarters of immigrants who arrived in 2000 were aged between twelve and forty-five, the authors estimate that the average immigrant will make a net contribution over their lifetime of $55,400. What's more, if Germany continues to admit 200,000 primarily young migrants a year and their impact on taxes and government spending is similar to that of current immigrants, immigration could reduce natives' net tax burden by around 30 per cent – and by as much as 45 per cent if the number of immigrants rose each year so as to keep the German population stable. Admitting 200,000 immigrants a year but selecting higher-skilled migrants who tend to pay more taxes and consume fewer social benefits could boost immigrants' net contribution even further, almost halving natives' net tax burden. (A study of Spain points to similar potential fiscal gains from immigration.[18]) In short, because Germany's population is set to age much more dramatically than America's, and because this will leave a huge hole in government finances given the generous pensions that the German government has promised its citizens, immigrants could potentially make a much bigger contribution to righting Germany's fiscal woes than would be the case in America, where one study finds that even a doubling of immigration would do little to improve pension finances.[19]

There's no cure for ageing

Immigration might help some countries with their transitional pensions problems, but it can't offset the ageing of their populations. After all, immigrants grow old too. The population of most rich countries is set to shrink and age over the first half of this century, because people are having fewer children and living longer. In 2000, the average American woman was having only two kids, below the 2.1 needed to sustain the population, while the average European woman was having a mere 1.4 (and the average Italian only 1.2). With fewer kids being born and more old people around, the number of people of working age (those aged 15–64) potentially able to support each old person (over 65) – technically known as the 'dependency ratio' – had fallen to 5 in the United States and 4 in the European Union. (In all of these projections, figures for the EU refer to the 15 countries in the Union as of 2000, not the 25 of today.)

If migration to rich countries stopped,[20] the populations of Europe and Japan would fall sharply by 2050, while America's would also begin to decline before that year, according to projections made in 2000 by the United Nations Population Division.[21] The population of the EU would shrink by 17 per cent, or 62 million people, between 2000 and 2050, with the French population edging up by 1 per cent (albeit declining between 2025 and 2050) to just over 59 million, the British population falling by over 5 per cent to less than 56 million and the German population slumping by over a quarter, to less than 59 million. Italy's population would plummet by over 28 per cent, to less than 41 million. The US population would be just 6 per cent higher than it was in 1995, at nearly 291 million (and would have declined between 2025 and 2050).

Some greens think that this would be a good thing, since having fewer people around would place less strain on the environment. Quite how few people they would like to see they rarely specify, however. Nationalists, though, would prefer a large and rising population, since it tends to boost a country's clout in the world. Companies worry, too: they do not like the idea of their domestic markets shrinking. The population in general might not mind, however, as long as their living standards keep rising. But will they? The potentially productive working-age population is set to fall, while the number of old people is set to rise sharply between 2000 and 2050: by 37 per cent in Italy, 39 per cent in Germany, 48 per cent in Britain, 62 per cent in France, 50 per cent in the EU as a whole, and 96 per cent in the US. As a result, the dependency ratio would slump from a little over 4 in each of Britain, France and Germany to 2.4, 2.3 and 1.75, respectively, from 3.7 to 1.5 in Italy, from 4.1 to 1.9 in the EU as a whole, and from 5.2 to 2.6 in the US. So even if everyone aged 15–64 in Italy was working – which is inconceivable – every 100 of them would also have to support 66 over-65s, while every 100 younger Americans would also have to support 39 US pensioners. Although there will be fewer children for adults to support, it costs around two and a half times more to look after a pensioner rather than a teenager. Welfare systems in rich countries will also come under increasing pressure as public pension payments rise: unless governments renege on their pensions promises, slash other government spending or raise taxes, public finances will deteriorate.

Of course, people in rich countries might start to have more children, but it is unlikely that procreation will recover enough to sustain the population. So if countries want to prevent their populations falling, they will have to promote immigration. And bringing in immigrants, who tend to be young and have more children, might also offset the ageing of the population. The first of these two goals might be realistic, but the second is not.

France and Britain do not need to admit many foreigners in order to maintain their populations. France has to let in about 1.5 million by 2050, a mere 27,000 a year; Britain 2.6 million, or 48,000 a year. Italy would need many more: 13 million, or 234,000 a year. Germany will require 17.8 million, or 324,000 a year. That is a large number, but fewer than it received on average in the 1990s. The EU as a whole needs 47.5 million, or 863,000 a year – fewer than it receives now. The US requires only 6.4 million, or 116,000 a year – much lower than current inflows. Europe's working-age population is set to start declining in 2007–8 and the United States' in 2020.[22] In order to keep this sector of the population stable, much greater immigration is needed. France needs a still relatively modest 5.5 million immigrants, or 99,000 a year; Britain 6.3 million, or 114,000 a year. Italy would need 19.6 million, or 357,000 a year. Germany would require 25.2 million, or 458,000 a year – which is still in line with its recent experience. The EU as a whole will need 79.6 million, or 1.4 million a year. The United States would require only 18 million, or 327,000 a year – again much less than it receives now.

Migration on this scale is perfectly feasible, but it would do little to ease the burden of supporting old people. Each old person would still be supported by only 2.25 people of working age in Italy, 2.4 in Germany (and the EU as a whole), 2.5 in France, 2.6 in Britain and 2.7 in the USA – and remember that not everyone aged 15–64 actually works. In order to offset the ageing of the population – that is, to keep the dependency ratio stable at its 1995 level – huge numbers of immigrants would be needed: Britain would need 60 million, or 1.1 million a year; France 94 million, or 1.7 million a year; Italy 120 million, or 2.2 million a year; Germany 188 million, or 3.4 million a year; the EU as a whole 701 million, or 12.7 million a year; and the USA 593 million, or 10.8 million a year. Such vast numbers are simply impossible to achieve. They would imply soaring populations, most of whom would be post-1995 migrants and their descendants: a population of 136 million people, 59 per cent of them recent migrants, in Britain; 187 million (68 per cent) in France; 194 million (79 per cent) in Italy; 299 million (80 per cent) in Germany; 1.2 billion (75 per cent) in the EU; and 1.1 billion (73 per cent) in the US. It will not happen – and it *should* not happen. It would, in any case, be only a temporary fix, since migrants grow old too. What's more, they tend to adopt local habits, so they will probably have fewer children once they settle in rich countries.

But just because immigration does not hold the key to the pensions crisis, that does not mean it should be halted. Without immigration we would certainly face shrinking populations and a much higher burden on working people. Women in rich countries, in Europe in particular, would somehow have to be persuaded to have more babies – no easy task. If that proved impossible, the retirement age would have to rise to over 72 in Britain, nearly 74 in France, over 74 in the US, nearly 76 in the EU as a whole and over 77 in Germany and Italy to keep the dependency ratio in 2050 at its 1995 level.

Offsetting the impact of ageing will require a combination of measures. Irrespective of whether rich countries choose to admit more migrants, they will have to raise their retirement ages to some extent. They will also need to ensure that more people of working age actually work (although it is inconceivable that all will, since some of them must also study, women will have children, and some will be physically unable to work). Working-age people will most likely have to save more (to provide for their own retirements) and pay higher taxes (to pay for others' pensions). But immigration could also help.

In the case of Australia, for instance, Glenn Withers' research leaves little doubt as to the best policy. If immigration were to continue at its historical average of 80,000 a year, the dependency ratio in Australia would fall from around 5.5 in 1999 to around 2.6 by 2050. However, with a constant immigration rate of 1 per cent of the population (amounting to roughly 200,000 in 2006), it would fall much less, to 3.5. 'It would save the government about 5 per cent of GDP in health and retirement support,' he says. The government should also encourage family-friendly workplaces to encourage larger families. And he points out that while raising the retirement age is an important part of the package, it doesn't have the same impact as bringing in young immigrants: 'The economy needs a mix of young, vital, recently trained workers too: a mix of experience and freshness.'[23]

To prevent the dependency ratio falling below 3 would require an annual inflow of nearly three million migrants each year into the EU. In the US, it would take just under a million immigrants a year (or about two-thirds of the current inflow).[24] In any case, rich countries with ageing populations will certainly attract immigrants from poor countries. As we have seen, the demand from older people for labour-intensive services in rich countries is already soaring – but the number of native young people who want to care for them is not. In poor countries, meanwhile, the number of workers is set to swell by nearly a billion by 2025.[25] Letting some of them in would make eminent sense. And although none of the papers discussed in this chapter allow for it, if immigration also helps spur faster productivity growth, it will increase the size of the economic pie available to everyone.

8

'Our Heroes'

How migration helps poor countries

Every year at Christmas the government of the Philippines prepares a special welcome for its returning heroes. World-beating sports stars? Globe-trotting businessmen? No: Filipinos working abroad who are coming home for the holidays. At the airport of Manila, the country's capital, prizes are handed out to lucky workers. And on Migrant Workers Day, the president awards the 'Bagong Bayani' (modern-day hero) award to twenty outstanding migrant workers who have demonstrated moral courage, hard work and a track record of sending money home.[1] One government minister remarked that 'Overseas employment has built more homes, sent more children of the poor to college and established more business enterprises than all the other programmes of the government put together.'[2]

Unlike most developing-country governments, the Philippines actively encourages its citizens to work abroad. It tries to place workers overseas and also licenses and regulates private recruitment agencies to do so. They typically work on two-year contracts that are usually open to renewal, primarily in Saudi Arabia, but also in Hong Kong, Taiwan, Singapore, Japan and the United States. They tend to go alone because they are not permitted to bring family members with them. Such temporary-work programmes are a model for what developing countries such as India are seeking to achieve through negotiations at the World Trade Organization, and they could be applied more widely to the benefit of rich and poor countries alike, without all the political and cultural issues that permanent settlement entails (see Chapter 10).

The government reckons that more than 7 million Filipinos, or 9 per cent of the country's population, work abroad.[3] They sent home $11.6 billion in 2004 through official channels – and perhaps twice that unofficially. This money represents at least 13.5 per cent – and perhaps as much as 40 per cent – of the economy, a more than fivefold increase since 1990. Remittances (the money that migrants send home) typically account for two-fifths of the household income of those with family members abroad. These not only allow Filipinos to enjoy a higher standard of living – televisions, home improvements and so on – but fund greater investment in education and enterprise. Studies show that as migrants earn more, they send more home – and this extra income allows their children to stay longer in school, reduces child labour and enables local people to start new businesses.[4] Remittances really came into their own during the Asian financial crisis of 1997 when the Filipino currency collapsed and the economy went into a tailspin. Receipts from workers abroad helped cushion the blow, as migrants sent home extra cash to help their hard-up relatives (and their dollar remittances now bought more devalued Filipino pesos).

The government encourages migrants to work abroad through official channels rather than illegally by offering them subsidised benefits, such as training on social and work conditions in other countries, life insurance and pension plans, medical insurance and tuition assistance for migrants and their families, as well as pre-departure and emergency loans through a government body called the Overseas Workers Welfare Administration (OWWA). The government has also made it easier for migrants to send money home cheaply and easily through private banks, and even offers tax-free investment programmes aimed at overseas workers.

The OWWA also helps returning migrants make the most of the savings and foreign know-how they have accumulated. Edgar Cortes worked as a casting operator overseas for fourteen years. When he returned to the Philippines, he set up a company to make aluminium wheels for tricycles, using his savings and a 100,000-peso loan from the OWWA to buy the machines and tools he needed. His shop, in one of Manila's most depressed areas, now employs four people. Sotero Owen was a welder in Saudi Arabia until a hefty pay cut persuaded him to return home. With his wife, he set up a weaving operation in Baguio City with the support of loans from OWWA. Using income from this business, he has been able to see his own children and some nephews and nieces through college. He was also able to build his house and buy a five-hectare property, on which he has started to farm.[5]

Mixed feelings

Most developing-country governments have mixed feelings about emigration. The departure of workers overseas is often seen as a sign of failure – and an exodus of scarce highly skilled graduates is viewed as particularly worrisome (see Chapter 9 for a discussion of the brain drain). Certainly, if African countries lose the few doctors they have, they will suffer – although, since governments do not own their citizens, preventing people from emigrating would grossly violate their human rights. But for the most part, emigration is a boon for developing countries. It can boost the wages of those who remain, while the remittances that migrants send back reduce poverty and can contribute to development. The Mexican government has started calling its citizens who work in the US 'heroes' or 'VIPs' in recognition of the huge financial contribution they make to the national economy.[6] When migrants return, as many do, they bring back the knowledge they acquired in rich countries. Half of the Turkish migrants who return from Germany start their own companies with money saved abroad within four years of coming home.[7] In the case of highly skilled workers, like the Indian internet entrepreneurs who have returned from Silicon Valley to set up world-beating companies in Bangalore, the circulation of brains from poor countries to rich ones and back can bring huge benefits. In fact, migration could do more to boost the economic prospects of many developing countries than either overseas aid or foreign investment.

If you doubt that migration can help poor countries close the gap with rich ones, consider Sweden. Not the super-prosperous high-tech Scandinavian powerhouse of today, but the grindingly poor, famine-stricken rural backwater of the 1850s. Then, wages in Sweden were lower than in Spain and half those in Ireland.[8] Over the next fifty years, though, Swedish wages quadrupled, so that by the eve of the First World War they were among the highest in Europe. In part, this was due to rapid industrialisation. But a great deal of Sweden's progress was also thanks to emigration. Between 1870 and 1910 one in six Swedes left for North America, along with millions of other Europeans.[9] Peasants fled the unproductive land in search of a better life across the Atlantic. They were welcome in America and the US economy boomed: living standards more than doubled between 1870 and 1913, as did productivity levels, while wages rose by half. During those years, the United States overtook Britain, which managed to increase its living standards by only half. Meanwhile, the poor countries that were sending migrants to

North America, such as Sweden, Italy and Ireland, also saw their economies prosper. Astonishingly, although the United States was in the midst of its industrial revolution, Swedish wages leapt from being only a quarter of America's in 1870 to three-fifths by 1913 – by which time they had equalled Britain's. In the case of Ireland, where nearly half the population emigrated, and Italy, where well over a third did, *all* of their catch-up in wages can be attributed to migration, according to Kevin O'Rourke of University College, Dublin and Jeffrey Williamson of Harvard University. In the case of Sweden, up to two-fifths of it was.[10] By relieving pressure on the land, emigration from Sweden drove up the productivity and wages of those who remained, helping to catapult Sweden from economic backwardness to prosperity in less than fifty years.

Counting the benefits

Except for some small islands in the Caribbean and the South Pacific, few countries nowadays lose as much of their population to emigration as Ireland did in the nineteenth century. In fact, developing countries' population is so huge (around 5.5 billion) and growing so fast (by over eighty million people a year) that emigration (around three million a year officially and perhaps another three million a year illegally) scarcely makes a dent in the overall numbers. But since, for instance, the average money wage that migrants earn in Europe is thirty-five times the average wage in sub-Saharan Africa, and since migrants tend to send back a sixth of their earnings, the remittances of even a relatively small number of migrants can make a significant difference, not only to their relatives, but to the prospects of their countries' economies as a whole. The money is spent in the local economy, boosting the demand for goods and services that locals produce. In countries like the Philippines, where remittances account for a substantial share of the economy, they can help alleviate poverty. And they can stimulate faster long-term growth in countries where poor people would otherwise find it impossible to borrow enough money to start their own businesses.

Estimates of how much money developing countries receive from their citizens working abroad vary. It is impossible to be sure how much money migrants send home, since they may transfer it in a variety of ways that are not recorded in official statistics. Transfers through banks are regulated and so relatively easy to track, but account for only a tiny share of the total flow. Most of the money is sent through wire-transfer agencies, like Western Union, which are lightly regulated. Another big chunk goes through channels that are not regulated at all. In Cuba, for example, the method of choice is a suitcase filled with cash. Complex networks of unregistered agents – known as *hawala* in the Arab world, *hundi* in India, *padala* in the Philippines and *fei-ch'ien* in China – leave no trace.[11]

But even according to officially recorded flows, remittances are huge – totalling $167 billion in 2005, according to World Bank estimates. The true figure, including unregistered flows, may be more than 50 per cent higher, the World Bank reckons,[12] or as much as three times higher, according to the Global Commission on International Migration.[13] Of that official total of $167 billion, $45 billion went to low-income countries such as India, $88 billion to lower middle-income countries such as China and the Philippines, and $33.8 billion to upper middle-income countries such as Mexico and Poland. The top developing-country recipients in 2004 were India ($21.7 billion), China ($21.3 billion), Mexico ($18.1 billion), the Philippines ($11.6 billion) and Morocco ($4.2 billion). Migrants in the US sent home the most money: nearly $39 billion in 2004. Migrants in developing countries sent home $24 billion to other developing countries in the same year.

The $160 billion that migrants sent home in 2004 is over

twice the $79 billion that developing countries received in aid from rich-country governments. It is also almost as much as the $166 billion of foreign direct investment – spending by foreign companies on factories, equipment and offices – which developing countries received. And it is more than the $136 billion of net purchases of developing-country bonds and shares by foreign investors.[14] Since the official flows underestimate the true figures, remittances are arguably by far the biggest transfer from abroad that poor countries receive.

In twenty developing countries, official remittances account for over a tenth of the economy.[15] The small Pacific island nation of Tonga tops the list: nearly a third of its economy comes from migrants' remittances. In thirty-six countries in 2004, remittances were larger than public and private capital inflows combined – government aid, foreign direct investment and net foreign purchases of bonds and shares. They were larger than total merchandise exports in twelve countries or territories,[16] and larger than the earnings from the biggest commodity export in another twenty-eight countries. In Mexico, remittances are larger than foreign direct investment; in Sri Lanka, they are worth more than tea exports; in Morocco, they bring in more money than tourism.

And they are rising fast. They are up by nearly three-quarters since 2001, with more than half of that increase occurring in China, India and Mexico. Of the thirty-four developing countries that received more than a billion dollars in remittances in 2004, twenty-six have notched up an increase of more than 30 per cent since 2001. In some countries, the increases were truly spectacular: Algeria and Guatemala reported more than a tripling of remittances, while Brazil, China, Honduras, Nigeria, Pakistan and Serbia and Montenegro recorded more than a doubling.

These official figures do not count the money that is transferred through informal operators (or suitcases of cash carried by travellers). Obviously, it is very hard to know how much money is transferred in this way, but it is likely to be a great deal. For a start, the fact that remittances doubled, tripled or quadrupled in some countries between 2001 and 2003 suggests that much of this 'increase' was actually due to governments keeping closer tabs on international transfers after 9/11. Household surveys also suggest widespread use of informal remittance channels. The World Bank estimates, for instance, that less than half of the money sent to Bangladesh – and only a fifth of the money sent to Uganda – goes through official channels. People are more likely to use informal transfers in countries where official money transfers are costly, where local banking systems are untrustworthy and where governments apply punitive official exchange rates that are much less favourable than black-market rates.

Remittances alleviate poverty

The beauty of remittances is that, unlike overseas aid, they end up directly in the pockets of the people they are designed to help. When they are spent in the local economy or used to set up small local businesses, they benefit the local community more generally. Although overseas aid can do a great deal of good – and rich countries ought to be more generous with it – it is often much less effective. For a start, it is typically channelled through developing-country governments. At best, these are bureaucratic and ineffective, so administrative costs gobble up a lot of the money donated, while even more may be wasted. More often, they are corrupt, so the aid is diverted into Swiss bank accounts or used to build grandiose presidential palaces. Even if foreign aid comes with strings attached – earmarked for healthcare or education, for instance – money is fungible, so that aid allows the government to divert money that it would otherwise have spent on health and education to other purposes, such as fancy new weapons for the army. Rich-country governments are not blameless either: many insist that their 'aid' be spent on products and services from their countries, such as hefty consultancy fees for their own citizens. In short, not enough aid gets through to ordinary people in poor countries who need it most.

Critics claim that remittances do little good to poor countries because they are frittered away on consumer goods such as televisions and video recorders rather than being invested more productively. But that's not true: some of the money is spent, some invested. In any case, what's wrong with consumption? If poor people prefer to spend their money on televisions, then it's up to them. Privileged Westerners, who all have televisions and video recorders, should not be criticising poor people's perfectly valid spending choices. Moreover, if remittances are sent to poor people who are struggling to put food on the table, or have just been hit by a natural disaster, they should surely spend the money on immediate consumption rather than invest it. Critics also point out, rightly, that those who migrate to rich countries are rarely the poorest in their home societies – because the poorest can't afford to move and lack even basic skills, such as being able to read and write – so that remittances may not help the worst off. But in fact, some very poor people do move and even relatively better-off migrants are poor by Western standards. Their remittances, moreover, benefit not just their friends and families but the whole local economy, including the very poorest people. According to one estimate, each dollar sent home by Mexicans boosted the local economy by $2.90 thanks to this multiplier effect.[17]

Study after study shows that remittances can transform the lives of poor people for the better. They alleviate poverty. They help cushion the blow, in countries where there is typically no social insurance, of potentially devastating events like a farmer's crop failing, or a worker losing his job or falling ill. They give farmers and small businesspeople precious access to funds that help them set up and expand their businesses. And they are often spent on education and health, which is good not just for the recipients but for the economy's development in general.

Start with the impact on poverty. The World Bank has calculated what would happen to poor people's incomes in a cross-section of thirty-seven developing countries if remittances dried up. In the countries where remittances account for a large share of the economy – 11 per cent of gross domestic product (GDP), on average – the share of the population living on less than a dollar a day would rise by half, from 24.8 per cent to 37 per cent.[18] In those where the poverty rate is high too – 38.9 per cent of the population, on average – ending remittances would cause the share of the population that is poor to skyrocket to 60.2 per cent. In other words, in countries where they account for a large share of the economy, remittances cut the poverty rate by a third. In the countries where remittances account for a smaller share of the economy – 2.2 per cent of GDP, on average – the poverty rate would rise by a fifth without remittances, from 25.6 per cent of the population to 30.6 per cent. In those where poverty is high too – 40.6 per cent of the population, on average – an end to remittances would cause the poverty rate to rise to 49.7 per cent. So even in countries that receive relatively small amounts from migrants, remittances can cut the poverty rate by nearly a fifth.[19] And since the true level of remittances is probably much higher than the official figures suggest, their impact on poverty is likely to be even greater.

Another study estimates that a 10 per cent increase in official remittances per person leads to a 3.5 per cent decline in the share of people living in poverty.[20] Household surveys suggest that remittances have reduced the share of people living in poverty by 11 percentage points in Uganda, 6 percentage points in Bangladesh and 5 percentage points in Ghana.[21] In rural Mexico remittances account for 15 per cent of household income.[22] In Guatemala, where half the population lives below the poverty line, remittances were found to be particularly helpful for the most poor: money from abroad accounted for three-fifths of the income of the poorest tenth of households, thus significantly alleviating their misery.[23]

Remittances also help protect poor people from harmful events from which people in rich countries are largely insulated. In poor countries, incomes are not only low but also often volatile. One year there is a bumper harvest, the next the crop fails. The price of copper soars one year, then plummets the next. One year the economy grows in leaps and bounds, the next a financial crisis destroys people's savings and throws millions out of work. Illnesses and crippling accidents are also much more common than in rich countries. What's more, people in poor countries are particularly vulnerable, because they generally have few assets to sell, or borrow against, to tide them through bad times, and because their governments rarely provide any kind of social insurance: no unemployment benefits, no handouts to needy families, no sick pay, disability allowance or free healthcare. People often have to rely on their extended family as a form of social insurance, but this is of little use if the whole community is hit by drought or a currency crisis.

Remittances help cushion the blow in several ways. They can provide poor people with a basic minimum when other sources of income dry up. They allow poor people to save more to tide them over bad times. And they can offset an unexpected financial blow: migrants typically send more money home if they know that their family has fallen on hard times. For instance, when Jamaica is hit by a hurricane, migrants tend to send home an extra $25 for every $100 in damage suffered, thus insuring local Jamaicans against a quarter of their losses.[24] In the Philippines, money sent home from migrants is estimated to replace 60 per cent of locals' income lost due to bad weather.[25] A study of a cross-section of countries found that $100 worth of hurricane damage leads to a $13 increase in remittances in the year of the hurricane and $25 more over five years.[26]

By making households richer, remittances can also affect their decisions about work. A study of Nicaragua found that remittances led to a fall in employment and a rise in self-employment: people take advantage of the extra cash to start their own businesses.[27] Even better, remittances to the Philippines have led to a fall in child labour, as families can afford to keep their kids in school.[28]

People in poor countries are rarely able to borrow money. But by providing a stable source of income, indeed one that typically rises when they need it most, remittances increase poor people's creditworthiness, because lenders perceive that they are more likely to be able to repay their debts, allowing them to borrow when they need to. When the recipients have incomes above the minimum needed to survive and when they have not just suffered an economic calamity, remittances tend to be channelled more into savings and investment than do other sources of income. This may be, for instance, because the migrant has earmarked the cash for his son's or niece's education, or for his brother to buy new farm equipment. It may be because remittances are generally sent to women, who tend to budget for the future better than men. Or it may be that households realise that investing in the future can be more rewarding than current consumption – if it allows them to start their own business, for instance. A survey of 6,000 small firms in Mexico found that nearly a fifth of their total capital came from remittances, rising to a third in the states with the highest rates of emigration to the US.[29]

A study of rural Egyptian households found that they spent only 12 per cent of their remittances on consumption, with most of it devoted to building and repairing their houses or buying land.[30] A study of Pakistan came up with similar results.[31] In Guatemala, households that receive remittances were found to spend a smaller proportion of their income on current consumption and more on education, health and housing than other households.[32] In El Salvador, which experienced massive emigration during its civil war in the 1980s and where one in seven households receive money from relatives or friends abroad, the children of families that receive remittances are much more likely to remain in school. Perhaps because the income from abroad is more regular, or because the sender insists that it is used for children's education, remittances do not just make families better off: compared with an equivalent increase in income from other sources, they have a disproportionately large impact – ten times as much in urban areas – on children's chances of remaining in school.[33] Remittances really can make a huge difference.

Hometown associations

The Miraflores Development Committee, which was set up to improve living conditions in a small town on the southern coast of the Dominican Republic, has made many improvements to local life. It has paid for an aqueduct, providing residents with a reliable water supply for the first time. It has funded renovations to the village school, health clinic and community centre. It is also paying for a funeral home and a baseball stadium. But this strikingly successful example of community development is based not in the Dominican Republic but in Jamaica Plains, a suburb of Boston, Massachusetts, where a large community of Mirafloreños now lives.[34]

This is typical: even while they are abroad, many migrants remain intimately involved with life back home. The largest Dominican agency in New York, Alianza Dominicana, which mainly provides social services to immigrants, also helps out with emergency relief when disaster strikes in the Dominican Republic. When the town of Jimaní was flooded in 2004, and over seven hundred people died or disappeared, the Alianza channelled aid from the US through local churches, bypassing the often-corrupt government authorities.

A website called conexioncolombia.com spreads information about Colombia among its expats around the world and channels their contributions to established charities in the country. 'With a simple click,' says Conexión Colombia's brochure, 'any person in the world can donate and contribute to the country's development. Connect yourself now!' Less than two miles away from the offices of *La Semana* magazine, which houses the headquarters of Conexión Colombia, Sor Irene of the Vicentine Sisters of Charity operates a refuge for the homeless of Bogotá, the 'street people', most of whom are mentally disturbed, retarded or addicted to drugs. Every night, Sor Irene and her helpers roam the dangerous neighbourhood to offer street people shelter, food and clothing at the refuge, as well as counselling and occupational therapy. All the equipment for learning new work skills – from manufacturing paper made from recycled waste to baking bread – has been paid for by donations from Colombians abroad. Living in the same convent is Sor Isabel, who helped found an asylum and school for orphans in the city of Tunja. The funds for buying the land for the asylum and building the dormitories and the school were provided, in large part, by the Foundation of the Divine Child (Fundación del Divino Niño), a charity established by a Colombian priest, a journalist born in Tunja and a network of immigrant volunteers in New York and New Jersey. The computers for the school were donated by IBM through the good offices of the foundation.[35]

Across the US and Canada, migrants have set up thousands of 'hometown associations' and similar grassroots organisations over the past decade, to help development projects in their home towns, mainly in Latin America and the Caribbean. France has a thousand or so *organisations de solidarité internationale issues de migrations* (international solidarity organisations stemming from migration – or OSIMs), and there are similar groups in Britain, such as the Sierra Leonean Women's Forum, which provides food and clothing for people back home.[36] Hometown associations focus on community needs mostly in rural areas, helping to make essentials such as health, education, roads and electricity more widely available. They can make a huge difference: their donations are often greater than the municipal budget for public works. 'Towns with a home town association abroad commonly have paved roads and electricity. Their soccer teams have better equipment, fancier outfits, and perhaps even a well-kept field where they practice,' one study found.[37]

Some hometown associations are moving beyond social projects and humanitarian aid to investing in economic infrastructure and community businesses – and developing-country governments are forming partnerships with them to leverage their benefits. For instance, under Mexico's 3-for-1 programme, started in 1997, local, state and federal governments all contribute one dollar for every dollar of remittances sent to a community for a development project. The 274 Zacatecan clubs in the US sent $2.5 million to the Mexican state of Zacatecas in 2001, and thanks to the 3-for-1 programme, Las Animas, a farming village of 2,500 people, obtained a $1.2 million drinking-water and drainage project with just $300,000 in club contributions.[38] By 2002, projects worth $43.5 million had been set up.[39] Between 2002 and 2004, more than 3,000 of these benefited a million people across Mexico.[40] El Salvador's government has set up a similar scheme to provide matching funds for community development, while OSIMs have been successful in extracting help from the French government for overseas development projects.

Globalisation from below

Most globe-trotting executives work for investment banks, management consultancies or big multinational companies. But much humbler migrants are now increasingly taking advantage of cheaper transport and communications to commute between countries. Their toing and froing is creating new businesses and trade links that span several countries: a kind of globalisation from below. For instance, the Otavalan indigenous community from the highlands of Ecuador have taken to travelling abroad to market their colourful ponchos and other woollens in major European and North American cities. Some have settled abroad, but they still earn a living by running garment workshops in their home towns in Ecuador, to which they travel regularly and from which they source their clothes.[41] In short, migration has allowed the Otavalan to access the global market rather than being constrained by their smaller and much poorer local one.

And they are not alone. Research by Alejandro Portes of Princeton University in the mid-1990s found that Dominican immigrants returning from the US had pioneered new businesses, such as fast-food delivery, software and video stores, selling and renting mobile phones, based on ideas and skills they had acquired there.[42] Construction industry bosses say that many firms could not survive without the demand for second homes and business space generated by Dominicans abroad. In El Salvador, immigrant capital funds new 'Tex-Mex' food stands in the capital, San Salvador, as well as software and video stores in provincial cities such as San Miguel. In turn, Salvadoran businesses have come to see the large immigrant community in the US as a big new market. The Constancia Bottling Company, a beer and soft-drinks firm, has set up a plant in Los Angeles to cater to the needs of the '*hermanos lejanos*' (distant brothers, as Salvadorans call emigrants). Others sell Salvadoran newspapers and the latest CDs and videos, or transfer goods and remittances across countries.

Portes and others have studied this phenomenon systematically, by surveying over 1,200 Colombian, Dominican and Salvadoran family heads in Los Angeles, New York and Washington, DC.[43] They found that transnational businesses were increasingly common – especially among immigrants who had been abroad for a long time, presumably because they had accumulated enough capital, know-how and contacts to get their businesses started.

The macroeconomic impact of remittances

Remittances can do more than just alleviate poverty and contribute to local development; they can also bring benefits to the economy as a whole. Just as money sent home by migrants can cushion the blow of a crop failure for an individual farmer, it can also help offset the impact of a natural disaster or financial crisis on the wider economy, as we saw for the Philippines during the Asian crisis of 1997. One study of thirteen Caribbean countries from 1980 to 2002 found that when the economy shrank by 1 per cent, remittances tended to rise by 3 per cent over the next two years.[44] In the two years after a devastating hurricane hit Haiti, for instance, remittances rose from 9.8 per cent of household spending to 15.5 per cent. Much as rich-country governments boost spending in recessions to help stabilise the economy – through public-works programmes, and because unemployed and needy people receive welfare benefits – remittances can have similar stabilising effects in poor countries.

Many poor countries find it hard to borrow abroad because their foreign-currency earnings are so small or volatile that lenders doubt that the debts will be repaid. But by providing a steady stream of foreign-currency earnings, remittances can improve a country's creditworthiness, allowing it to borrow more at lower interest rates. Developing-country governments are now even able to borrow using their country's expected future remittances as collateral – much like David Bowie issued 'Bowie bonds', borrowing money using his expected future royalties as security. Mexico was the first to do this, in 1994, and since then such 'securitisation' has taken off. Mexico, El Salvador and Turkey together borrowed $2.3 billion between 1994 and 2000. In the four following years, Brazil, Turkey, El Salvador, Kazakhstan, Mexico and Peru together raised a total of $10.4 billion. Even the poorest countries, which receive $45 billion in remittances a year, could eventually tap this relatively cheap form of finance, giving them the opportunity of faster growth.

Potentially the greatest benefit is that remittances could boost long-term economic growth. Putting children through school and paying for them to see the doctor aids the economy as a whole, because healthier, better-educated workers are more productive. If recipients of remittances start up new businesses or invest more in existing ones, this can provide jobs and boost growth. Of course, it is very hard to ascertain the precise impact of remittances on economic performance, but some studies suggest that they boost growth. Looking at a sample of seventy-three countries between 1975 and 2002, Paola Giuliano and Marta Ruiz-Arranz of the International Monetary Fund find that in countries with rudimentary financial systems where borrowing is difficult and costly, remittances allow people to bypass these problems, invest more (and more wisely), and thus increase economic growth. They claim that if remittances increase by one percentage point of GDP, growth rises by 0.2 percentage points. Therefore, in a country where official remittances amount to a tenth of the economy, economic growth is boosted by 2 percentage points a year.[45]

Thus, for developing countries, sending some of their workers abroad really can be a win-win. The migrants themselves end up much better off, as do their relatives back home, and the home economy as a whole can benefit, too. But what happens if a poor country loses its most talented people overseas?

9

Brain Drain or Brain Gain?

The costs and benefits of skilled emigration

Black Hawk Down, the Oscar-winning film about the firefight that followed the shooting down of a US military helicopter in war-torn Mogadishu in 1993, is the closest experience of Somalia that most Westerners have had. When the East African country descended into murderous anarchy in the early 1990s, its desperate plight briefly grabbed the world's attention, prompting the United States to send in troops to try to keep the peace – only to beat a hasty and humiliating retreat when eighteen American soldiers were killed in a gun battle on a single day, as immortalised in Ridley Scott's masterpiece. Since then, the rest of the world has largely ignored the place – but thankfully the large diaspora of Somalis dispersed around the world by the country's civil war has not.

Spearheaded by the Somali community in Britain, and with the help of Somalis in Australia, Sweden, Kuwait and the US, emigrants have clubbed together to help turn a dilapidated old school building in Hargeisa into a university that now educates eight hundred students a year. Hargeisa is the capital of Somaliland, the breakaway northern part of Somalia on the Gulf of Aden that was once a British colony. Because the rest of the world does not recognise Somaliland, it is being rebuilt without much help from Western donors. Remittances from abroad – estimated at around $500 million a year – are the main source of income for the three million or so people who live there.[1]

But foreign-based Somalis contribute more than just money. Expats in Sweden provided 750 tables and chairs for the University of Hargeisa, while those in Kuwait sent computers. Collaborating over the internet with a global network of Somalis, a steering group in London helped identify priority academic areas, wrote a curriculum and drew up a charter and a business plan for the university. The first vice-chancellor was an eminent Somali scientist who had worked in Canada for a number of years and who gave his time for free to oversee the university's crucial first few years. The university has even helped reverse the country's brain drain, with Somalis returning from the Gulf, Britain and Canada to attend. High-school graduates who would previously have had to leave Somaliland to continue their studies or do without further education now have the option of studying in their home country.[2]

Pros and cons

From a global perspective, it makes sense for highly skilled people like Harinder Takhar, whom we met in Chapter 4, to go work in countries like Canada, where their talents are used more productively. From an individual migrant's point of view, it is clearly a good thing too – or they would not move. But understandably, many developing countries are worried that their best-educated and most enterprising people might be leaving.

Remzi Lani, director of Albania's Media Institute, bemoans the brain drain that has stripped his country in the past decade. 'All three AIDS experts have gone to Canada,' he says. 'The best brains go and don't come back. We have lost one in six of the population – almost one person per family. There are 8,000 Albanians studying in Italian universities – more than in Tirana University. How many will return? Not more than 5 per cent.'[3]

A brain drain can harm developing countries in a variety of ways. Talented and enterprising people create jobs and prosperity for others: they start companies, spark off other talented people, train and mentor bright younger workers, and boost the productivity of less skilled ones. When they emigrate they deprive their country not only of their own skills and experience but also of these positive by-products. In industries where companies need a wide pool of talent to be competitive, their departure may leave fewer opportunities for local firms to achieve the necessary economies of scale. If highly skilled workers all move to work in clusters in rich countries, there is less chance that poor countries will develop their own clusters. The price of services that require skilled workers, such as accountancy or law, may rise. Governments may lose out financially from the departure of the country's highest earners, especially if they had previously subsidised their education. And a country's political, judicial and administrative systems may also suffer if too many educated people leave.

Yet the costs of high-skilled emigration from poor countries are not always huge. India, for instance, produces more engineers than it could profitably employ, so it loses little when some of them leave. Private medical schools in the Philippines advertise for students, who pay for their own training, guaranteeing them jobs in the US once they graduate. In countries that are desperately poor and badly run, the skills and education of highly skilled workers may be wasted – although their departure may make it less likely that the situation will improve. Some countries, moreover, are simply too small to be able to sustain a large number of skilled professionals. Many may thus face a choice between a 'brain drain' and 'brains in the drain' – and for the individuals involved, moving to a rich country may therefore be a 'no-brainer'.

More importantly, developing countries can also gain from exporting some of their brainpower. For a start, this may boost the wages of the highly skilled workers who remain, because there are now fewer of them. Moreover, since highly skilled migrants typically earn more than low-skilled ones, they are likely to send home more money. For instance, an engineer who earned $5,000 a year in a poor country may move to a rich country to earn $30,000 a year and send $5,000 of this home to his elderly parents. Also, many migrants eventually return home, bringing with them new skills and ideas acquired abroad. And a global diaspora can create networks that stimulate trade and investment and spread knowledge and technology, as Silicon Valley highlights. Just look at how Peter Jackson, the director of *Lord of the Rings* and *King Kong*, has injected new life into the film (and tourism) industry in his native New Zealand, not least by filming those 'Hollywood' movies there. The possibility of working abroad and earning higher wages may also encourage more people in developing countries to acquire skills and education – and not all of them will end up migrating. One study finds that an increased opportunity for migration increases investment in education and skills and that this gain outweighs the loss of brainpower from migration.[4] All these benefits may boost economic growth and more than compensate developing countries for the loss of some of their highest-skilled workers.

Countries such as China, Cuba, India, the Philippines, Sri Lanka and Vietnam all have programmes to encourage highly skilled workers to emigrate, which suggests that their governments believe the benefits outweigh the costs. India, which produces more highly qualified people than it can employ, is pressing at the World Trade Organization for rich countries to grant more temporary work visas to its skilled workers. But in order to ensure that their brain drain turns into a brain gain, developing countries need to make the most of their networks of emigrants, as Somaliland has done with the University of Hargeisa.

Even so, while some high-skilled emigration may be a good thing, too much may not be. The good news is that most poor countries suffer from relatively low brain-drain rates. The bad news is that the most acute problem involves a shortage of doctors in African countries devastated by AIDS.

Small isn't beautiful

Emigration of highly skilled workers from developing countries to rich ones has soared since 1970 and risen by two-thirds between 1990 and 2000.[5] They are attracted by the higher wages, better career opportunities and higher standard of living, and increasingly they are being courted by rich-country governments too. As we saw in Chapter 4, Australia and Canada are at the forefront of efforts to recruit highly skilled migrants from developing countries. Even European governments are overcoming their deep-seated antipathy towards immigration in general and looking to poor countries for talented workers. And governments have not only made it easier for highly educated migrants to come work; many have also offered tax breaks and other incentives to lure them.

Of the twenty million or so immigrants in rich countries who have some university or further education, just over half are in the US, 13.4 per cent in Canada, 7.5 per cent in Australia, 6.2 per cent in Britain, 4.9 per cent in Germany and 3 per cent in France.[6] Many highly educated people from rich countries work in other rich countries, too – within the EU, for instance – so that net brain migration to the EU is close to zero.[7] Britain in fact registers a small brain loss: around 1.6 million high-skilled Britons have emigrated – including Ridley Scott, who was born in South Shields – while 1.4 million highly skilled foreigners work in Britain. (Britain's Royal Society first coined the expression 'brain drain' to describe the outflow of scientists and technologists to North America in the 1950s and early 1960s.[8]) Some countries have even become stepping-stones in a brain-drain chain. Australia and Canada not only lose some of their own brightest people to the US; many of the most skilled immigrants merely stop off there to acquire citizenship and qualifications before moving on to the States.

In terms of raw numbers, most of the highly skilled emigrants from developing countries are from South and East Asia: over a million each from the Philippines and India, over 900,000 from Mexico, over 800,000 from China, 650,000 from North and South Korea, half a million from Vietnam, 450,000 from Poland.[9] But the countries with the highest brain-drain rates are in the Caribbean, Central America, the South Pacific and Africa. Nearly nine in ten highly skilled workers from Guyana have emigrated, as have over eight in ten from Grenada, Jamaica, Saint Vincent and the Grenadines, and Haiti, over seven in ten from Trinidad and Tobago, St Kitts and Nevis, Samoa, Tonga and St Lucia, over six in ten from Cape Verde, Antigua and Barbuda, Belize, Dominica, Barbados, the Gambia, Fiji and the Bahamas, over half from Malta, Mauritius, the Seychelles and Sierra Leone, and over four in ten from Surinam, Ghana, Mozambique and Liberia.[10] The problem is particularly acute for small, poor countries: twenty-five of the thirty countries with the highest brain-drain rates have a population of less than five million people. Among larger countries, those with a population of over five million, Haiti, Ghana, Mozambique and Kenya have lost the highest proportions of their skilled workforces, followed by Laos (37.4 per cent), Uganda (35.6 per cent), Angola (33 per cent), Somalia (32.7 per cent), El Salvador (31 per cent), Sri Lanka (29.7 per cent), Nicaragua (29.6 per cent), Hong Kong (28.8 per cent), Cuba (28.7 per cent), Papua New Guinea (28.5 per cent), Vietnam (27.1 per cent), Rwanda (26 per cent), Honduras (24.4 per cent), Guatemala (24.2 per cent), Afghanistan (23.3 per cent) and the Dominican Republic (21.6 per cent).[11] On average, middle-income countries have higher brain-drain rates, because emigration is costly and people in the poorest countries don't have the means to move abroad, but the poorest countries saw a sharp increase in their brain-drain rates in the 1990s.

For most of the developing world, the brain drain is not a serious problem. Most of the developing countries that have high brain-drain rates are very small. Although twenty-eight countries have more than three in ten of their workers with further education living abroad, those countries account for only 3 per cent of the developing world's population. A further sixteen countries have between two and three in ten of their highly skilled workers living abroad, but they too account for only 3 per cent of the developing world's population. Thirty-three countries have a brain-drain rate of between 10 per cent and 20 per cent, and together they account for 19 per cent of the developing world's population. So the seventy-seven countries with a brain-drain rate over 10 per cent account for only a quarter of the developing world's population.[12] Moreover, around half of these people live in developing countries in the bottom quarter of the United Nations' Human Development Index, where living conditions are so poor that highly skilled workers may not even be able to practise their professions effectively. When Somalia collapsed into anarchy, for instance, the emigration of its lawyers and university professors caused little additional harm, since there was no work for them to do.

Given that some skilled emigration may be good for a country, but that too much may be harmful, some studies have tried to estimate an optimal brain-drain rate. By one reckoning, developing countries with a brain-drain rate above 20 per cent would benefit from reduced skilled emigration. If that study is right, countries accounting for only 6 per cent of the developing world's population are suffering an excessive brain drain. The other 94 per cent would gain from more skilled emigration.[13]

Of course, such figures don't distinguish by profession – the loss of a doctor may be more keenly felt than the loss of a literature professor; or by quality – the doctors who emigrate may be the very best, leaving only mediocre practitioners behind. More importantly, what really matters is not how many people go abroad, but whether enough people with the right skills are left behind.

Can you find a doctor when you need one?

Dr Agyeman Akosa, the head of Ghana's health service, is in despair. 'I have at least nine hospitals that have no doctor at all, and twenty hospitals with only one doctor looking after a whole district of 80,000 to 120,000 people,' he says.[14] Dr Akosa reckons his country's public health system is virtually collapsing because it is losing not just many of its doctors, but its best ones. Ghana, with only 6 doctors for every 100,000 people, has lost 30 per cent of the doctors it has educated to the United States, Britain, Canada and Australia, each of which has more than 220 doctors per 100,000 people.[15]

Of the twenty countries that export the highest share of physicians they train, nine are in either the Caribbean or sub-Saharan Africa. Other studies estimate that Pakistan loses around half its medical-school graduates every year,[16] as does South Africa.[17] More Ethiopian doctors are said to be practising in Chicago than in Ethiopia.[18] Jamaica apparently has to train five doctors, and Grenada twenty-two, to keep just one.[19]

High emigration rates are not necessarily a problem – the Philippines, India and Cuba have all deliberately trained more doctors and nurses than they need in order to export them to rich countries – but shortages of medical staff are. Among the 47 sub-Saharan African countries, 37 do not have the minimum 20 doctors per 100,000 people recommended by the World Health Organization. Malawi filled only 28 per cent of vacant nursing positions in 2003, while South Africa had up to 4,000 doctor vacancies.[20] But the brain drain is by no means the sole – or even the main – cause of Africa's healthcare problems: the principal cause of attrition among health workers in Malawi is not migration but AIDS-related death, while South Africa has 35,000 registered nurses documented as being in the country who are inactive or unemployed, despite 32,000 vacancies in the public sector. Even so, in sub-Saharan Africa, where the AIDS epidemic has contributed to a dire need for health workers, emigration has certainly aggravated existing shortages.

Those most likely to migrate are the brightest and most experienced, who might otherwise be managing and training others. While remittances help fill the financial hole left by departed medical staff, whose training is estimated to have cost South Africa, for instance, $1 billion, they cannot fill the gaps left by the absence of trained staff in hospitals and clinics. And since a country's economic wellbeing is tightly linked to its citizens' health, the resultant devastation may be huge. But what to do?

The problem with healthcare in Africa is primarily that demand is huge, because of the AIDS epidemic in particular, while pay and conditions are terrible, especially in rural areas. So health workers seek better opportunities in cities, in other professions and abroad. Moving to rich countries is particularly attractive, because salaries are much higher and conditions much better. One survey found that monthly salaries for physicians in Africa range from $50 in Sierra Leone to $1,242 in South Africa – while salaries in Canada and Australia are around four times those in South Africa, not to mention the better facilities, career opportunities and improved prospects for their children.[21] Rich countries, in turn, have a growing shortage of healthcare professionals, especially those who can provide assistance to the elderly. The US Department of Health and Human Services projects a potential domestic shortfall of 275,000 nurses by 2010. The US produces only 17,000 medical-school graduates each year for the 22,000 vacancies that arise.[22] The shortfall is filled from abroad. One in four US doctors were schooled elsewhere – and 60 per cent of them hail from low-income countries. In Britain, 28 per cent of doctors graduated overseas, three-quarters of them from poor countries.

Given that migration is only part of the reason why there is a shortage of medical staff in some countries, preventing healthcare workers from emigrating would most likely be ineffective as well as unethical. The freedom to emigrate is a fundamental human right, according to the Universal Declaration of Human Rights.[23] Of course, rich countries could agree to not actively recruit healthcare workers in Africa. Britain has already implemented a 'code of practice' that bans the National Health Service from recruiting health workers from certain countries. However, while the code has been well respected in the public sector, it is not binding on the private sector – so the number of nurses recruited abroad has continued to increase. Other countries have bilateral agreements that either permit or prohibit recruiting healthcare workers from overseas. For instance, Norway's public healthcare sector is not allowed to recruit from most developing countries, but has signed agreements allowing Poles and Filipinos to work there. Some have proposed that an international agreement should regulate the migration of healthcare workers. But however well-meaning, such regulations make little sense. If both poor and rich countries suffer from a shortage of healthcare workers, then the global solution must surely lie with higher wages and other incentives so that more young people train as doctors in both rich countries and poor. Local shortages of healthcare workers could then be improved through increased financial aid from rich countries to poor ones, to pay for higher salaries and better conditions in African clinics – and from African governments making healthcare spending a greater priority. Indeed, several countries suffering from health-worker shortages, such as Botswana, Kenya, South Africa and Zimbabwe, have used foreign volunteers and recruited doctors from India, Pakistan, Cuba and elsewhere to work in the most disadvantaged and rural areas.

More generally, the blame for a brain drain cannot lie with rich countries alone. Poor countries have no automatic right to their citizens' labour – or indeed their allegiance. If poor countries are to retain, or attract back, their highly skilled workers, they need to foster their sense of national allegiance, make them feel wanted and provide them with better wages and conditions and a minimum of self-fulfilment. It is no surprise that so many Africans, skilled and unskilled, are fleeing their countries when their rulers are corrupt and show more commitment to lavish lifestyles than their countries' development. Those leaders can hardly expect others to sacrifice themselves when they set such a poor example. Would you stay working for a company if you felt your efforts were unappreciated and the boss was creaming off all the profits? Many of the countries with the worst brain drains are not just poor but also unfree. It is only natural that people want to leave – and that scientists, academics and researchers, for whom intellectual freedom is vital, are particularly keen to do so. It is certainly a tragedy that in Zimbabwe, three-quarters of all doctors emigrate within a few years of completing medical school[24] – but if you lived in a country ravaged by a despot like Robert Mugabe, wouldn't you?

'When the entrenched elites in developing countries see the highly educated young people emigrating, does that steel their resolve to make the changes necessary to stanch the brain drain or does it just reduce the pressure on them to give up the privileges that are barriers to development and that lead to the brain drain in the first place?' asks David Ellerman, a consultant to the World Bank.[25] Good question. Obviously, the answer is: it depends. But although the departure of highly educated people may harm their country's political, as well as economic, prospects, their individual freedom must come first. The alternative – to decree that people must remain in their country of origin, however loathsome, in order to try to change things for the better – is morally intolerable. In any case, poor countries can do little about it. Just as rich countries find it almost impossible to prevent unwanted immigrants getting in, poor countries cannot easily prevent people they want to retain from leaving. If the mighty Soviet Union couldn't stop its people emigrating, a tinpot dictatorship like Zimbabwe or a desperately poor country like Haiti certainly can't.

Making the most of the diaspora

Yet the brain drain has an upside, even for those countries that, according to the 20-per-cent rule of thumb, need to stem the outflow. There is plenty that developing countries can do to turn it into a brain gain. Some suggest that they should tax their citizens who live abroad,[26] but that is impractical, since it would require the cooperation of all rich countries. Moreover, it would probably be counterproductive, since it would give emigrants an incentive to give up their citizenship rather than remain involved in the affairs of their home country, let alone eventually return home. The best way for developing countries to make the most out of a global network of talent lies not with sticks, but with carrots. They should start viewing a well-educated and well-connected global diaspora as a brain bank to which countries contribute talented people and from which they can receive remittances, know-how and contacts – and perhaps ultimately migrants who return home. As we saw in the previous chapter, the money that migrants send home from abroad can give a big boost to recipients' lives as well as to the economy as a whole. But talented emigrants can provide much more for their country of origin than just cash.

Take Cecilia Ruto, for example. A Kenyan entrepreneur who ran a postal business that was forced to close because of government regulations, she set off for Australia seeking new work opportunities. However, put off by the strict immigration rules there, she decided to try New Zealand instead. There she discovered that while Kiwis had a passion for tea, the markets seemed to stock only poor-quality brands. 'I managed to organise with connections back home to import some tea for a trial run and the locals who tasted it were very impressed. They loved it. Then I knew that I was on to a winning idea,' she says. Thus emigration has created a new market for Kenyan exports that had previously been unexplored.[27] Since most small and middling businesses in Africa cannot afford to send staff abroad to find distributors and marketing partners for their goods, African expatriates can often do that vital work for them.

Expatriates' role in promoting trade is nothing new, of course. Trade among South-east Asian countries has long been dominated by the ethnic Chinese diaspora scattered around the region. One study found that the presence of a Chinese community in a country boosted trade with another country with a Chinese minority by over 150 per cent.[28] The tight-knit Chinese diaspora helps match buyers with reliable suppliers and enforce international contracts that would otherwise rely on the vagaries of dodgy national legal systems.

More recently, India's diaspora has been central to the stunning growth of its IT sector. Nineteen of the top twenty Indian software businesses were founded by, or are managed by, professionals from the Indian diaspora.[29] The industry relies for new ideas, new technologies and new markets on diaspora-led professional organisations in India and abroad, such as TiE (see Chapter 4), and diaspora-led subsidiaries in key markets, such as the US. Meanwhile, Filipinos working in the States provide professional and financial support for medical services in the Philippines. And a growing number of internet-based, diaspora networks, such as the Worldwide Indian Network, the Global Korean Network, the Philippines' Brain Gain Network and Thailand's Reverse Brain Drain Project, provide valuable sources of expertise and business contacts, while the Lebanese Business Network, the Armenian High Tech Council of America and the South African Diaspora Network help create new trade and investment links.[30] East Timor's ETRA is carrying out research and advocacy to improve treatment and prevention of endemic diseases such as tuberculosis and dengue fever. As Mercy Brown of the University of Cape Town explains, 'The aim of the diaspora option is to encourage highly skilled expatriates to contribute their experience to the development of their country of origin, without necessarily returning home.' She helped set up the South African Network of Skills Abroad (SANSA), an internet-based network which has been widely emulated in more than forty countries.[31] Some internet networks – such as Digital Partners' Digital Diaspora Networks, which has projects in India and Africa – have even developed virtual mentoring programmes that allow skilled expats and others to train their counterparts at home.

Migrants who return can also make a big difference. In 1993 Sylvain Zongo graduated top of his class in computer science at the University of Rennes in France. Job offers flooded in, but he chose to take his skills home instead. On 9 April 1996, sitting at his desk at the Institute of Research in Ouagadougou, the capital of Burkina Faso, he made a historic phone call – the country's first internet connection. After running the institute's computer department for several years, he decided to take the internet to the people. He and an old university friend pooled all their savings and opened Cyber Frites, an internet café that was soon very popular. In 2002 he launched Burkina Faso's first internet telephone service. The fledgling company made $100,000 in its first year. Thanks to Sylvain Zongo, landlocked and poor Burkina Faso is now better connected to the world.[32]

Governments in some developing countries, notably China, the Philippines and Taiwan, offer a wide range of incentives, including research funding, access to foreign currency and study opportunities, to encourage migrants to return. If there are plenty of opportunities to invest, and returning migrants are welcome, they are obviously more likely to come home, as they have in South Korea, than if countries place taxes and regulations in their way.[33] Given opportunities and political stability, good leadership and the rule of law, many of those who would otherwise leave a developing country will stay – and some of those who have left will return.

Brains on the move

As a globalising economy creates new links that cut across national borders, the concept of a brain drain is becoming increasingly outdated – in the technology sector, at least. I already discussed in Chapter 4 how Silicon Valley is not an American success story but a global one: the crucible where Indians, Chinese, Taiwanese, Americans and others combine to form world-changing new companies. I return to it here because the impact of brains on the move around the world highlights how poor and rich countries can both gain from skilled migration. A survey by AnnaLee Saxenian of more than 1,500 first-generation Indian and Chinese immigrants in the US found that half go back at least once a year to their home countries on business, and 5 per cent return at least five times a year. Even more telling, three in four Indian respondents and over half of the Chinese said they hoped to start a business back home.

Many already have. Saxenian has documented how Silicon Valley has created new networks of trade, investment and enterprise that span the Pacific:

> Talented immigrants who have studied and worked in the US are increasingly reversing the brain drain by returning to their home countries to take advantage of promising opportunities there. In so doing they are building technical communities that link their home countries to one of the world's leading centres of information and communications technologies, Silicon Valley. As the brain drain increasingly gives way to a process of brain circulation, networks of scientists and engineers are transferring technology, skill, and know-how between distant regional economies faster and more flexibly than most corporations.[34]

In the 1960s and 1970s, the dominant companies in the computer industry were behemoths like IBM that controlled all aspects of hardware and software production in house. But the rise of personal computers and then the internet has fragmented the industry's structure, which is now organised around networks of increasingly specialised producers. In the semiconductor industry alone, for example, independent producers specialise in chip design, manufacture, packaging and testing, while the manufacture of the materials and equipment needed to make semiconductors is itself split between several companies. Other firms specialise in devising improved modules rather than entire chip design. This fragmentation of the industry has provided opportunities for new companies from developing countries. But although these companies are independent, they need to work closely together. Migrant entrepreneurs can thus play a vital role in setting up new companies in developing countries, while maintaining ties to Silicon Valley to monitor and respond to fast-changing markets and technologies. Saxenian says:

> First-generation immigrants, like the Chinese and Indian engineers of Silicon Valley, who have the language and cultural as well as the technical skills to function well in both the United States and foreign markets are well positioned to play a central role in this environment. By becoming transnational entrepreneurs, these immigrants can provide the critical contacts, information, and cultural know-how that link dynamic – but distant – regions in the global economy. They can create social networks that enable even the smallest producers to locate and maintain mutually beneficial collaborations across great distances and facilitate access to foreign sources of capital, technical skills, and markets.[35]

For example, Taiwan's leading personal-computer suppliers – including Acer, the world's fastest-growing computer company – secured their initial contracts for IBM-compatible PCs in the early 1980s from Chinese entrepreneurs in Silicon Valley. Senior Indian engineers in large US companies were similarly among the first to outsource software services to India, thereby helping to establish the reputation and credibility of producers in regions like Bangalore. In my research for my first book, *Open World*, I witnessed how Azim Premji, a graduate of Stanford University in California, had transformed Wipro, an Indian high-tech company based in Bangalore, from a tiny firm selling cooking fat worth $2 million into a global IT services company worth nearly $2 billion.

In the 1970s and 1980s, around a fifth of Taiwanese college

graduates went abroad to complete their studies, and few returned. This brain drain generated a great deal of anxiety back home, but did not stop the country's economy from growing at a remarkable rate. Now, the brain drain has slowed and partially reversed. Migrants come home with high levels of education, some of it subsidised by foreign governments and universities, and many also have significant business experience. The expertise they bring has fuelled a boom in the domestic high-tech sector.

A close-knit community of return migrants, 'astronauts' (those who commute between Taiwan and the US), and US-based Taiwanese engineers and entrepreneurs have become the bridge between Silicon Valley and the comparably sized region that extends from Taipei to Hsinchu Science Park. The park attracted more than 5,000 returning scientists in 2000 alone. Companies there employed 102,000 people and generated $28 billion in sales in the same year. Of the park's 289 companies, 113 were started by US-educated Taiwanese; 70 of the companies also have offices in Silicon Valley, and many rotate their personnel between the two sites.[36] By transferring technical know-how, business models and contacts, they have accelerated the upgrading of Taiwan's technological infrastructure – and increased the importance of its suppliers to global production networks. Taiwan is now the world's largest producer of laptop computers and a range of related PC components including motherboards, monitors, scanners, power supplies and keyboards. And where Taiwan has led, India and China are now following.

Only a few countries have so far tapped the full potential of their diaspora network, and its impact has generally been limited to certain sectors. Its role in a country's development should not be taken for granted. Developing countries need to make big efforts to build links with their émigrés: relying on emotional bonds and nostalgia is not enough. They not only need to be open to the world but also to possess well-run economies, good government, basic infrastructure and a generally favourable investment climate.

Critics will scoff that while Taiwan may benefit from its foreign brainpower, Africa cannot. For sure, a country like Zimbabwe – which was richer than Taiwan as recently as 1960 – is currently ill-placed to do so. But if even Somaliland, which doesn't officially exist as a country, can successfully tap into its global diaspora, every country could.

10

It Needn't Be Forever

The case for temporary migration

Hang on a minute. All this talk about the economic benefits of migration is all very well, but what about the political and cultural consequences? Man does not live on bread alone, and while opening our borders to lots of foreigners might make us richer, it would also transform our societies. For the better, mostly, I would argue; but many would disagree. But leave that debate for later. Because many of the economic benefits of migration – workers to fill the jobs that need doing in rich countries, higher wages for migrants, more money sent home to poor ones – can be had through the temporary movement of workers, while most of the political and cultural consequences that critics fear could only result from migrants settling permanently, not coming to work for a few weeks, months or even years. Of course, some migrants who intend to live temporarily in a foreign country ultimately stay for good – think of Madonna marrying Guy Ritchie and settling in London. However, most don't want to stay and won't, especially if they are given incentives to leave.

Temporary-worker schemes have lots of things going for them. They would give rich countries the flexibility to allow in people as and when the economy needed them: if labour demand fell, foreign workers' contracts would simply not be renewed. Fears about the burden that immigrants might place on the welfare state could be assuaged by allowing in migrants to work but denying them access to social benefits or the right to bring their children with them. What's more, if enough temporary work visas were available to low-skilled workers, the pressure to migrate illegally could drop dramatically: why risk death or exploitation in the black economy if you can come to work legally instead? Poor countries could benefit too, since those working abroad temporarily without their families are likely to send home a bigger share of their earnings. Indeed, if the poor-country migrants working in rich countries rotated every few years, the benefits of migration could be more widely spread. And if temporary-worker schemes make it politically feasible for rich countries to allow in more unskilled workers legally, then migrants will benefit too, since they are better off working for a while in rich countries to save up a nest egg than being stuck at home or migrating illegally.

Certainly, temporary-worker schemes aren't perfect. If rich-country employers would prefer to hire someone on a permanent basis, having to hire a succession of workers on temporary contracts, each of whom needs training, may be more costly. Temporary migrants are also less likely than permanent ones to acquire useful skills, such as learning the local language – though the wage gap between rich and poor countries is so big that even on a short-term visa they may still find it profitable to do so.

Some critics object to creating a new class of foreign workers with fewer economic, social and political rights than national citizens: unlike natives, they could stay only for a fixed period of time, and they could not claim benefits or vote. That's a fair point: ideally, it would be better if everyone had the right to move, work and settle freely around the world. But in practice, they can't, and until this is politically acceptable it is surely better to allow in temporary workers who choose to come voluntarily than to try to shut them out entirely, leaving them poorer if they stay at home and with even fewer rights if they enter the country illegally.

Others object that such schemes won't work, because some migrants will decide to stay and rich countries won't be able to get rid of them. Indeed, some supposedly temporary migrants have proved decidedly permanent. Between 1942 and 1964, Mexicans were allowed to work in the US for up to six months a year under the Bracero programme. Although most returned home at the end of their seasonal jobs, some found ways to stay on, and the entry of hundreds of thousands of farmworkers to pick cotton and sugar beet in Texas and California provided camouflage for a substantial flow of undocumented labour.[1] Likewise, although three-quarters of the 18.5 million foreigners who came to Germany as 'guest-workers' between 1960 and 1973 left, over 4 million stayed – and thanks to judicial rulings that allowed them eventually to bring over their families, much unwanted permanent settlement has resulted. Inevitably, under any scheme, some workers will remain, but better-designed programmes could give migrants greater incentives to go home, as I shall discuss later in this chapter.

In any case, temporary-worker programmes are coming back in vogue. Rich countries are competing to lure highly skilled workers on temporary visas as well as permanent ones, and some are also starting to respond to the pressure for greater unskilled migration. For instance, the US, Canada, Germany, France and Britain all run schemes to allow in seasonal labour in agriculture and a few other sectors. Spain's amnesty for illegal immigrants in 2005 offered them temporary work permits instead of permanent residence rights. And most notably, in

January 2004 President Bush proposed the US's biggest-ever temporary-worker scheme.

Canada's seasonal-farmworker scheme, which is run by the Canadian and Mexican governments together with Canadian farmers, is particularly elaborate and hands-on. Over 18,000 farmworkers are flown in each year from the Caribbean and Mexico for an average of four months at a time. Farmers have to offer at least 240 hours of work over six weeks, free approved housing as well as meals or cooking facilities, and whichever is highest out of the minimum wage, the prevailing hourly rate or the piece-rate paid to Canadians doing the same job. Farmers advance migrants the cost of flying from Mexico to Canada, but recover it from their wages; they also deduct payroll taxes and insurance costs from their pay. Workers have a fourteen-day probation period after arrival, and farmers prepare a written evaluation of each one and place it in a sealed envelope. On returning to Mexico, migrants give this evaluation to the authorities. Farmers can specify the names of those they want, and they often do; the typical worker interviewed in one study had seven years' experience in Canada. Mexican consular officials meet arriving migrants at Canadian airports, inform them of their rights, and are entitled to inspect housing and solicit any grievances. Despite suggestions that the consular officials are sometimes ineffective advocates for them, most migrants report that they prefer the security of contracts in Canada to the insecurity of unauthorised status in the US. The migrants tend to be isolated on farms, so they do not spend much money, and they save an average C$1,000 a month from their C$345 (£160) pay for a fifty-hour week. Many Canadian and Mexican government officials think the seasonal-worker programme is a best-practice model, although there have been protests by migrants, notably because farmworkers (Canadian as well as foreign) don't have the right to strike in Ontario.[2]

President Bush's proposed programme – to 'match willing

foreign workers with willing American employers to fill jobs that Americans will not do' – is far more ambitious and much less interventionist. It would offer three-year visas, renewable for an unspecified number of times, to new workers applying from their home country as well as, initially, to the twelve million or so illegal immigrants already in the US – a clever way of regularising illegals' status. Unlike previous temporary-worker schemes, the visas would not tie migrants to a specific employer or sector – a big plus that would make the labour market more flexible and reduce the chance of workers being exploited. Nor would bureaucrats try to second-guess how many workers the US economy needs: the number of visas would be determined by the number of available jobs rather than a pre-set quota. Illegal immigrants applying from within the country would have to pay a fee and prove they were currently employed, while prospective migrants applying from abroad would require a job offer from a US employer for a post that the employer could not fill with a domestic worker. Temporary workers would be free to leave and re-enter the US at will – another big plus – but once their temporary visa was no longer renewable, they would have to return home permanently. An electronic database would also be set up to help match eligible foreign workers to US employers after verifying that a reasonable effort to hire a US citizen has been made. Temporary workers would be able to apply for permanent residence (the cherished green card), but only through existing channels, by being sponsored by an employer or a relative. Last but not least, to give temporary workers an incentive to go home eventually, the US government would try to set up tax-free savings accounts that workers could access only when they returned to their country of origin, as well as giving returning immigrants credit in their home country's social-security system for the work they had done in the US.

Money talks

The Bush proposal is a big improvement on previous temporary-worker schemes. It is economically and politically astute. But it could be even better. Martin Ruhs of Oxford University proposes that rather than forcing employers to go through the motions of pretending to look for local workers who might, for instance, pick fruit, it might be better to charge them a monthly fee for each foreign worker they employ.[3] This would give employers a proper incentive to find out if there really are any local workers willing to pick fruit, as well as to consider alternatives, such as mechanisation or outsourcing. The fees would also reassure locals that they are gaining from employing foreign workers, he argues. But care would have to be taken to ensure that some employers don't illegally deduct work-permit fees from migrant workers' wages.

In Singapore, the government sets and regularly revises flexible 'foreign-worker levies' that employers must pay to hire an immigrant. The levies differ by industry and by skill. To hire a skilled foreigner in construction, for example, an employer must pay S$80 (£27) a month. To hire an unskilled migrant, the employer must pay S$470.[4] With these levies, the government can try to fine-tune demand for immigrant labour. The idea of employer levies may be sound, but fine-tuning is not. Since governments are not in a good position to do this, it would be better if they set a flat-rate tax – which could be reduced over time as countries become more relaxed about immigration – and let the market decide how many foreign workers are needed.

The other big issue is how to ensure most temporary workers eventually go home. Under the Bracero programme, 10 per cent of migrants' wages was withheld and went to the Mexican government, to be given back to the workers when they returned. Unfortunately, few workers ever saw this money again, and their claims for deferred wages have been under investigation for decades. In South Korea, temporary workers contribute to a special account that is refunded to them if they leave on time or forfeited if they linger. The British government is thinking of asking some migrants to post a bond, like a defendant on bail, which they will lose if they choose not to return home. Philip Martin of the University of California at Davis argues that the social-security contributions migrants have paid in rich countries – which account for 10 to 20 per cent of their earnings – could be refunded when they leave. This would give them a strong incentive to return home and would ensure they left with a substantial nest egg.

Since developing-country governments also have an incentive to encourage workers to return home, they might cooperate to make temporary-migrants schemes work. For instance, the government of the Philippines regulates migrant recruitment agencies and assists with the return of workers who have been apprehended and deported. Another option is to give 'labour mobility brokers' licences to supply a given number of workers for specific occupations. Thus recruitment, matching workers to jobs and returning them once their contracts run out would all be the responsibility of a domestic firm, not individuals. 'In many cases this is how it is done currently in practice, but the fact that it is mostly illegal means that workers are at even more risk of being exploited and abused,' says Lant Pritchett of the World Bank.[5]

Dani Rodrik of Harvard University has suggested creating a global temporary-worker scheme. Under his proposal, skilled and unskilled workers from poor countries would be allowed to work in rich countries for three to five years, to be replaced by a new wave of migrants when they return home. As well as financial incentives for migrants to return home, he suggests penalties for home governments whose nationals failed to comply with return requirements. 'For example, sending countries' quotas could be reduced in proportion to the numbers that fail to return,' he argues. 'That would increase incentives for sending governments to do their utmost to create a hospitable economic and political climate at home and to encourage their nationals' return. In the end, it is inevitable that the return rate will fall short of 100 per cent. But even with less than full compliance, the gains from reorienting our priorities towards the labour mobility agenda remain significant.'[6]

So far, most international migration agreements have been between two countries rather than among many. But some suggest that agreement at the World Trade Organization could open the door to more short-term work abroad. The WTO's services agreement – the General Agreement on Trade in Services (GATS) – could allow countries to negotiate a relaxation of rules on admitting temporary workers. Mode 4 of the agreement covers the temporary movement of people across borders to supply a service – potentially anything from building work to nursing – but explicitly excludes permanent migration and workers in non-service sectors, such as agriculture and manufacturing. Mode 4 service suppliers enter a country to fulfil a specific contract for a generally specified period of time, and are usually confined to one sector or one job. They include business visitors coming to do deals, people transferred from country to country within a company, and foreign labour contractors. Although it has so far been limited to the highly skilled and hedged with many restrictions, it could potentially be applied more liberally and to low-skilled workers.

Alan Winters of Sussex University advocates starting with subcontracting schemes for low-skilled workers: 'With well-defined parties on both sides of the transaction – incorporated firms – the enforcement of the conditions imposed for mobility is much easier than it is for individual workers.'[7] He points out that Germany's existing bilateral subcontracting schemes place a duty on both local companies that hire foreign workers and overseas (subcontracting) firms to ensure that workers leave at the end of their contracts, backed up by financial incentives for them to comply.

A serious international discussion about migration at the WTO would be a big step forward. A limited initial agreement covering some service-sector workers could serve as a template for broader liberalisation. But in the short term, national, or bilateral, schemes are likely to offer a better way forward. Few countries want to make permanent commitments at the WTO when domestic labour conditions might change. Nor do they want to open their labour markets equally to citizens of all countries (as they would have to at the WTO): they prefer to privilege countries that they trust. And with the Doha Round of negotiations indefinitely suspended, liberalising at the WTO might prove to be slower than doing so unilaterally.

11

Alien Nation?

Does immigration threaten national identity?

The mass immigration so thoughtlessly triggered in 1965 risks making America an *alien nation* – not merely in the sense that the numbers of aliens in the nation are rising to levels last seen in the nineteenth century; not merely in the sense that America will become a freak among the world's nations because of the unprecedented demographic mutation it is inflicting on itself; not merely in the sense that Americans themselves will become alien to each other, requiring an increasingly strained government to arbitrate between them; but, ultimately, in the sense that Americans will no longer share in common what Abraham Lincoln called in his First Inaugural Address '*the mystic chords of memory, stretching from every battle field and patriot grave, to every living heart and hearth stone, all over this broad land . . .*'

Peter Brimelow, *Alien Nation*[1]

> I do not deny that people who speak the same language, were born and live in the same territory, face the same problems, and practice the same religions and customs have common characteristics. But that collective denominator can never fully define each one of them, and it only abolishes or relegates to a disdainful secondary plane the sum of unique attributes and traits that differentiates one member of the group from the others. The concept of identity, when not employed on an exclusively individual scale, is inherently reductionist and dehumanizing, a collectivist and ideological abstraction of all that is original and creative in the human being, of all that has not been imposed by inheritance, geography, or social pressure. Rather, true identity springs from the capacity of human beings to resist these influences and counter them with free acts of their own invention . . . The notion of 'collective identity' is an ideological fiction and the foundation of nationalism.
>
> Mario Vargas Llosa, 'The Culture of Liberty'[2]

'We will decide, and nobody else, who comes to this country' – so said John Howard, Australia's prime minister, to a baying crowd of supporters as he launched his campaign for re-election in 2001. His anti-foreigner rhetoric certainly did the trick: by declaring war on asylum seekers, mainly Afghans and Iraqis, heading for Australia from neighbouring Indonesia – infamously refusing hundreds of refugees rescued from their leaking boat by a container vessel called the *Tampa* permission to land in Australia – he turned around a campaign that he had seemed certain to lose. But was his bald assertion correct? Is immigration purely a political choice for Us to make? And who are We anyway?

People are increasingly on the move, yet the world is organised on the basis that people stay put in one place. It is split into independent strips of territory called states whose people, known as citizens, are ruled by – and in democracies, elect – a 'sovereign' government that recognises no higher outside authority within its borders. States derive part of their political legitimacy simply from controlling territory within boundaries that other states recognise, but they get most of it from being the means through which groups of people who feel a common bond towards each other – also known as 'nations' – govern themselves. In theory, then, the world is neatly divided into sovereign nation states: separate self-governing groups of people each controlling a specific piece of land.

In practice, though, the world is much more complicated. For a start, states' freedom of action is constrained in many ways. In part, they tie their own hands voluntarily: for instance, through international treaties committing them to allow in political refugees and allow out any citizens who wish to emigrate; or, if they are in the EU, by pledging to allow the citizens from any of the twenty-five member states to move freely to any of the others. In part, others force their hand: for instance, illegal migrants highlight the fact that states do not control their borders absolutely; while other states and multinational organisations, such as pressure groups, increasingly assert a right to intervene in states' affairs in the name of a higher good – such as protecting human rights deemed to apply universally – and, when they are sufficiently powerful, they can make a big difference. National laws also constrain what governments can do to foreigners: in liberal democracies, unwanted migrants cannot simply be deported; on the contrary, courts often assert foreigners' rights to stay and to bring over their families to boot. Rich countries have also foresworn immigration policies that discriminate explicitly on ethnic or racial grounds, so, for instance, John Howard's government could not exclude migrants who meet Australia's immigration criteria on the basis of their race or nationality alone. Political pressure from an established immigrant community, or from self-interested employers, may also constrain governments' freedom to remove illegal immigrants at will.

So states are not unconstrained and all-powerful. Nor are nations as clearly defined as some people think. Start with an obvious but often overlooked observation: even without immigration, the people in a country are forever changing, because some die, others are born and every individual changes over time, as do the conditions around them. So the people who make up the American and British nations of today are wholly distinct from those of just over a century ago, and they are substantially different from those of fifty years ago. Moreover, the changes in a nation are largely outside the control of the nation as a whole: nations do not generally dictate who has children, how many they have or how they will turn out. Thus, to cultural conservatives' despair, some people continue to grow up gay; to white supremacists' annoyance, black Americans tend to have more children than whites; while the puritanical tenets cherished by one generation might be rejected wholesale by the next. The notion of a single, unchanging national community – America as 'one nation under God'; Britain united in love of Queen and country, church bells, the Union Jack, cricket, warm beer, and so on – is a myth. Irrespective of immigration, nations change – and many in the older generation will inevitably lament about decline. Surely, though, immigration poses a particular challenge to our notions of what defines Us?

In *Alien Nation*, Peter Brimelow argues that: 'The word "nation" is derived from the Latin *nescare*, to be born. It intrinsically implies a link by blood. A nation in a real sense is an extended family. The merging process by which all nations are created is not merely cultural, but to a considerable extent biological, through intermarriage.'[3] This idea of nations as extended families, or modern-day tribes, is widespread – but except perhaps for Icelanders, it is nonsense. It goes without saying that Spain is at most a conglomerate of ethnicities – Catalans,

Basques, Galicians and others – under Castilian rule. But look too at Britain, a union of at least four ethnic groups (the English, the Scots, the Welsh and the Irish), which themselves are complex products. In the case of the English, we have an agglomeration of Normans, Vikings, Angles, Saxons, Huguenots and many more that are subdivided even today into Yorkshiremen and Lancastrians, Liverpudlians and Londoners, Cornish people and Northumbrians, Northerners and Southerners, and so on, their local languages and dialects surviving as different accents and regional words, with different foods and supposedly different characters. Or consider France, which embraces Celtic Bretons, Germanic Alsatians, Basques, Catalans and Corsicans, the people in the Midi (the south) who speak *la langue d'oc* and those in the north who speak *la langue d'oïl*, and so on. As for Peter Brimelow's single-handed attempt to create an ethnic American nation – he asserts that 'As late as 1960, nearly 90 per cent of the US population was European, the great bulk of it closely related, from the British Isles, Germany and Italy,' as if Sicilians and Scots were second-cousins – it is an almost farcical delusion, but worthy of someone who also thinks that 'the peoples of Britain merged, eventually'.[4] Tell that to a Scot in a Glaswegian bar – and then duck. 'In reality, nations are quite unlike families,' Nigel Harris rightly observes, 'since they are far too large (and past mixtures far too great) to pretend to anything except a fictional common descent – they are necessarily mongrel rather than pedigree.'[5]

If there is a British, French or American nation, it is largely a civic construct – not an ethnic one – and an unfinished one at that. Far from being clans whose origins lie in the mists of time, nations have in large part been forged by states in their own image. Governments have set out more or less consciously to mould the population under their rule together through a standardised language and common laws, a single educational system, a web of roads, railways and administration, and sometimes an official religion too. In the nineteenth century, for instance, the French republic united a hodge-podge of local laws and customs into a single national legal system; taught a single version of 'French' history and the French language through compulsory schooling for all; and imposed the ideals of the Revolution and the secular state (*l'état laïc*) as the official 'religion'. Similarly, the British government sought to foster a sense of Britishness through the common endeavour of the British Empire, the 'white man's burden', a special calling to greatness (and opportunity to advance oneself) reserved for Britons. Of course, these attempts at nation-building were not starting with a blank canvas – there is an ethnic component to most nations – but neither were they just a question of connecting the dots, nor were the pictures ever completed. Even when an ethnic nation supposedly predates the nation state in which it came together – as in the case of Germany – the reality is far more complex: Germans include Bavarians, Prussians, Saxons and so on, while the German nation state has always played host to minorities such as Poles, Sorbs and Jews. In short, the nation is a slippery concept, only loosely related to ethnicity, while the notion of a world divided into nation states is even more questionable: every so-called nation state has within it minority groups; some groups of people who consider themselves nations, such as the Kurds, have no state to call their own; and increasingly, citizens belong not just to one nation state but to several, possessing dual (or multiple) citizenship and allegiances. Immigration may complicate this mix, but it is not muddying any ancient national purity.

Nations have always been far more diverse – and divided – than nationalists like to claim. Moreover, people have never identified themselves wholly and exclusively with a nation: a century ago, for instance, a single British person might also be from Whitechapel, from East London, a Londoner, a Southerner, Jewish, white, working class, a tailor, Harry Goldstein son of

Benjamin, husband of Jessica and father of Isaac, and so on. Even in the heyday of national unity after the Second World War, British society was fractured along lines of class, ideology, region and religion. But while class divisions may now be less apparent, individualism and globalisation have combined to undermine the bonds of nationality. Since the 1960s, individuals and groups – women, gays, greens and so on – have increasingly asserted their right to be different and belong. Globalisation, in turn, has created a new global consciousness and new chosen communities of common interests and values that cut across national borders, while also helping to revive regional and local identities. Thus, many people in Scotland place more emphasis on feeling Scottish and/or European than on feeling British. Many Londoners feel that being from the capital defines them more than being from Britain. Muslims may feel that their ties to their co-religionists trump their attachment to country or place. Greens may place more weight on their environmentalism and feel a stronger bond to environmentalists in other countries than to their neighbours. Above all, people assert their right to define themselves, and to define themselves differently according to whom they are with: for instance, an Arsenal fan will be a Gooner during a game against Chelsea, English at a football match against France, European during the Ryder Cup golf competition against America, and simply himself when he is with friends.

More than ever, people have multiple, overlapping identities that are not limited by national borders. Thus someone may identify herself as a British Muslim, of Pakistani origin, of Kashmiri origin, born in Bradford, living in London, European, Asian, middle class, of working-class origin, university-educated, gay, a lesbian, a woman, single, best friends with Jane and Samira, a Leeds supporter, a Labour voter, on the left, a liberal, a human being – herself. These changes force people to consider what they really have in common. Is Britishness defined by a passport, a group of institutions, a set of values, or a shared history and geography? To what extent is Britishness even relevant nowadays? Although immigration has undeniably added another layer of complexity, expelling non-Western immigrants would not turn the clock back to the 1950s, still less to the mythical 1950s that some hark back to.

Let me be clear: I am not claiming here that nations do not exist; nor that they no longer matter. I am saying that they are not neatly defined and that the simplistic idea of nations as extended families – and therefore by definition at odds with the mixing of people through international migration – is incorrect. There may, for instance, be a set of characteristics that we might identify as English, and is typical of what many, but not all, English people are like. The English are said to have a stiff upper lip, for instance, though viewers of daytime TV may doubt this. One can also identify common values and institutions that unite many English people: some claim that there is a distinctive English sense of 'fair play', for instance (though foreigners may disagree), while polls show that most English people treasure the National Health Service and support the monarchy. But these characteristics, values and support for institutions do not define the English nation, since one does not need to have them in order to be English and one can possess them and still not be considered English: there are fair-minded foreigners and English cheats; Scots generally love the NHS too, while English right-wingers hate it; many Australians want Queen Elizabeth II as their head of state, while English republicans do not want her for theirs. The only definition of a nation that is consistent with reality is that it is a group of people who believe that they form a distinct political community called a nation. To a large extent, then, a nation defines itself. Or to put it another way, a nation is broadly speaking the widest group of diverse people who accept being ruled by a government that a majority of them has elected.

If a nation is not woven from a single piece of cloth, immigrants need not tear apart its fabric; they may instead add new threads to its rich tapestry. A nation state may admit immigrants, and lots of them, without dissolving its citizens' sense of nationhood, if the forces that create bonds between strangers still operate; and conversely, one can exclude immigrants altogether and still see other forces tear nations apart. France, for instance, absorbed millions of Italian immigrants in the 1920s without subverting the idea of Frenchness, so perhaps it could absorb millions of North Africans now without weakening the French nation. It cannot easily expel them, so it ought at least to try to help them find their place. Or perhaps the French nation is destined to fall apart anyway under the impact of globalisation and the cultural revolution of the 1960s, even if it puts a halt to immigration. And so much the better, the Bretons or the Basques might say, while the Parisian elite might lament it. Or perhaps a new idea of Frenchness could emerge, possibly a less restrictive and rigid form of Frenchness, one better suited to the times, one that was compatible with, indeed reinvigorated by, immigration. It could, for instance, preserve the French language as a common means of communication – not in aspic, but evolving with the times – while recognising France's rich heritage of regional languages and the new ones that immigrants from North Africa and elsewhere have brought. It could replace the simple untruths of '*nos ancêtres, les Gaulois*' (our ancestors, the Gauls) with a nod towards not only France's great regional diversity but its even greater ethnic diversity nowadays: as Gaston Kelman puts it in a recent book, France could recognise that '*Je suis noir et je suis bourguignon*' (I'm black and I'm from Burgundy).[6] It could reinvigorate the tradition of *laïcité*, the peculiarly French anticlerical form of secularism, with a more tolerant acceptance of religious difference that does not intrude on the impartiality of the state. It could celebrate the ideals of the Revolution of 1789 – *liberté, égalité, fraternité* – while acknowledging that the modern republic falls far short of them and endeavouring, by violating a few revolutionary taboos, if necessary, to make all Frenchmen more truly free and equal brothers.

Rather than viewing immigration as a threat to our national identity, we ought to see it as an opportunity to redefine our national identity in new, more appropriate ways. Even if there were no British Muslims, for instance, few British people would nowadays wish to place Christianity at the heart of Britishness. Likewise, although speaking English is clearly an important part of being British, speaking other languages – Welsh, Gujarati or French – is also compatible with it. Placing more importance on our shared present – we live in the same country, vote in the same elections, use the same NHS, and so on – and our common aspirations for the future, such as greater prosperity and security, is also preferable to harking back to a past that some do not share and others resent. Moreover, the ambivalence that some immigrants feel towards their host country – the desire to fit in while at the same time being different – is increasingly felt more widely: people are individuals, women, lesbians, Scots, Europeans and citizens of the world, as well as British. And like immigrants, natives increasingly have friends and partners from different countries, study abroad, travel round the world, chat on the internet to friends in far-flung places, and so on. Instead of seeing the immigration of those with different cultural backgrounds as 'diluting' our national identity, we should in part define ourselves through our cultural diversity, seeing our differences as a source of strength rather than as a weakness.

After all, if nations can be created, they can be recreated – all it takes is people, time and a common desire. In countries that have already admitted immigrants – such as Britain, France and Germany and others – some will remain permanently excluded and society will fracture unless the nation is redefined in a way that embraces different cultures and ethnicities. Immigrants too need to feel that they belong if they are to develop any national allegiance. Redefining, and thereby giving new life to, nationhood is not impossible. Although some forces are fragmenting nations – such as globalisation and individualism – states retain many of their nation-building powers. We still elect national governments that act on behalf of all of us; there are still national laws, national education systems, national newspapers, radio and television and national football teams; and although people move around more, they still tend to live in one place most of the time. And if nations can be recreated to better reflect reality and make them more robust to a changing world, opening the door more widely to immigration need not endanger them; it could even strengthen them.

The new American nation

Peter Brimelow is keen to assert that America is not just an idea, embodied in a set of institutions, but a nation (with a large ethnic component). So he rubbishes the notion that what might define the American Us is the obvious, such as respect for a document penned three centuries ago, the US Constitution – along with the ringing assertion in the Declaration of Independence that 'We hold these truths to be self-evident, that all men are created equal, that they are endowed by their Creator with certain unalienable Rights, that among these are Life, Liberty and the pursuit of Happiness' – a devotion to an ancient sacred text that seems quaint to non-Americans, along with the shared reality of living in the US today with its common fear of terrorism, common experience of televised elections and shared sense of global self-importance. This glue is not enough, he fears: 'America must be kept American,' he asserts, approvingly quoting President Calvin Coolidge, the man who fiddled while his country was devastated by the Great Depression.

'The American experience with immigration has been a triumphant success,' Brimelow admits – the US allowed him into the country, after all.

> But there are very clear reasons why the American nation has been able to absorb and assimilate immigrants. In considering further immigration, its enthusiasts must ask themselves honestly: *do these reasons still apply*? One reason America could assimilate immigrants . . . is that there were regular pauses for digestion. Another reason is that the American political elite *wanted the immigrants to assimilate*. And it did not hesitate to ensure that they did . . . Almost a century ago, the last Great Wave of immigrants were met with the unflinching demand that they 'Americanize'. Now they are told that they should retain and reinforce their diversity.[7]

He points to 'bilingualism', which he describes as 'foreign language-ism'; 'multiculturalism', which he describes as 'non-Americanism', in the education system; 'affirmative action', or 'government-mandated discrimination against white Americans'; and a 'systematic attack on the value of citizenship', by making it easier for non-citizens to vote, receive social benefits, and so on.

Start with bilingualism. Why is the fact that many Americans are actively encouraged to – and increasingly do – learn and speak another language as well as English corrosive of American nationhood, or indeed a bad thing in any way? Surely it is beneficial for many people to speak two or more languages. People in every other country are forever being encouraged to learn another language: it broadens the mind, introduces you to a different culture, helps you better understand your own, and is useful for business and travel. And even though people around the world are increasingly learning English as their second language, they are not forgetting their mother tongue or losing their sense of nationhood. Why then should the American nation crumble if some – or many – Americans speak Spanish as well as English? There is no evidence that Americans are speaking Spanish *instead* of English (see Chapter 12); indeed, if the incentive to learn English is so strong that Chinese and Russians are doing it, surely Mexicans who live and work in the US will do so too.

Move on to multiculturalism, by which Brimelow means that 'immigrants are officially not expected to assimilate'.[8] The question is: assimilate to what? If assimilation means respecting the same laws as other Americans – and all the cultural specificities that those laws embody – then immigrants are clearly still expected to assimilate. If assimilation means believing in the 'American dream' of achieving greater things through hard work and merit, then the overwhelming majority of immigrants subscribe to it with gusto. If assimilation means changing the colour of their skin, then that is impossible. If assimilation means adopting American values and cultural customs, then should all immigrants watch *Seinfeld* or *Oprah*; worship in a church, a synagogue, at home or not at all; support a woman's 'right to choose' or oppose abortion; believe in free markets or the New Deal? The reality of modern America is its great diversity, irrespective of immigration. So when Brimelow advocates a vast Americanisation campaign, to purge America of diversity, multiculturalism, foreign languages and hyphenated identities, how exactly, and with what, does he intend to scrub blacks, Asians and Latinos clean?

He does have a point about the pernicious impact of well-meaning affirmative action – the preferential hiring and promoting of minorities such as native Americans, blacks, Asians and Hispanics. There is no denying that giving some people privileges at others' expense damages national unity and gives those in the majority a legitimate interest in how many people enjoy those privileges. As Brimelow puts it: 'Because of affirmative action quotas, it absolutely matters to me as the father of a white male how large the "protected classes" are going to be. And that is basically determined by immigration.'[9] But he is wrong to finger immigration for exacerbating the problem. And his solution – that 'No immigrant should count as a member of a "protected class" for the purposes of US affirmative action programs'[10] – is unworkable, because one cannot legally distinguish between immigrants and native-born Americans once immigrants have become citizens without creating two classes of citizenship, which would be even more divisive.

Regardless of how many newcomers arrive in America, and regardless of the grounds, historic or otherwise, for trying to help some people more than others, giving privileges to those who identify themselves as separate minorities is corrosive of national unity. To attack immigration because of affirmative action is politically expedient but intellectually incorrect – affirmative action is causing American society to splinter regardless. Short of purging the United States of everyone but whites – something even Brimelow does not have the temerity to suggest – there is no escaping the noxious impact of affirmative action. And even if there were only whites in the US, minorities would still have an incentive to distance themselves from the majority: Italian-Americans seeking redress from Scots-Americans, Irish-Americans from German-Americans, and so on. Affirmative action is indeed a problem; but immigration is not. As for the 'systematic attack on the value of citizenship' that Brimelow bemoans, if anything this has gone into reverse as social benefits that were once available to all US residents are now reserved for US citizens.

Brimelow's histrionics have little foundation. He asks: 'Is America still that interlacing of ethnicity and culture we call a nation – and can the American nation-state, the political expression of that nation, survive?'[11] He doubts it: 'There is no precedent for a sovereign country undergoing such a rapid and radical transformation of its ethnic character in the entire history of the world.'[12] In fact, there are at least two: one next door; and one on the other side of the globe.

Canadians do it better

It is shocking, truly shocking that one in eight Americans is now foreign-born, and that most of these immigrants are from Latin America and Asia rather than from Europe. Disaster surely beckons. But what is one to make of the fact that one in five Canadians was born abroad and that the US's northern neighbour adds nearly 1 per cent a year to its population through immigration, mostly from Asia, with hardly any coming from Europe? Americans are notoriously nonplussed by what happens north of the border: perhaps Canadian society has collapsed already without Americans even noticing. As for Australia, well, it is half a world away, but it is much like America – a vast country colonised initially by white Anglo-Protestant settlers. Or at least it was. Now, nearly a quarter of Australians are immigrants, half of them non-European, and two-fifths of the population has a foreign-born parent. Even so, if a conservative like John Howard still thinks there is an Australian society he wants to defend, it cannot have disintegrated entirely.

Canadians make a virtue of their diversity. 'Sharing our community values with new Canadians of diverse origins lies at the heart of our citizenship,' says Joe Volpe, Canada's minister of citizenship and immigration. 'There are no degrees of "belonging" or classes of "membership". You don't get bonus points if your ancestors arrived 200 years ago, and you harvest maple syrup, and play hockey on weekends.' How is immigration changing Canada's idea of itself?

> Our concepts of citizenship and immigration have always been interlinked. By now, we could even consider them to be interlocked . . . In Canada, we define our core values simply: respect your neighbour, obey the law, embrace equality, and become involved in the day-to-day life of your community. Share our bounty, share our obligations, but share our values too – as would new members of any family, congregation or community. The people who choose to come to Canada are an energetic and highly skilled force of nation-builders. The very notion of 'Being Canadian' is constantly transforming itself thanks to newcomers' unique skills, work ethic, and the heritage traditions they add to what we call our 'multicultural mosaic'.[13]

Where the United States once had a melting pot, Canada has an ethnic mosaic in which the pieces increasingly consist of 'visible minorities' (as the government puts it) – visibly different, in other words, from the white Europeans who dominate Canada's older generation. Canadians are taught to celebrate their diversity: the Canadian Multiculturalism Act of 1988 aims to 'encourage and assist the social, cultural, economic and political institutions of Canada to be both respectful and inclusive of Canada's multicultural character'. And Canada's sense of itself as a nation, though always loosely defined, has survived – indeed, now thrives on – the country's ethnic transformation.

While groups such as Canada First oppose non-European immigration, most Canadians – 51 per cent, according to an Ipsos Reid survey in January 2006 – believe immigrants are having a 'good influence' on the way things are going in their country, although 40 per cent disagree. The country is evenly split on whether the number of immigrants it accepts each year – a whopping 235,000 in a population of 32 million – is 'too much' (44 per cent) versus 'too low' (10 per cent) or 'just right'

(34 per cent).[14] But what can bring this motley crew together as a nation?

An American journalist, Richard Starnes, once remarked that 'Canadians are generally indistinguishable from the Americans, and the surest way of telling the two apart is to make the observation to a Canadian.' But jokes aside, what does define Canadians' national identity? According to the late Pierre Berton, arguably the country's best-known writer, 'One of the unifying forces of Canada is the long debate about who we are. No other country debates the way we do, and that is because of the presence of the [United] States.' On the basis of extensive polling on Canadians' 'silent but deep patriotism', Anthony Wilson-Smith, a leading journalist, argues that 'Canadians are convinced there is such a thing as a unique national identity – even if they are unable to agree on what constitutes it.' Three in four respondents thought Canadians have a distinct character, with 30 per cent saying a tendency towards non-violence and 29 per cent saying a tolerance of others made them distinct. But interestingly, three in four thought that the way they view themselves revolves largely around the work they do, rather than anything specifically Canadian. At the same time, Canada rated third, after Ireland and the US, among twenty-three countries polled in 1995 on a series of questions designed to test civic pride in areas such as the economy, culture, the military and sports.

If national identity is about shared values, what values do Canadians share? When they were asked to say what 'most ties us together as a nation', the top response (although given by only 7 per cent of the sample) was 'our system of government'. When specific suggestions were offered, there was broader agreement on healthcare and ice-hockey. One observer remarks that

> The rather fatuous notion of old, that Canadians sometimes are, well, nicer, is not entirely hogwash. Canada's human rights legislations are a codified form of

> public conscience . . . Perhaps the unifying vision for Canada is civility. Fairness to others is a modest aspiration when compared with the dreams of world leadership implied by America's soaring eagle or Japan's rising sun but many advantages would accrue [to] a nation that becomes renowned for a patriotic duty to be kind.

An editorial in the *Globe and Mail*, Canada's leading newspaper, sought to give voice to 'the Canadian idea', what 'we stand for as a nation':

> Most of us already know in our hearts. We are against the idea that people should be treated differently because of their skin colour, language, religion, or background. We are for the idea that all Canadians should be treated as full citizens. We are against the idea that any person is more purely Canadian than another, no matter how far back his or her Canadian ancestry goes. We are for the idea that everyone should have an equal chance to succeed on his or her merit. We are against ethnic nationalism, in which people of common ethnicity rule themselves – masters in their own house. We are for civic nationalism, in which people of different backgrounds come together under the umbrella of common citizenship to form a community of equals. Ours is a modern nationalism: liberal, decent, tolerant, and colour-blind. That is what Canada represents to the millions of people who come here from other countries. That is the idea of Canada.[15]

In a very real sense, the debate about 'Canadianness' captures the ineffable nature of modern nationhood: Canadians are sure they have a unique national identity, without being quite sure what it comprises. Stripped of the myths of ethnic nationhood and confronted with the reality of the diversity of globalised individualism, Canada's debate leads the way for others to follow. Perhaps British and French people should stop kidding themselves about their national myths too. They might discover what Canada's example illustrates: that the very nebulousness of twenty-first-century national identity can be a strength, not a weakness, and that its elasticity can allow nearly everyone to find a place if they want to. It is a concept of a nation as an open rather than a gated community; one defined by diversity, not masquerading as uniform; one united not by common ethnicity, but by common institutions and the principles they embody. This may explain why Canada can absorb so many immigrants without developing an underclass or too great racial tensions. And it shows that the United States, whose national identity is primarily based on a set of ideas and institutions tied to a specific place, could also absorb many more immigrants without the nation falling apart.

It sounds almost perfect. Except for one big thing: what about separatist-minded Quebec? Or to frame it in terms of America's debate about immigration, doesn't Latino immigration to the US risk creating America's very own Quebec problem? Could, as Samuel Huntington fears, Hispanics in the US become a nation within a nation?

12

Huntington and Hispanics

Is Latino immigration splitting America in two?

Mexican immigration is heading towards the demographic *reconquista* of areas America took from Mexico by force in the 1830s and 1840s, Mexicanizing them in a manner comparable to, although different from, the Cubanization that has occurred in southern Florida. It is also blurring the border between Mexico and America, introducing a very different culture, while also promoting the emergence, in some areas of a blended society and culture, half American and half Mexican. Along with immigration from other Latin American countries, it is advancing Hispanization throughout America and social, linguistic, and economic practices appropriate for an Anglo-Hispanic society.

Samuel Huntington, *Who are We?*[1]

With their own radio and TV stations, newspapers, films, and magazines, the Mexican Americans are creating an

> Hispanic culture separate and apart from America's larger culture. They are becoming a nation within a nation.
>
> Patrick Buchanan, *The Death of the West*[2]

> These population dynamics will result in the 'browning' of America, the Hispanization of America. It is already happening and it is inescapable.
>
> Henry Cisneros, former mayor of San Antonio, Texas[3]

> I hope very much that I'm the last president in American history who can't speak Spanish.
>
> Bill Clinton[4]

With her greying hair and old-fashioned knitwear, Miriam Mejia looks more like a kindly grandmother than a menace to American society – but if you believe one of America's most influential intellectuals, Hispanic immigrants like Miriam could turn out to be a bigger threat to the United States than Osama bin Laden. Nobody is suggesting that people like Miriam are going to kill anyone, but Samuel Huntington does believe that Latin American immigrants could tear America apart. The Harvard academic shot to fame in the 1990s by warning of the threat to the US from a global 'clash of civilisations' with the Islamic world. Now he has caused a storm by warning of the peril from an enemy within: a domestic clash of civilisations between its Anglo-Protestant majority and its growing Latino minority:

> The persistent inflow of Hispanic immigrants threatens to divide the United States into two peoples, two cultures, and two languages . . . Unlike past immigrant groups, Mexicans and other Latinos have not assimilated into mainstream US culture, forming instead their own political and linguistic enclaves – from Los Angeles to

> Miami – and rejecting the Anglo-Protestant values that built the American dream. The United States ignores this challenge at its peril.[5]

One such enclave is Washington Heights in New York City, home to a large community of people originally from the Dominican Republic, the country which shares the Caribbean island of Hispaniola with Haiti. Based there is the largest provider of social services to Dominican Americans, the Alianza Dominicana – its Spanish name alone doubtless an affront to Huntington – which Miriam Mejia runs. Her husband had come to visit someone in the US in 1986 and ended up staying, initially illegally. She followed him in 1988, starting work at the Alianza the following year and getting her US residency the year after that. 'To be healthy mentally, I have to go back to the Dominican Republic twice a year,' she says, our discussion flipping freely between English and Spanish. 'I have my mother there, a sister and a brother. I call them three times a week, sometimes more. Here I have one brother and three sisters . . . Why do I have to go back? To see my country, to see the sea and blue sky, to feel the weather, to see my old friends – and then to come here with new energy and continue working.' What could possibly be wrong with that?

A great deal, according to Huntington. He believes that the United States is based on the Anglo-Protestant culture of its first settlers and the 'creed' – the set of beliefs embodied in the Declaration of Independence penned by Thomas Jefferson in 1776, such as Americans' inalienable rights to 'life, liberty and the pursuit of happiness' – that it produced. These are under assault, he says, from a battery of heavy artillery:

> the popularity in intellectual and political circles of the doctrines of multiculturalism and diversity; the rise of group identities based on race, ethnicity, and gender over

> national identity; the impact of transnational cultural diasporas; the expanding number of immigrants with dual nationalities and dual loyalties; and the growing salience for US intellectual, business, and political elites of cosmopolitan and transnational identities.

Of these many threats, he says the greatest is Latin American immigration. In effect, he argues, millions of people like Miriam – Spanish-speaking, one foot still in their country of origin, asserting their right to be American *and* Latino – are splitting America into two peoples with two cultures (Anglo and Hispanic) and two languages (English and Spanish). Really?

'Human beings can go from one place to another and we change in the process,' counters Miriam. 'Your vision immediately changes, because you are at least in touch with another culture.' She may not be a Harvard academic, but she certainly knows a thing or two about life. 'I'm fifty-something, and I'd like to go back to my country one day, but my children have already graduated from university and they want to stay here – and I want to be with my children.' She pauses. 'Maintaining your roots is not easy. My children feel Dominican but they like to be here, too. They eat Dominican, they know the music, but they don't travel there as frequently as me. My eldest daughter goes once a year, the second and youngest ones less. They speak fluent Spanish and English, but the second has an accent since she went away to university.' She pauses again. 'I'm proud of them.' Another pause. 'I work with a lot of young people, so they don't lose the Dominican connection . . . I run a folkloric dance group so that young people can experience Dominican culture as well as talk about it.' I ask her whether she feels Hispanic. 'I don't like the term "Hispanic",' she replies. 'Latin Americans are all different. Each country has its own ways. Latin American immigrants are not like a block. But our vision is to work together with other communities. We share the Spanish language.'

In many respects, Miriam is remarkably integrated into mainstream American life. She runs an organisation that has to work closely with the New York City government, federal agencies, private funders and service providers. In a very real sense, then, she is plugged in to American society. And unlike many immigrants (especially women) who arrived in America a century ago, she speaks good English. That she can call and travel to the Dominican Republic regularly certainly allows her to stay in touch with her home country in a way that immigrants a century ago could not, but earlier immigrants could still maintain a strong connection to their country of origin without any direct contact. My grandfather was never able to return to his beloved homeland, because he died in 1989 while Estonia was still under Soviet rule, but that did not stop him maintaining strong ties to it in his heart and through the Estonian community in California.

But what about the children and grandchildren of Latino immigrants? How are they adapting to America? Whereas Miriam has a foreign accent when she speaks English, Griselidys Polanco sounds like a New Yorker – unsurprisingly, since she was born in New York City twenty-two years ago. She is already married, to a Dominican American, and has a daughter, aged four. Her father, an assistant chef, immigrated in 1979; her mother, a housewife, in 1982. Griselidys studied business and veterinary science at college and aims to set up her own animal clinic. She speaks fluent Spanish, also with no accent. I ask if she maintains contact with the Dominican Republic. 'I went there three and a half years ago,' she replies. 'I still have family over there, but it feels like a foreign country: the laws are different, what you buy is different, the TV and music are different. I watch Dominican TV here, but it's made here. Dominicans treat you like an American. But after a couple of days you feel comfortable.' The Dominican Republic is clearly her parents' country rather than her own: 'My parents came here for a reason: a better life for us,' she says. 'My true heritage is

Dominican. I wouldn't like to lose it. Out of love and respect for them, I owe it to them to keep it going.' Whereas Miriam calls the Dominican Republic her 'country', Griselidys refers to her Dominican 'heritage', one which she has to make an effort not to lose. How will her daughter, twice removed from the Dominican Republic, end up feeling?

Alejandra Malave is thirty-one, and she too was born in the US. Her parents came to work, but they've now retired and returned to the Dominican Republic. She has been there only a few times. 'As I was growing up I felt Dominican,' she says.

'I was the only member of the family born in the US. I am a US citizen, but I felt Dominican. It was not until I went to college that I embraced both. I'm not Dominican or American, I'm both. I speak fluent Spanish but people say I have an accent. In the Dominican Republic people ask me where I'm from. I want to keep my cultural tradition without limiting myself.

'I also embrace my African background. People ask me why I don't straighten my hair, why my hair is so short. There is a lot more discrimination and racism in the Dominican Republic: two of the three nightclubs I tried to go to said I couldn't come in because of the colour of my skin. Here they'd have got a lawsuit. I'd never experienced discrimination so upfront: it was very blatant . . . I've now made it my business to be black.'

Alejandra is a social worker and a psychotherapist. She studied sociology and African studies at college, and has a masters degree in social work. I ask why she works for the Alianza Dominicana. 'I grew up in the community. There's a connection and I want to make a change in Washington Heights. It's not an ethnic thing, it's geographic.'

She has a ten-year-old daughter, who is what academics call a 'third-generation immigrant': the grandchild of someone born abroad. 'She didn't know what being Dominican meant until we travelled there in 2003,' says Alejandra. 'She didn't know how to speak Spanish. When we were over there, she wanted to go out and play with the other kids but she didn't dare join in because she didn't speak Spanish. She is now learning it at school. Her Spanish is fairly good.'

I am not claiming for a second that I can disprove Huntington's fears about America splitting in two through a few personal interviews, however representative. In fact, Dominicans are notorious for maintaining stronger links with their home country than other Latino immigrants, travelling home more often and speaking more Spanish. Rather my aim is to highlight how Huntington's concept of how immigrants adapt, or *should* adapt, to America – all or nothing, you're either American or you're not; or, to put it more starkly, you're either with us or against us – is hopelessly simplistic and unnecessarily restrictive. If you believe that 'assimilation' is a black-and-white issue, then you can interpret shades of grey as a failure to assimilate; but if you conceive of cultural identity in a more realistic and less restrictive way, you will see that it is all shades of grey, so the shades that immigrants display may be much less distinctive or worrying. Immigrants are not aligning themselves with a single definition – Anglo-Protestant or otherwise – of what it means to be American: they are fitting into a broad spectrum of Americanness. They are not alone in this: in a globalising world, more and more non-Latino Americans also have foreign connections and express a wide variety of values.

Anglo-Protestant?

Huntington's argument is wrong in so many ways that it is hard to know where to start. Take the assertion that America is based on an Anglo-Protestant culture and creed, and that immigrants must adopt this wholeheartedly as their own – or 'assimilate' – in order to become American. 'Key elements of that culture include the English language; Christianity; religious commitment; English concepts of the rule of law, including the responsibility of rulers and the rights of individuals; and dissenting Protestant values of individualism, the work ethic, and the belief that humans have the ability and the duty to try to create a heaven on earth, a "city on a hill",' he argues. Undeniably, most Americans are Christian and religious: 81 per cent describe themselves as Protestant or Catholic, and the same number say that prayer is an important part of their daily lives.[6] But these are not prerequisites of being American. It will be news to Jews (2 per cent of the US population) that their religion is incompatible with being American, while non-religious people (9 per cent) are hardly un-American. In any case, Latino immigrants are overwhelmingly practising Christians, albeit mostly Catholic – as indeed are a quarter of the US population. But the fact that Huntington is comfortable that being Catholic is compatible with being American – unlike those who argued that John F. Kennedy shouldn't be president because he would take orders from the Vatican – suggests that the cultural components of American identity are remarkably elastic, and have evolved over time, as he himself admits. Moreover, if Huntington believes America is still fundamentally based on Anglo Protestant values despite a quarter of its population being Catholic, then those values would appear to be remarkably robust – and his fears about their fragility in the face of much smaller Latino immigration unfounded.

The notion that America's political values are inherently Anglo or Protestant is also incorrect. It would surprise the Chinese, for instance, to hear that the work ethic is a uniquely Anglo-Protestant trait. As Tamar Jacoby of the Manhattan Institute, a think-tank in New York City, points out:

> Many of the Enlightenment ideas upon which the US Constitution is based originated in the British Isles, but that does not make them inherently British – any more

> than Christianity, which originated on the shores of the Mediterranean, is inherently Middle Eastern or Italian . . . Americans long ago appropriated Enlightenment ideals and used them to shape distinctively American institutions, which have been subtly influenced and improved by input from a long succession of immigrant groups.[7]

To what, then, do immigrants have to subscribe in order to become American? They do not have to try to ape George Bush and transform themselves into WASPs (White Anglo-Saxon Protestants). As Donna Shalala, Secretary of Health and Human Services in the Clinton administration, remarked, 'My parents came from Lebanon. I don't identify with the Pilgrims on a personal level.'[8] But immigrants do have to learn English, which is America's dominant – if not official – language. Also, says Tamar Jacoby,

> We ask newcomers to buy into our political values by understanding and embracing the Constitution and its ideals. We require that they identify with the United States by swearing loyalty to the nation and committing to its defense when necessary. But we have never demanded that newcomers adopt any particular cultural habits, Anglo Protestant or otherwise. As long as they adopt our ideas about freedom, tolerance, and equality before the law, we have left them to do as they pleased in the private sphere. We have always been confident that US political values – the very act of living in this republic – would eventually transform their attitudes toward matters as deeply personal as the role of the individual, ambition, opportunity, self-reliance, responsibility, how merit and initiative should be rewarded, and the proper place of ethnicity in the larger

commonweal. And transform them our free and tolerant way of life always has.[9]

Mexican wave

Huntington claims that Latin American, and in particular Mexican, immigration is more threatening to America's integrity than previous immigration (and current immigration from other countries) because of a combination of six factors. First, Mexico is poor and next door. 'Contiguity enables Mexican immigrants to remain in intimate contact with their families, friends, and home localities in Mexico as no other immigrants have been able to do,' he says. Second, whereas Filipinos accounted for only 4.3 per cent of the US's foreign-born population in 2000, Mexicans accounted for 27.6 per cent. They made up more than half of Latin American immigrants to the States in the 1990s, and by 2000 Hispanics totalled around half of all migrants entering the country. Hispanics accounted for 12 per cent of the US population in 2000, and may be as much as a quarter of it in 2050, Huntington reckons, due to continuing immigration and higher birth rates. Third, illegal immigration continues unabated – it may now be as high as half a million a year, and surpass twelve million people in total. Huntington reckons that over two-thirds of illegals are Mexican.

Fourth, Hispanic immigrants tend to concentrate regionally: Mexicans in southern California, Cubans in Miami, Dominicans in New York. For instance, in 2000 46.5 per cent of Los Angeles' residents were Hispanic – nearly two-thirds of them of Mexican origin – while 29.7 per cent were non-Hispanic whites. It is estimated that Hispanics will make up more than half of LA's population by 2010. By 2002, more than 70 per cent of the students in the Los Angeles Unified School District were Hispanic, again predominantly Mexican, with the proportion increasing steadily; only one in ten were non-Hispanic whites. In 2003, for the first time since the 1850s, a majority of the babies born in California were Hispanic. 'The more concentrated immigrants become,' argues Huntington, 'the slower and less complete is their assimilation.' In 1998 'José' replaced 'Michael' as the most popular name for newborn boys in both California and Texas. But, comparing Latino immigration to an invading army, Huntington warns that Hispanics are also establishing 'beachheads' elsewhere in the US. Fifth, the current wave of Mexican immigration shows no signs of ebbing – and it is unlikely to, Huntington reckons, while US living standards, adjusted for differences in purchasing power, are four times higher than in Mexico. Sixth, Mexicans can lay claim to a large part of the US territory where they are now settling: almost all of Texas, New Mexico, Arizona, California, Nevada and Utah was part of Mexico until the US annexed them in the 1830s and 1840s. The South-west could therefore, he thinks, become more than just a separatist province like Quebec; it could be claimed by Mexico itself. In short, Mexican immigration is large, sustained, in large part illegal, and concentrated in areas to which the US's next-door neighbour has a historical claim.

These fears echo those of the right-wing politician Pat Buchanan:

> The numbers pouring in from Mexico are larger than any wave from any other country in so short a time . . . Mexicans not only come from another culture, but millions are of another race . . . Millions of Mexicans are here illegally . . . Unlike the immigrants of old, who bade farewell forever to their native lands when they boarded the ship, for Mexicans, the mother country is right next door . . . Today, ethnic enclaves are encouraged to maintain their separate identities, and in the barrios ethnic chauvinism is rife.[10]

Huntington is right that this combination of six factors is unprecedented in US history, but each of the points he makes is questionable. 'In the past, immigrants originated overseas and often overcame severe obstacles and hardships to reach the United States,' he says – whereas now they just have to risk death in the Arizona desert or the shark-infested waters between Cuba and Florida. Nor does the fact that Mexico is next door necessarily make it easier for Mexicans to stay in touch with their country of origin. Unlike, say, Filipinos, most Mexican immigrants are illegal – and without documents, they cannot readily travel back and forth to Mexico – and it is as cheap and easy for a Filipino to call home as it is for a Mexican. Nor is the scale and persistence of Mexican immigration without precedent when compared to the size of the US population. In the 1990s, an estimated 4.2 million Mexicans immigrated to the United States, both legally and illegally. 'That represents 1.5 Mexican immigrants per 1,000 US residents each year. In comparison, the nation absorbed an average of 3.6 Irish immigrants per 1,000 US residents annually in the 1840s and 1850s – more than double the current inflow of Mexicans,' Daniel Griswold of the Cato Institute, a think-tank in Washington, DC, points out. Moreover, 'For half a century, from 1840 to 1890, the rate of German immigration was greater in every decade than the current inflow of Mexicans. From 1901 to 1910, Russian, Italian, and Austro-Hungarian immigration each surpassed the current rate of Mexican migration. Yet US society successfully absorbed each of these groups, despite fears at the time that they were too alien to assimilate.'[11]

In order to make the Hispanic threat seem greater, Huntington lumps together Mexicans who have just crossed over into California with the grandchildren of Dominican immigrants in New York. But just because they are both categorised as 'Hispanic' – a label that those with even the slightest link to Latin America have an incentive to claim, because it entitles them to privileged access to jobs and other benefits – does not mean they form a monolithic block, still less a threatening one. In reality, Hispanics – a hodge-podge of people whose origins lie, more or less distantly, in Mexico, Cuba, El Salvador, the Dominican Republic, Colombia and other Latin American countries, some of them Indian-language rather than Spanish speakers – are a varied bunch that are blending into the rest of American society. In the 2002 National Survey of Latinos, the overwhelming majority (85 per cent) of 'Hispanics' said Latinos from different countries had different cultures, while only 14 per cent said Latinos shared one Hispanic/Latino culture.[12] And while those who classify themselves as Hispanic accounted for 12.5 per cent of the US population in 2000, Mexican-born immigrants account for a much smaller share: 27.6 per cent of the 12 per cent of Americans who are foreign-born – roughly 3 per cent of the population, in other words. If one also includes the children, grandchildren and other descendants of Mexican immigrants, the number of Mexican-Americans rises to 8 per cent of the US population – far less than the 12.3 per cent who describe themselves as black or African-American.[13] The question is: are these people of Mexican origin remaining apart from the American mainstream? Huntington claims they are.

Speaking Spanish

'The size, persistence, and concentration of Hispanic immigration tends to perpetuate the use of Spanish through successive generations,' claims Huntington, before admitting that: 'The evidence on English acquisition and Spanish retention among immigrants is limited and ambiguous.' It is not even that: there does not appear to be much to worry about. Admittedly, among the 262 million people in the US aged over five, 28.1 million speak Spanish at home; but of those, 14.3 million also speak

English 'very well' and a further 5.8 million speak English 'well'.[14] And while those who speak Spanish at home and English less than 'very well' total 13.7 million – 5.2 per cent of the population – 9.5 million of them were born abroad. So only 4.2 million of those born in the US – a mere 1.8 per cent – speak Spanish at home and English less than 'very well'. Just 1.2 million – one in 200 – speak English poorly or not at all.[15]

Huntington asserts that 'The continuing huge inflow of migrants makes it increasingly possible for Spanish speakers in New York, Miami, and Los Angeles to live normal lives without knowing English.' But in fact, nearly all Spanish speakers born in the US also speak English, indeed predominantly so. Among the children of Latino immigrants, 46 per cent predominantly speak English, 47 per cent are bilingual and only 7 per cent primarily use Spanish. And among Latinos whose parents were also born in the US – the crucial third generation and higher that particularly concerns Huntington – 78 per cent predominantly speak English, while only 22 per cent are bilingual, leaving an insignificantly small number who predominantly speak Spanish.[16] That is unlikely to change: nine in ten Latinos (89 per cent) say that they believe immigrants need to learn to speak English to succeed in the US.[17]

But Huntington's worry is not just that Latinos are failing to learn English – a fear that is clearly not justified by the facts – but that they are continuing to speak Spanish at all. 'If the second generation does not reject Spanish outright,' he frets, 'the third generation is also likely to be bilingual, and fluency in both languages is likely to become institutionalized in the Mexican-American community.' Perhaps, but so what? To bastardise George Orwell, 'one language good, two languages better'. Surely it would be a good thing if more Americans were bilingual. Huntington agrees, up to a point, but adds: 'It is quite different to argue that Americans should know a non-English language in order to communicate with their fellow citizens.' But his argument does not convince at all: if many Americans speak Spanish *and* English, all citizens – those who speak only English and those who are bilingual – can still communicate with each other in English. It is only if many Americans speak Spanish but not English – which is not the case – that Americans would also need to know Spanish to communicate with each other.

Huntington also inveighs against Mexicans and other Latinos trying to maintain their cultural heritage. But what's wrong with that? Being American does not require you to give up your roots – and if there is no problem with Irish-Americans celebrating St Patrick's Day (indeed, with American presidents of non-Irish origin officially celebrating it too), what is wrong with Mexican-Americans celebrating Mexico's national holiday on 5 May? Having two or more cultures is a plus, not a handicap. And it is perfectly possible, as Jews everywhere can testify, to maintain distinct cultural traditions and emotional ties to another country while remaining a loyal citizen of the country in which you live. 'A disproportionate number of the names on the military casualty lists from Iraq and Afghanistan are Hispanic,' points out Roger Daniels of the University of Cincinnati, Ohio.[18] And ironically, so are many US Border Patrol agents.

Yet Huntington warns that many parts of the United States could soon resemble Miami, where two-thirds of the population are Hispanic, mostly of Cuban origin, and where, he claims, English is being driven out. He quotes a Cuban-born sociologist who says, 'In Miami there is no pressure to be American. People can make a living perfectly well in an enclave that speaks Spanish.' Yet Huntington is also dismayed by a study which finds that in Miami families who speak only Spanish have average incomes of $18,000, those who speak only English earn an average of $32,000, but bilingual families take home over $50,000 on average. It is outrageous that people who speak an extra language earn more than those who speak only one. Whatever next? People with a college degree earning more than those without one? Huntington seems not to appreciate that if bilingual families earn three times as much as those who speak only Spanish, that is a powerful incentive for Spanish speakers to learn English – as indeed they are doing.

Latinos, it seems, can do nothing right. Huntington lambasts them both for remaining concentrated in ethnic enclaves – as most immigrants have typically done at first – and for starting to spread out around the country, as immigrants tend to do once they become better established. Indeed, according to a study by the Pew Hispanic Center and the Brookings Institution, Latinos are dispersing geographically at a faster rate than the great waves of European immigrants a century ago. As Ricardo Hausman, a colleague of Huntington at Harvard, sarcastically remarks:

> Huntington argues that Hispanics are a problem because they are poor and uneducated, except in Miami, where they are excessively rich and powerful and make it too difficult for Anglos to succeed. If this problem is not remedied, imagine the consequences: Mississippi, Alabama, and West Virginia could end up as backward and destitute as Florida and California, where the Hispanic epidemic has apparently done the gravest damage.'[19]

Not long ago, in *The Clash of Civilizations*, Huntington claimed that 'the cultural distance between Mexico and the United States is far less than that between Turkey and Europe', and that 'Mexico has attempted to redefine itself from a Latin American to a North American identity'. But now he argues that 'profound cultural differences clearly separate Mexicans and Americans', such as Mexicans' belief that their lives are at the mercy of unpredictable events and their lack of initiative, self-reliance and ambition. Certainly, Mexicans in Mexico are not like Americans in America. But Mexicans in America change: indeed, the very fact that they have uprooted themselves in search of a better life for themselves and their families – in many cases risking death crossing the border – suggests a great deal of initiative, self-reliance and ambition. It is fanciful to argue, as Huntington does, that most Mexican-Americans don't believe in education and hard work to get ahead. Why, then, are Californian schools bulging with Mexican-American children and Californian fields crammed full of their parents doing back-breaking work in the blistering sun? As for the matter of fatalism, Roberto Suro, the director of the Pew Hispanic Center, points out that whereas the 2002 National Survey of Latinos found that 'Among Spanish-speaking Latinos, a clear majority . . . said they agreed with the statement "It doesn't do any good to plan for the future because you don't have any control over it" . . . three-quarters of English-speaking Latinos disagreed, which is about the same response that came from the non-Hispanic population.'[20]

Huntington warns of 'the creation of a large, distinct, Spanish-speaking community with economic and political resources sufficient to sustain its Hispanic identity apart from the national identity of other Americans and also able to influence US politics, government, and society'. Pat Buchanan fears that 'California could become another Quebec, with demands for formal recognition of its separate and unique Hispanic culture and identity – or another Ulster.'[21] In his book *Mexifornia*, Victor Davis Hanson asks: 'So are we now a Mexifornia, Calexico, Aztlán, El Norte, Alta California, or just plain California with new faces and the same old customs?'[22] But even in areas where Latinos predominate, America's defining institutions remain intact. The US Constitution is still in place. Democracy and other aspects of the American political system remain the rule. Capitalism is thriving. People are still free, the media uncensored, private property protected, the courts uncorrupted. Nothing like Mexico, in fact.

So what are the scaremongers worried about? In 1994 some Mexican-Americans demonstrated against California's Proposition 187, which aimed to restrict the welfare benefits available to the children of illegal immigrants, by marching through the streets of Los Angeles waving Mexican flags and carrying US flags upside down. A year later the president of the National Council of La Raza, a Hispanic lobby group, claimed that Hispanic values were superior to American ones. In 1998 some Mexican-Americans booed the US national anthem at a soccer match between Mexico and the USA. 'Such dramatic rejections of the United States and assertions of Mexican identity are not limited to an extremist minority in the Mexican-American community,' claims Huntington. 'Many Mexican immigrants and their offspring simply do not appear to identify primarily with the United States.'

Nonsense. Although only one in three foreign-born Latinos describe themselves as American, this rises to 85 per cent among their US-born children – and 97 per cent among the US-born kids of US-born Latino parents.[23] Moreover, successive generations are blending in with the rest of US society. Like most immigrants, foreign-born Latinos tend to marry within their ethnic or racial group. But their children and grandchildren do not: whereas only 8 per cent of foreign-born Hispanics marry non-Hispanics, 32 per cent of their US-born children do and 57 per cent of their grandchildren and great-grandchildren do.[24]

Huntington's broader fear is that the US as a whole will become bilingual and bicultural. In May 2001, President George Bush celebrated Mexico's Cinco de Mayo national holiday by inaugurating the practice of broadcasting the weekly presidential radio address to the American people in both English and Spanish. In September 2003 one of the first debates among the Democratic Party's presidential candidates also took place in both English and Spanish. 'If this trend continues, the cultural division between Hispanics and Anglos could replace the racial division between blacks and whites as the most serious cleavage in US society,' asserts Huntington. But again this is ridiculous: Bush has not switched from English to Spanish; he is using both. That is not causing division, it is spanning differences. And if having a big Spanish-speaking population encourages many more Americans to learn a second language, then they will be all the richer for it.

In short, Huntington's argument does not stand up. Its premise – that America is based on a core Anglo-Protestant culture to which Latinos ought, but are failing, to assimilate – is incorrect. America is not threatened by Mexicans and other Latinos hanging on to the Spanish language and their broader cultural heritage – but in any case, by the third generation, Latinos mostly speak English, mostly marry non-Latinos and mostly believe in the values and institutions on which America is based. More generally, as Roberto Suro points out, 'Assimilation is not and never has been the quick, zero-sum, one-way process that Huntington postulates. A richer, slower give-and-take between newcomers and natives has always been part of the American experience and thankfully remains so today.'[25] America's core identity has not remained fixed since the Puritans arrived on the *Mayflower*. Successive waves of immigrants have not simply become new-model Puritans: they have adapted to America, but also changed – and enriched – it. Moreover, immigrants are quite capable of embracing more than one culture – of being Mexican at home and Anglo at work – just as we all behave differently in different circumstances. Undeniably, Latino immigrants will change America, as well as being changed by it, but this is not exceptional, and it need not fracture America's constantly changing national identity.

13

Stranger, Can You Spare a Dime?

Does immigration threaten social solidarity?

Ever since the invention of agriculture 10,000 years ago, humans have been used to dealing with people from beyond their own extended kin groups. The difference now in a developed country such as Britain is that we not only live among stranger citizens but we must share with them. We share public services and parts of our income in the welfare state, we share public spaces in towns and cities where we are squashed together on buses, trains and tubes, and we share in a democratic conversation – filtered by the media – about the collective choices we wish to make. All such acts of sharing are more smoothly and generously negotiated if we can take for granted a limited set of common values and assumptions. But as Britain becomes more diverse that common culture is

> being eroded. And therein lies one of the central dilemmas of political life in developed societies: sharing and solidarity can conflict with diversity. This is an especially acute dilemma for progressives who want plenty of both solidarity (high social cohesion and generous welfare paid out of a progressive tax system) and diversity (equal respect for a wide range of peoples, values and ways of life).
>
> David Goodhart[1]

> The basis on which you can extract large sums of money in tax and pay it out in benefits is that most people think the recipients are people like themselves, facing difficulties that they themselves could face. If values become more diverse, if lifestyles become more differentiated, then it becomes more difficult to sustain the legitimacy of a universal risk-pooling welfare state. People ask: 'Why should I pay for them when they are doing things that I wouldn't do?' This is America versus Sweden. You can have a Swedish welfare state provided that you are a homogeneous society with intensely shared values. In the United States you have a very diverse, individualistic society where people feel fewer obligations to fellow citizens. Progressives want diversity, but they thereby undermine part of the moral consensus on which a large welfare state rests.
>
> David Willetts MP[2]

Worries about immigration undermining the nation are typically greater on the Right, particularly among cultural conservatives. But some on the Left – I won't stoop to calling them national socialists – hold similar fears about the impact that greater diversity might have on national solidarity. 'We feel more comfortable with, and are readier to share with and sacrifice for, those with whom we have shared histories and similar values,' says David Goodhart, the editor of Britain's intellectual magazine *Prospect*. 'To put it bluntly – most of us prefer our own kind.' While some on the Right fear that greater diversity means that people will no longer be willing to die for their nation, some on the Left fret that it will undermine their willingness to cough up for the poor.

Can increasing diversity be reconciled with the sense of common identity that is said to underpin a generous welfare state? Goodhart stirred up a hornet's nest – he was soon accused of being a racist and worse – when he highlighted what he calls the 'progressive dilemma'. I am convinced that he is an honest and honourable man – but I am equally convinced that he is mistaken. That the source of his 'dilemma' was a Conservative politician should have alerted him to the fact that it is a political ploy: the Right putting the Left on the rack by insisting that it must choose between two things it cherishes. But neither the Left nor society in general need choose. Contrary to what Goodhart and Willetts argue, support for the welfare state does not rest solely, or even mainly, on a feeling of kinship for one's fellow-citizens; nor is a more ethnically diverse society necessarily one with less social solidarity. A simplistic juxtaposition of America and Sweden proves nothing: London, New York and Canada are all incredibly diverse while displaying much higher support for social spending than more uniform places like Surrey, Wyoming or Ireland.

Racist or not?

I don't think that it is necessarily racist to support immigration controls. Greens may support immigration controls because they believe that an extra influx of people would put a strain on the environment. Trade unionists may worry about the impact on the jobs of their members, black and white. Others may worry that immigration undermines the financial basis for traditional welfare systems, which grant free or subsidised benefits and services to people primarily on the basis of residency rather than financial contributions. Those who believe these things may or may not be racists; but the beliefs themselves are not racist.

Nor is it racist to worry that immigration *might* undermine social solidarity for reasons other than foreigners' foreignness. It is not racist to point out that if immigrants *happen* to be a bunch of thieves and villains, they might cause many problems. It is only racist to assume that foreigners tend to be thieves and villains. It is not racist to argue that if immigrants *happen* to have very different tastes and characteristics that clash with those of natives, they might also undermine solidarity. If millions of white American libertarians were to pitch up in social-democratic Sweden, support for its cradle-to-grave welfare system might fall.

A non-racist might also observe that immigration could undermine social solidarity if most other natives themselves are racist, although this is slippery ground because it can allow racists to support racist positions on the basis of others' purported racism while pretending not to be racist themselves: hence the common claim by British politicians, some of them doubtless racist, that immigration controls are needed for 'good race relations'.

Undeniably, immigration could conceivably pose a political challenge to universal welfare provision. White Britons might be less willing to pay for social insurance for blacks – or for white Poles. But the issue is not whether it *could*, but whether it *does*. And if it does, can the welfare state be reformed in such a way that it is compatible with greater diversity?

It's not purely altruistic

It is worth recalling that the driving force behind the establishment of the welfare state in Europe was not just the concern that socialists and others had for their poorer fellow-citizens; it also came from enlightened elites who wanted to buy off the masses to avert a potential revolution. Bismarck, for instance, the founder of Germany's welfare state, was hardly progressive, but he did worry that capitalism without a safety net was socially unsustainable. Support for the vast expansion of Britain's welfare state in 1945 was not just the product of social solidarity, strengthened by the sense of community in adversity engendered by the Second World War; it was also born of fear of a Soviet-style revolution. And it is surely no coincidence that the twin bursts of welfare expansionism in the US – Franklin Roosevelt's New Deal in the Depression era of the 1930s and Lyndon Johnson's Great Society project in the Civil Rights era of the 1960s – coincided with periods of great social and economic upheaval. In short, even if the rich don't care about the poor, they may still be willing to help them if they fear them. If so, even if immigration does undermine social solidarity, it need not undermine political support for the welfare state. Quite the reverse: French society's fear of its potentially threatening immigrant underclass may actually stimulate more social spending, not result in less.

The universal welfare state not only provides the rich with security against the poor – it also provides everyone with security against becoming unemployed, sick or old. Social insurance is not simply a means of providing the poor with, for instance, decent healthcare – that could be done through a government programme targeted at the poor, such as America's Medicaid; it is also arguably a more efficient way of financing healthcare provision for all than private insurance markets. That the much richer US spends twice as much as Britain on healthcare as a proportion of its economy without making Americans noticeably healthier certainly suggests as much – and people in most rich countries except for the States certainly believe it to be so. In short, people support the NHS not just out of concern that everyone should have access to healthcare, but mainly out of self-interest – because they believe a government-funded healthcare system works out cheaper and better for them than a private insurance system would. A society with less solidarity could still support the NHS.

You may loathe and despise your jobless neighbour but still be willing to pay for unemployment benefits if you fear that you might one day end up out of work yourself, or if you are terrified that your penniless neighbour might otherwise rob you. The welfare state does not rest on solidarity alone. Even so, Goodhart is clearly right that people are often willing to be more generous towards those for whom they feel a sense of solidarity – and that one basis on which they might do so is shared kinship. But here the discussion begins to mirror the one about ethnicity and nationhood in Chapter 11: ethnically homogeneous societies need not be full of brotherly love – they may very well be dog-eat-dog – while diverse societies may be more liberal and compassionate; and solidarity can be based on much else besides ethnicity. If immigrants are generally seen as honest, fair and hard-working, why should their presence undermine political support for the welfare state? (But conversely, if legal channels to immigration are closed, so that migrants resort to illegal ones, they may be perceived negatively, thus undermining social solidarity.) An increase in diversity may boost solidarity if different minority groups support each other: a rainbow coalition of gays, blacks, feminists, immigrants and others may combine to press for more welfare spending. Canada makes a virtue of its diversity, which thus enhances Canadians' solidarity with each other. Moreover, echoing the discussion about the economic impact of immigration on the welfare state in Chapter

7, if young, healthy immigrants are net contributors to strained public finances, their arrival will actually make generous welfare provision, such as higher state pensions, more affordable. And if immigrants are seen as a drain on the public purse, they can be denied social benefits, while welfare systems can also be reformed more generally: for instance, by making more benefits dependent on previous contributions.

Nothing to fear

It is an open question whether immigration undermines political support for the welfare state: it might, but it need not. But a look at the evidence gives little reason to believe that it does. Goodhart claims that 'Scandinavian countries with the biggest welfare states have been the most socially and ethnically homogeneous states in the west. By the same token, the welfare state has always been weaker in the individualistic, ethnically divided US compared with more homogeneous Europe.' Now the reason why Sweden, for instance, has a generous welfare state may be that Swedes are more compassionate than others: Sweden is also a world leader in giving aid to poor people overseas and it has a long tradition of welcoming political refugees. Swedes may also be more egalitarian and more risk-averse. But more importantly, Sweden is no longer ethnically homogeneous: one in eight of the population is foreign-born, the same proportion as in the US. Even if one excludes those born in the other twenty-four EU states – and there is no particularly good reason why one should, since although they are mostly white, they are clearly not ethnically Swedish – 5 per cent of the Swedish population was born outside the EU. And yet the Swedish welfare state has hardly collapsed: Sweden's government takes half of its citizens' income in tax.

Consider next the US. A more plausible reason why the Americans have not developed a generous welfare state is surely that they are generally more individualistic and suspicious of government intervention than most: even the poor believe in self-reliance and the American dream. This was true even in the early nineteenth century, when the country was mostly Anglo-Protestant; if anything, the more diverse America of today places greater calls on government than the more homogeneous America of yesteryear. Note too that the last big expansion of the welfare state, LBJ's Great Society, took place even as America's repressed diversity was bursting into view during the more permissive 1960s. And just look at New York, the most diverse city in America, which is also a bastion of high taxes and government social programmes.

More substantially, Goodhart marshals in evidence a paper by Alberto Alesina and Edward Glaeser, both at Harvard, and Bruce Sacerdote of Dartmouth College entitled 'Why Doesn't the US Have a European-Style Welfare System?'. This does not purport to explain why the pattern of social provision differs across countries: it simply seeks to explain why America did not develop a European-style welfare state. Goodhart claims that the paper argues that 'the answer is that too many people at the bottom of the pile in the US are black or Hispanic'. In fact, it concludes, 'Americans redistribute less than Europeans because (1) the majority believes that redistribution favors racial minorities, (2) Americans believe that they live in an open and fair society and that if someone is poor it is their own fault, and (3) the political system is geared towards preventing redistribution.' In the case of race, Americans' antipathy towards welfare does not spring from a lack of concern towards immigrants in general, but towards blacks in particular. This is more likely to be the product of the US's distinct history of slavery and segregation than a point from which one can draw more general conclusions. So it does not follow that, for instance, allowing more immigrants into Britain would undermine support for the welfare state. Note too the importance of other US peculiarities: Americans typically perceive the poor as lazy, while Europeans generally perceive them as unfortunate. 'Americans essentially believe that anyone can work their way out of poverty by dint of hard work and that the poor only remain poor because they refuse to put in this effort,' the authors say – the American dream is alive and well. Moreover:

> Political variables including the electoral system (in particular, proportionality and the US two-party system) and the role of the courts, are important. The two-party system, and the lack of proportionality, created obstacles that blocked the formation of a strong and lasting Socialist party in the US. The upheaval in continental Europe over the last century has meant that there were no durable institutions which could protect property against popular demand for redistribution. Monumental differences in history such as the US Civil War and the open frontier with the West contributed to create a different climate and attitudes toward the relationship between the individual and the state.[3]

In short, Goodhart's star witnesses scarcely buttress his claims about a general trade-off between diversity and solidarity.

In truth, there is no obvious correlation between ethnic homogeneity and the size of the welfare state: America is diverse and does not have a welfare state, while Belgium is split between Flemish and French speakers, but has a big government; Sweden *was* ethnically homogeneous with a huge welfare state, while South Korea and Japan are still ethnically homogeneous but do not have European-style welfare states. Perhaps the best counter-example is Canada, which is far more ethnically diverse than the United States – and increasingly so. Yet far from this undermining solidarity, it enhances it: Canadians make a virtue of their diversity, which is now seen as an essential part of what unites them, and sets them apart from other nations. Far from lurching towards an American-style sink-or-swim attitude, Canada's ever more diverse population prides itself on its socialised healthcare system and its more redistributive taxation. Indeed, three Canadian researchers who looked at the relationship between immigration and the welfare state over time in many rich countries found that:

> There is no relationship between the proportion of the population born outside the country and growth in social spending over the last three decades of the twentieth century, controlling for other factors associated with social spending. There was simply no evidence that countries with large foreign-born populations had more trouble sustaining and developing their social programs over these three decades than countries with small immigrant communities.[4]

However, social spending did rise more slowly in countries that saw a big increase in immigration over that period.

Keith Banting and Will Kymlicka, both at Canada's Queen's University, also tested a related question: whether multicultural policies weaken the welfare state. In essence, multicultural policies (discussed in greater detail in the following chapter) go beyond protecting the basic civil and political rights of all individuals by giving some public recognition and support to minority groups to maintain and express their distinct identities and practices. Critics claim that these policies may exacerbate any underlying trade-off between diversity and redistribution, by causing disadvantaged groups to focus on cultural issues rather than economic ones, for instance, or by corroding trust among various groups in society. Supporters say that they can ease inter-communal tensions and strengthen mutual respect, trust and support for redistribution. Banting and Kymlicka find:

> no evidence here of a systematic tendency for multiculturalism policies to weaken the welfare state. Countries that adopted such programs did not experience an erosion of their welfare states or even slower growth in social spending than countries that resisted such programs. Indeed, on the two measures that capture social policy most directly – social spending and redistributive impact of taxes and transfers – the countries with the strongest multiculturalism policies did better than the other groups, providing a hint that perhaps multiculturalism policies may actually ease the tension between diversity and redistribution.[5]

Looking at Canada in particular, the posterchild of ethnic diversity and multiculturalism, researchers find that although ethnic diversity may erode feelings of trust in one's neighbours, this does not weaken support for social redistribution.[6] 'There is no evidence of majorities turning away from redistribution because some of the beneficiaries are "strangers",' concludes Banting.[7] The Canadian government continues to provide socialised healthcare for all and to redistribute from rich to poor.

Obviously there is potentially a conflict between ethnic diversity and solidarity, and this could potentially undermine the welfare state. But it need not – and there is little evidence that the two clash in practice. White Americans' unwillingness to pay for welfare for poor blacks does not prove that higher immigration will undermine the welfare state. And even if it did, reforms to the welfare state could shore up public support for it. Already, most rich countries do not allow immigrants to claim most social benefits when they initially arrive. If immigrants cannot make use of the welfare state, they clearly cannot undermine support for it. Second, to the extent that some people are perceived to be lazy or undeserving recipients of assistance, welfare rules can be tightened, for instance by making unemployment benefits conditional on actively looking for a job. Since taxpayers are more likely to object to anyone – not just immigrants – abusing the system, such reforms make political (and economic) sense in any case. Third, to the extent that permanent immigrants are deemed to be a net burden on public finances – something for which there is little evidence – social benefits can be more closely linked to contributions.

There is no denying that immigration requires the political acquiescence of voters – not because natives may be 'right' not to want foreigners in their midst, but because they may prefer to live in a closed society and may react with hostility to unwanted strangers. If immigration is to be a success, locals need to be persuaded that it is a good thing. Their fears, warranted or not, must be allayed. Some countries, such as Japan, may prefer to keep out foreigners at any cost. You or I may not wish to live in such a closed society, but others may – and they are entitled to form a political community apart. But the issue is rather different in countries that have already admitted a considerable number of immigrants. The case for excluding foreigners cannot rest on their ethnic or racial difference, because the national community already includes people of diverse ethnicities and races: you cannot, for instance, legitimately exclude blacks from Britain on the basis that Britain is a wholly white country, because it no longer is. Instead, the basis for exclusion must be their foreignness, which in turn implies a Britishness that is based not on race or ethnicity, but on a broader sense of community expressed through a willingness to obey the same laws and accept government by a majority. That community may be very diverse, not only ethnically but in values terms, yet still bound together by a common identity, common habits and common interests. That immigrants have expressly chosen to join it, rather than being born into it, may only increase their feeling of belonging. The more open, more freely chosen communities of today may be very different from the closed, coerced communities of old – but they are no less real and are in many respects preferable.

14

Learning to Live Together

How to integrate immigrants into society

It is hardly possible to overrate the value, for the improvement of human beings, of things which bring them into contact with persons dissimilar to themselves, and with modes of thought and action unlike those with which they are familiar . . . it is indispensable to be perpetually comparing [one's] own notions and customs with the experience and example of persons in different circumstances . . . there is no nation which does not need to borrow from others.

John Stuart Mill[1]

The mélange of culture is in us all, with its irreconcilable contradictions. In our swollen, polyglot cities, we are all cultural mestizos. In the age of mass migration and the internet, cultural plurality is an irreversible fact; like it or dislike it, it's where we live, and the dream of a pure monoculture is at best an unattainable, nostalgic fantasy and at worst a life-threatening menace.

Salman Rushdie[2]

'Mami's youngest sister – my tía Yrma – finally made it to the United States that year. She and tío Miguel got themselves an apartment in the Bronx, off the Grand Concourse, and everybody decided that we should have a party. Actually, my pops decided, but everybody – meaning Mami, tía Yrma, tío Miguel and their neighbours – thought it a dope idea. On the afternoon of the party Papi came back from work around six. Right on time. We were all dressed by then, which was a smart move on our part. If Papi had walked in and caught us lounging around in our underwear, he would have kicked our asses something serious.'[3]

It's raw, it's real, and if it wasn't for immigration, it wouldn't have been written. Savour a slice of Junot Díaz, born in the Dominican Republic and now living in New York. Whether it is a curry from London's Brick Lane, the triumph of France's *black–blanc–beur* (black–white–Arab) football team in the 1998 World Cup, or Cuban-born Gloria Estefan performing at a concert for the US military, nearly everyone can appreciate some of the cultural benefits of immigration. 'Every time I see and hear Gloria Estefan sing, it makes my heart feel better,' says George Bush. It's not just the wider choice of ethnic food, music or sporting talent that people enjoy; it's also the new cultural cross-breeds that immigration produces: Salman Rushdie's Anglo-Indian writing, fusion cuisine, American hip-hop picking up Caribbean reggae and Indian bhangra beats. More generally, immigration brings us into contact with different cultures and ways of thinking, making our lives more varied and rewarding, broadening our minds, and enabling us all to learn from others.

Yet there is no denying that immigration can also cause friction. Miguel and Yrma's party might have annoyed their neighbours, for instance. What for some is a harmonious melody is to others a discordant din, while one man's sweet smell is another's foul stench. As France's president, Jacques Chirac, once infamously remarked, people may dislike '*le bruit et les odeurs*', the noise and smells, of foreigners. White Londoners might love a curry but still resent living next door to Indian immigrants. Many people dislike or feel threatened by immigrants' different ways – that they talk, look and pray differently – and many immigrants in turn feel excluded and discriminated against. The 2004 film *Crash* depicts Los Angeles as a city of alienated people struggling to connect across vast barriers of language, class and culture. The multicultural unity of France's football heroes jars with the country's deep racial divisions. The black-and-white images of Mathieu Kassovitz's *La Haine* (1995) captured the bleakness of life for the outsiders who live in Paris's largely immigrant suburbs; they end up rioting. While the hearts of conservative Americans might flutter along with their president's when they hear Gloria Estefan sing, they may also rage at the impact of Cuban culture on Miami. And, as I shall discuss in the following chapter, many Europeans worry that Muslim immigrants will not be able to fit in to their societies – especially now that Islam is associated in many minds with terrorism.

How can people of diverse ethnic backgrounds, races, religions, cultures, habits and values learn to get along? Where people value diversity – a wider choice of ethnic restaurants, for instance – there is no problem. But where they don't, or where they feel it clashes with something they cherish – such as national cohesion, social solidarity, traditional behaviour norms, local culture or liberal values – it becomes much trickier. In Chapter 11, I argued that unless national identity is redefined in a way that embraces the diversity within today's societies, many people will be left feeling that they don't belong, and nations will fracture. In Chapter 12, I suggested that the US was primarily based on the principles in the Declaration of Independence and the US Constitution rather than Anglo-Protestant culture, and that fears that Latinos were forming a nation within a nation were unfounded. In Chapter 13, I showed that greater diversity need not undermine social solidarity or the welfare state: just look at London and New York. In this chapter, I shall look at broader issues that relate to the three previous chapters and the following one. How far should immigrants adapt to society, and to what extent should society adapt to them? Are there limits to how much diversity a society can embrace? Do people need shared norms, a common culture and shared values in order to live together peacefully and productively? If so, what are they? Should immigrants be left to their own devices, potentially to lead separate lives in splendid (or bitter) isolation, or should they be encouraged, perhaps even forced, to mingle? To what extent should cultural groups as well as individuals have rights? And if groups should have rights, should these be equal rights, special rights or limited rights?

Consider language. Should immigrants be forced to learn the local language, be encouraged to do so, be offered free language classes or be left alone? If some fail to learn (or don't yet know) the local language, should the government produce leaflets for them in their own language, or is this divisive and a deterrent to incomers learning the local language? Should immigrants' children be encouraged to learn their parents' language or should their schooling be solely in the local language? At one extreme, France insists that all immigrants must learn about 'our ancestors, the Gauls' and 'assimilate' to local ways; at the other, extreme multiculturalists argue that Western societies should bend over backwards to respect immigrants' cultural traditions, such as forced marriages, even when these clash with basic tenets of a society's values and laws, such as the equality of women.

For sure, such issues do not arise simply because of immigration: they apply to each individual and group that must find a place for themselves in society. Society has long had to try to accommodate traditional moralists as well as gays, nationalists as well as speakers of regional languages, and adherents of different faiths as well as atheists. But because immigrants begin as outsiders and may be more different than most, their integration may be particularly tricky.

Models of integration

Whatever approach countries take, integration is a two-way street. If immigrants are willing to assimilate to local ways, natives must also be willing to treat them like locals. If society is racist, or even simply indifferent, then with the best will in the world, immigrants will not be able to fit in. Conversely, even if immigrants are accepted into society without being forced to conform, they must also be willing to participate in it. If immigrants want to remain apart, then even the most liberal society will not succeed in integrating them. It takes two to tango.

Integration is also a dynamic process, with vicious as well as virtuous circles. If society broadly welcomes immigrants, who are keen to embrace its ways, a society can become steadily more diverse without becoming fractious: consider Canada, which I shall return to in greater depth at the end of this chapter. A tolerant and diverse society can more readily accommodate not only people who want to fit in but also those who are keen to be different. Like most people born in rich countries, the children of immigrants increasingly want to choose their own identities – some want to emphasise their cultural roots, others want to blend in to the society in which they live, still others just want to define themselves as individuals, while most prefer to emphasise different aspects of their overlapping identities in different circumstances – while also wanting to be accepted by other members of society and have the same opportunities as them. It is easier for immigrants' children to find a place in a society that balances their roots, their individualism and their desire to belong when a broad spectrum of acceptable ways of life already exists and is tolerated – and conversely, it is easier for a diverse and tolerant society to accept that immigrants' children can be different and still belong. In a city like London that treasures its diversity, a friend of mine who is a British-born gay Muslim doctor has no problem combining going out to gay clubs, praying in his local mosque and working for the National Health Service.

But if society initially rejects immigrants who want to fit in, their children may in turn become resentful or even hostile, even if society has subsequently become more welcoming. Likewise, if immigrants do not want – or are unable – to fit in, society may become hostile to them, making their children (who might otherwise have been keen to fit in) feel excluded. In both cases, society may then conclude from this resentment that immigrants and their children are an ungrateful lot who have no desire to fit in at all, and so attack, exclude or clamp down on them, thus causing a new cycle of resentment and misunderstanding. That has often happened in many European countries that have struggled to accept the non-white, frequently Muslim, immigrants that they drafted in to work in the 1950s and 1960s.

Europe's experience of immigration since the Second World War has often been traumatic because immigrants with little knowledge of their new homes and no role models to show them how to adapt were thrown into countries that did not consider themselves places of immigration and took a long time to accept – and then often only grudgingly – that the newcomers were there to stay. For instance, many immigrants who came to England in the 1960s to work in the now-closed textile factories in Oldham were from isolated rural areas of Bangladesh and Pakistan, spoke no English, brought their feudalism with them – and were expected to go back eventually.[4] The town erupted into violent white–Asian riots in 2001.

Germany saw its mostly Turkish immigrants as temporary guest-workers, which they were initially, and so has taken particularly long to realise that it needs to find a place for them in German society. It treated them as foreigners, separate from the rest of society, with fewer social rights. Even their children born and raised in Germany had little chance of becoming German citizens; imagine how they must have felt when over 1.5 million people of German descent with only remote historical links to Germany arrived from the former Soviet Union in the 1990s and immediately became citizens. Unsurprisingly, Germany's Turks have tended – and were left – to live in separate communities, socialising, shopping and praying with each other, reading their own Turkish-language newspapers and watching their own satellite TV programmes. But things are starting to change, albeit slowly. Since 2000, a new citizenship law has granted children born to foreigners in Germany the automatic right to German citizenship, so long as one parent has been legally resident for at least eight years. And under a new law adopted in 2005, the government is making greater efforts to integrate immigrants culturally, with publicly financed courses in German language, history and so on. Even so, most Germans continue to think of the country's residents of Turkish origin as foreign – and the two communities still lead largely separate lives.

France has pursued a very different tack. It has long been a country of immigration and has sought to integrate post-war immigrants from North Africa as it did earlier ones from Italy and Spain: by asserting that anyone who speaks French, adopts French culture as their own and shares republican values can become French. Immigrants can easily become French citizens, with full political and social rights – indeed, anyone born in France used to acquire citizenship automatically – but they must 'assimilate' to French ways, jettisoning their own cultural heritage. The French state does not recognise that its citizens differ according to their ethnic or cultural backgrounds: they are all just French. In theory, then, foreigners can become fully fledged members of French society, but only if they do all the adapting. France even has an official High Council for Integration, designed to ensure that the process takes place.

But what France has failed to recognise is that even when immigrants have tried to conform, society has not accepted them as truly French, due to the colour of their skin, for instance. This rejection has in turn caused immigrants to reassert their differences, compounding the problem. As the riots in late 2005 highlighted, many non-whites, despite being French citizens, continue to be discriminated against and still feel excluded from the rest of society. 'They harass you, they hassle you, they insult you the whole time, ID checks now, scooter checks next. They call you nigger names,' Karim, a seventeen-year-old on an estate in Sevran just north of Paris, said of the interior ministry police. Asked whether he felt French, his friend, who refused to give even his first name, said: 'We hate France and France hates us. I don't know what I am. Here's not home; my gran's in Algeria. But in any case France is just fucking with us. We're like mad dogs, you know? We bite everything we see.'[5] This is more than just teenage rebellion. Research by the Institut Montaigne, a Paris-based think-tank, showed that replies to job ads with identical CVs received five times as many responses when a 'traditional' French name rather than an Arab name was used. Ethnic minorities are scarcely represented among chief executives, judges, civil servants, journalists and national politicians. Aziz Senni, a Moroccan-born businessman and author of *The Social Elevator Is Broken, I Took the Stairs*, blames widespread segregation for the violence and frustration. 'We cannot eternally keep a whole part of the French population in this closed circuit without hope,' he says.[6] The French model of assimilation exacts a heavy toll on personal freedom, by striving to erase cultural differences, without delivering the equality and national cohesion it espouses. Its one-size-fits-all homogenisation seems neither desirable nor achievable.

The US has traditionally taken a third way – the so-called 'melting-pot' approach – which involves give and take on both sides. Immigrants have to pledge their allegiance to the United States and sign up to the values in the Declaration of Independence and the US Constitution, but they don't have to adopt any particular cultural habits, Anglo-Protestant or otherwise. Over time, each influx of immigrants changes and enriches American culture, while they adapt freely to American ways, although they may retain some of their cultural heritage. Irish-Americans celebrate St Patrick's Day; Mexican-Americans have a fiesta on 5 May; Korean-Americans watch Korean-language TV. This approach has worked remarkably well until now. But America's affirmative-action laws, which discriminate in favour of minority groups, are contributing to an increasingly fractious assertion of group rights. As Stepan Kerkyasharian, who runs the Sydney-based Community Relations Commission for New South Wales in Australia, points out, 'specific laws giving specific privileges to specific people force citizens by legislation or inducement to make a conscious choice: do you belong to the majority or do you want to belong to an identified minority so as to enjoy the privileges of that minority, while contracting out of the privileges of the majority? It's a formula for disaster.' In practice, then, the US has veered towards a multicultural approach – and a fractious one at that.

Multi-multiculturalism

Multiculturalism means different things to different people, in part because countries such as Australia, Canada, Britain, the Netherlands and now the US have embraced different variants of it. Indeed, many people – Tony Blair included, apparently – are not even sure what it means. Basically, though, it involves a 'live-and-let-live' approach, which recognises that society is culturally diverse and that individuals and groups need to tolerate each other's differences in order to live together. Immigrants are allowed to keep their language and culture while still becoming citizens, and anti-discrimination laws aim to ensure that everybody is treated equally (or, in the US case, laws discriminate in favour of minorities). But except perhaps in Canada, governments are beginning to dilute their commitment to multiculturalism as they question the limits to how much diversity a society can embrace.

A Labor government committed Australia to multiculturalism back in 1989. Given that two in five Australians have a parent who was born abroad, it was bowing to reality. It asserted that immigrants had a right to hold on to their cultural traditions and that the government had a duty to help them integrate socially and economically. In return, immigrants had to declare a primary allegiance to Australia and accept such basic structures and principles as the Australian Constitution, freedom of speech and equality of women. But social conservatives, epitomised by Pauline Hanson's briefly successful One Nation party, lamented what they saw as the dilution of the Anglo-Celtic heritage of Australia's original colonists – and when it took office in 1996 the National government led by John Howard took up many of Hanson's themes. It has rowed back on Australia's multicultural policies, closing key federal agencies that promoted them and cutting funding for community agencies for ethnic minorities. Even so, as Abul Rizvi points out, Australia's migration programme is run by an Indian-born Muslim – Rizvi himself – and Australia continues to 'respect people's beliefs, so long as they are not contravening Australian laws'. But 'people are expected to mix and send their kids to local schools. And we try to disperse migrants around Australia rather than letting them concentrate together.'

Multiculturalism has suffered at a state level too. In 2001, the New South Wales Ethnic Affairs Commission was renamed the Community Relations Commission as part of a government strategy to remove the word 'ethnic' from official documents. But the friendly and thoughtful man who runs it, Stepan Kerkyasharian, remains committed to the cause, his life an eloquent illustration of the merits of multiculturalism. 'I was born in Cyprus, my parents were refugees living in a slum who survived the Armenian genocide of 1915,' he explains. 'I started working when I was eight, in a garage. I moved to England when I was seventeen with £10 in my pocket. I found a job in an electrical shop, paid for high school and ended up managing a nightclub called Omar Khayam by the age of twenty. Then I got married to my half-Irish, half-Armenian wife. We went on our honeymoon to Australia and loved the weather so much we decided to move here. It wasn't hard to fit in as we spoke English. I was an electronics engineer: I designed blood-pressure monitors. Then in 1976 I started a volunteer Armenian radio programme and from then on helped set up community radio stations and television.'

He strongly believes that 'Whilst the notions of loyalty and commitment to a state by a citizen should not relate to the individual's race, religion, language and ethnicity, an individual should have the right of self-identification by any of those identifiers . . . Citizens should also have the right to form communities based on any or all of the identifiers. The notion of a community of communities should form part of the accepted foundation of a nation or a state.'[7] And where tensions arise between communities, governments have to be 'pro-active and interventionist' in defusing them, he says. 'For instance, multicultural street festivals generate lots of goodwill. We target Anglo areas. People have to work together to put on a festival. It helps to create a new hybrid identity. We also brought together religious and community leaders to defuse tensions when the Iraq war started.'

Dam break

Multiculturalism has been a way of life in the Netherlands for centuries, but the country has undergone a sea change in recent years. Over a coffee in The Hague, the Netherlands' tranquil seat of government, Chris Huinder of Forum, the government-funded but independent Institute for Multicultural Development, explains how his country has long recognised its cultural and religious differences:

> Dutch society has for centuries been a society of minorities – Huguenots, Belgians, Germans – and diverse religious beliefs – Catholic, Protestant, Jewish. So we built a 'pillar' system: each group had its own churches, schools, even football clubs. Society was fragmented, but we tolerated our differences and we were all Dutch.
>
> When migrants from our former colonies arrived in the 1960s and 1970s, with their different skin colour, conduct and customs, we tried the same approach as with other minorities: we gave them their own institutions, paid for by government money. But in the 1980s, economic crisis caused many migrants to lose their jobs as well as leading to cuts in government

subsidies. By the 1990s, we realised that lots of things were going on, such as forced marriages, that we couldn't accept.

Pim Fortuyn, the outspoken gay politician, struck a chord with Dutch voters in the 2002 election campaign by railing against immigration and Islam. He argued that Moroccans and Turks in the Netherlands lived in a world apart that was not Dutch: in separate communities, watching Turkish and Moroccan television, contemptuous of 'Western' values such as the equal treatment of women. He was murdered just before the election was due to take place – by a white left-winger who said he acted to stop Fortuyn turning Muslims into society's 'scapegoats'.

But what really sent Dutch society into a tailspin was the murder in November 2004 of a famous filmmaker, Theo Van Gogh. He was stabbed to death on the street in Amsterdam by a Dutch-born Muslim extremist, Mohammed Bouyeri, who considered one of Van Gogh's films to be blasphemous towards Islam. Rita Verdonk, the Netherlands' hardline minister of integration and immigration, immediately made the murder an integration issue, not least by speaking at a noisy rally organised in Amsterdam on the evening of the murder, and saying bluntly, 'It has gone this far, and it goes no further.'[8] Over twenty religious schools, mosques and churches in Holland were subsequently burned down in tit-for-tat attacks. A dam had broken – and it looked as if support for multiculturalism had been swept away.

'The right and centre say immigrants have to assimilate, they have to accept our ways,' Chris Huinder explains. 'Dutch culture must be the leading culture and immigrants have to discard their backward ways.' Not everyone agrees with this, though.

> The liberals and the left say integration is a two-way street. There should be two pillars: Dutch and Muslim. Muslims should be given their own institutions. After all, if someone is active in their own community, they can become active in Dutch society and act as a bridge between the two. Muslims should be able to wear headscarves, have their own mosques, and so on, but they have to comply with Dutch laws: no forced marriage, no blood revenge, respect for women's rights . . . We say: 'You are entitled to be Moroccan, but please be aware you are a Moroccan in Dutch society with Dutch laws, values and so on. At the end you have to accept that you are living in the Netherlands. If not, you are free to go back.'

For the moment, assertions that immigrants must assimilate are drowning out more liberal voices. Yet the Dutch are in danger of throwing the baby out with the bathwater. Eduard Nazarski, the director of the Dutch Refugee Council, argues that although the Dutch model is far from perfect, it has been much more successful than the government now thinks. 'In 1998 a new law was passed saying integration was a two-way street and that newcomers had duties to try to fit in and be good citizens,' he explains.

> By 2002 politicians expected this to have solved all the problems. They are a bit impatient. Of course, there are problems, which Pim Fortuyn revealed. People are dissatisfied and don't feel at ease. They felt the government didn't understand how difficult it was to live in a community where sixty per cent were newcomers. And the government has lost public trust by pledging each year to reduce the number of asylum seekers without actually doing so. Also, even when asylum was restricted,

> Turks and Moroccans could still come here freely on family-reunion visas, and the public does not distinguish between foreigners, asylum seekers, legal migrants, illegal migrants and so on.

But Dutch xenophobia is as much to blame for the country's problems as immigrants' different ways. 'What was labelled as Dutch tolerance wasn't: it was indifference,' says Nazarski. 'If immigrants just worked and didn't cause too many problems, they could just be ignored.' In effect, then, although the Dutch claimed they were being multiculturalist – tolerating different cultures within Dutch society – they were actually treating immigrants like the Germans did: as temporary guests separate from the rest of society.

Hikmat Mahawat Khan, a Muslim born in the former Dutch colony of Surinam who leads the liberal Islamic organisation Ulamon and the Contact Group Islam, a moderate group that advises the Dutch government, recognises that Muslims need to change, but insists that Dutch society must, too. 'People believed that they lived in an ideal, very tolerant multicultural society,' he explains.

> But now the underlying tensions have been exposed. The ice is thinner than we thought: it cracked at the first test. People and even politicians still treat you as if you were a temporary guest. One politician said, 'Muslims should not demand a lot of rights. If I went to Saudi Arabia, I wouldn't dare ask for a holiday on Easter.' But that's totally different: I'm not an expat here.
>
> The second and third generations were born here. They know only Holland, and yet the white Dutch still expect them to adopt the habits and values of the days when it was completely white. But Holland has changed, whether you like it or not. It belongs to all races now. If the white

> Dutch don't accept Muslims, it creates frustration and resentment, which causes a counter-reaction, which leads the white Dutch to say, 'I told you so'. It's a chicken-and-egg scenario. Both sides need to come together and acknowledge the need to change. Government needs to play an orchestrating role rather than play politics with the issue.

The Dutch government insists that immigrants have to adapt to Dutch ways. They have to learn Dutch (many speak English instead), abandon some of their culture and habits, dress differently. Even a liberal, open-minded guy like Eduard Nazarski admits to feeling discomfited by women wearing the veil. I ask him whether he is more shocked by a woman in a veil or by one wearing hardly any clothes? 'I don't feel at ease with women wearing a veil. You can't have contact or communication with them. It's also worrying because it's a sign of protest and resistance. The veil says: this is the identity I want to broadcast. Many Muslim girls want to wear headscarves to make clear where their historical roots are. Basically, they are saying, "You Dutch made clear you don't like us, so we are rejecting you."'

Nazarski agrees that immigrants ought to learn Dutch, work, be aware of Dutch norms and values and practise them. But he maintains the government is wrong to think that there is a single Dutch culture to which immigrants can conform. 'The government has an image of all Dutch people having the same aims, a shared identity and culture,' he says. 'There are proposals for a historical canon and a literature canon that all need to know. But Dutch society isn't like that any more. People now pick and choose their culture, and their friends live all over the world.' Moreover, he says, the Dutch are unfairly focusing their fears about change on foreigners: 'People feel uncomfortable with the very fast change in society. Neighbourhoods are not neighbourhoods any more: people don't know their neighbours. Cultural differences are growing. It isn't like it used to be. There is a nostalgia for the 1950s. People direct their anxieties about all of this at foreigners.' He is worried that the Dutch overreaction against multiculturalism risks repeating the mistakes of the past. 'The government has failed to prepare people for the fact that we will have newcomers. The prime minister thinks we can close the borders, but we can't. He thinks the onus is on the individual to adapt, not society. But we mustn't make the same mistake as with the guest-workers. We have to make people welcome and integrate them.'

Criticisms of multiculturalism

Britain did not initially perceive itself as a country of immigration: the newcomers from the Caribbean, India and Pakistan were seen as isolated aberrations, legacies of empire and the regrettable consequences of a misguided labour-recruitment policy. But gradually, Britain has come to embrace multiculturalism in practice, without developing an overarching strategy for how immigrants should be integrated. Ethnic minorities are not only left alone by the state to practise their faith, language or culture, but are actively encouraged and subsidised to do so. The Muslim Welfare House in Finsbury Park, for instance, provides English-language and Arabic lessons, advice on looking for a job, and youth and homework clubs, as well as holding weekly prayers – all with the help of an annual grant from the British government. It serves newcomers such as Algerians and Albanians as well as longer-established Pakistanis and Bangladeshis. 'We do the grass-roots job the government can't,' says an official.[9]

Strict anti-discrimination laws seek to ensure the equal treatment of minorities, with the onus now on employers to prove that they have not discriminated, rather than on employees to show that they have been treated unfairly. Many urban local authorities publish documents in several languages (although others don't). When the Pakistani and Indian cricket teams visit, they are cheered on by their ethnic cousins, most of them British-born and thus British citizens, without this worrying most people and prompting fewer still to suggest doing anything about it. It is broadly accepted that society is now multicultural, multi-ethnic, multi-racial and multi-faith, but the government has done little to help, or encourage, immigrants to integrate. The model seems to work remarkably well. People from ethnic minorities are becoming more prominent in all walks of life, from TV news-reading to politics, as well as in the arts and sport. Despite riots in the northern cities of Oldham, Burnley and Bradford in 2001, racial tensions seem to be diminishing: London, where a third of the population is now from an ethnic minority, has not seen a big race riot for many years. Even so, the mood is changing: the government wants newcomers to take English-language classes and has brought in a 'Britishness' test that prospective citizens will have to pass.

Certainly, one danger with multiculturalism is that it may give group rights primacy over individual ones. Respect for cultural and religious differences can veer into defining people exclusively by their cultural or religious background and giving community leaders an apparent mandate to speak and act on their behalf. In effect, dividing society into distinct cultural blocks is like creating a set of mini-nations within it. And splitting people into fixed communities – British Muslims, say, or blacks – that are said uniquely to define them is not just harmful to society; it is as limiting, and as factually incorrect, as asserting that there is a single and indivisible French nation. While people may be part of a community, they are above all individuals with multiple, overlapping identities. Mixed marriages further blur these boundaries. Respecting people's ancestry should not imply trapping them in it; within a multicultural society, individuals should be free to choose their future. Thus some Muslims are non-practising, some are secular, some are religious but do not view the leaders who speak on their behalf as representative, some would prefer to make their voices heard as a parent or through their MP, some prefer to define themselves as British first, or individuals first, and so on. How many Christians feel that the Archbishop of Canterbury or the Pope should speak for them? As Nobel prize-winner Amartya Sen rightly says, 'Multiculturalism can be understood in terms of making it possible for people to have cultural choice and freedom, which is the very opposite of insisting that a person's basic identity must be simply defined by the religious community in which he or she is born, ignoring all other priorities and affiliations.'[10]

Another worry is that instead of leading to a harmonious feast of cultural mixing, letting people do their own thing can fail to do enough to bring people together, leading to segregation and isolation, with immigrants forming closed, resentful and potentially hostile communities. Strictly speaking, the issue is not multiculturalism itself – France and Germany have ethnic ghettoes; Canada does not – but whether more needs to be done to integrate outsiders socially and economically.

A third criticism is that although diversity may generally be a good thing, too much of it may not. Surely immigrants in Britain, for instance, need to be encouraged at least to learn English? Social conservatives claim society still needs a common culture and social norms in order to hold together. Liberals argue that tolerance of cultural diversity can only go so far: society cannot accept cultural traditions that trample on fundamental values such as the equality of women. The growth of Muslim extremism and the threat of home-grown Islamic terrorism have given a new edge to the debate. As Salman Rushdie puts it, 'the British multiculturalist idea of different cultures peacefully coexisting under the umbrella of a vaguely defined pax Britannica was seriously undermined by the July 7 bombers and the disaffected ghetto culture from which they sprang'.[11] In short, the worry is that multiculturalism may degenerate into a harmful cultural relativism – anything goes and is equally valid – and that society requires some common norms and values and a common culture to hold together. But what might they be?

Core values?

Immigrants are forever being urged to conform to local ways. But conform to what? Fifty years ago, many would have argued that the core norms of society included traditional codes of behaviour and morality. Happy (or not-so-happy) families with dad at work, mum at home and kids who put up and shut up were viewed as good; divorce, single parents, working mums, unmarried couples, independent teenagers: bad. Gays? Ugh! Christianity was good; Judaism and atheism less good, but tolerated. Thankfully, times have changed. The pendulum has swung dramatically from social conformism in personal behaviour towards what critics call 'rampant individualism' and what supporters might call 'doing your own thing'. The notion that people should conform to a set way of behaving, that they should all think in the same way or have the same set of values is increasingly rejected. And even though a vocal minority disagrees, society broadly accepts a diversity of family values, while outlawing discrimination on the basis of sex, race, sexuality and so on. Society is now a church broad enough to include nuns as well as sexually liberated women, straights, gays, bisexuals and transsexuals, stay-at-home dads and career women, Marxists and libertarians, eco-warriors and corporate big-wigs, people who think Western civilisation is the bee's knees as well as those who see it as the root of all evil. And all of them rub along together pretty well. While there is no denying that people need some things in common in order to coexist peacefully, the remaining moral norms are not too hard for most outsiders to observe: broad, common standards of right and wrong and no polygamy, for instance.

An even trickier question is what a common culture might comprise. A national language is generally desirable, but not indispensable: Canada and Belgium have two; Switzerland four. But it is generally in immigrants' as well as society's interests that they learn the local language – although there is no good reason why they should have to abandon their own. Trying to inculcate notions of a shared history are either laughable – Moroccan immigrants scarcely have a shared history with the native Dutch – or deeply contested: France views its colonial history differently to people from its former colonies in North Africa. More promising is educating everyone about common institutions that bind all members of a society together: the system of government; social programmes, from healthcare and education to welfare; the laws of the land more generally. Immigrants might be persuaded to learn these by being required to pass a language and civic-knowledge test in order to obtain citizenship, for instance. If so, though, such basic requirements of citizenship should also be taught in schools to all children. If we believe it is essential for immigrants to know how our system of government works in order to vote, then surely the same ought to apply to natives. But in practice, governments' efforts in this direction are likely to overstep the mark. The new Britishness test has rightly been ridiculed; the Dutch government has introduced mandatory courses for new migrants on cultural understanding and language skills; the US plans to include rigorous testing of language and culture as a precondition for gaining citizenship.

'This idea that there is a singular way of life which all immigrants need to sign up to assumes that Britishness is something frozen and fixed, whereas it is and always has been a work in progress, a continuing historical narrative in which we all play our part,' argues Sarfraz Manzoor, a journalist for the *Observer*.

> Fifty years ago, 'our way of life' would not have included Bengali restaurants, Pakistani doctors and Indian shop owners; each has contributed to and changed Britain. When politicians speak about 'our way of life', they play into the hands of those who would like to use the tragedy of the London attacks to pursue an agenda that is not simply about debating the value of multiculturalism as it is about retreating to outdated notions of Britishness.[12]

A BBC poll in the aftermath of the 7 July bombings found that 62 per cent of respondents agreed that multiculturalism had made Britain a better place to live. It also found that Muslim respondents were more enthusiastic than others in agreeing that new immigrants ought to learn English and pledge primary loyalty to Britain.

While trying to compel immigrants to behave in a certain way is unhelpful, efforts to promote cultural understanding should, of course, be encouraged. Fatima Hennouch, a cultural mediator at Málaga Acoge, a group that helps immigrants in the southern Spanish town of Malaga, explains how problems can arise. 'In Spain, if you avoid someone's glance when you are talking to them, it means you are lying; in Africa, it is a sign of respect.' In another case, she dealt with 'a man from the Ivory Coast who was working for a local charity. To show her appreciation for his hard work, an older Spanish woman touched him kindly. But he didn't like it: where he was from, only prostitutes touched men.' In another case, 'a Spanish boss said to a hard-working immigrant: "If you are tired, you don't have to come to work tomorrow, we'll be fine without you." The immigrant was offended: he thought his boss was saying, "If you don't come in, you can get lost." Here in Spain we say things directly; in Africa they say things in a more roundabout way.' Fatima's aim is not to get everyone to behave the same: it is to defuse the tensions that arise through misunderstandings.

But what about shared values? At one level, it's hard to see what values our diverse societies have in common: people have different views on nearly everything – the environment, abortion, capitalism, you name it. But our societies are in fact based on a set of common principles – secularism, constitutional democracy, respect for the rule of law – which all must accept. Laws are made by man, not by God; the men and women who make our laws are elected; everyone must abide the laws they enact. But their ability to make laws is constrained by certain fundamental principles, which some call 'core human rights', such as individual freedom within the law, equality of all before the law and tolerance of differences. These principles are often incorrectly described as 'Western' or 'universal', when they are really 'liberal'. Thus even a democratically elected government cannot arbitrarily trample on people's freedom.

This does not mean everyone in a society has to believe in democracy, equality or tolerance – fascists, male chauvinists and bigots do not – but they do have to accept the laws that flow from them. Likewise, immigrants who believe that religious law trumps civic law must still respect civic law when it clashes with religious edicts. Thus immigrants must accept gay rights, just as gays (and everyone else) must accept immigrants' freedom to worship religions that condemn homosexuality; immigrants must accept the equality of men and women, just as women (and everyone else) must accept the equality of people of different races, ethnicities and faiths; immigrants must accept the principles of constitutional democracy, and in turn they have the right to be protected as a minority and by the due process of law; immigrants must tolerate different values and behaviours that they abhor, just as natives must tolerate immigrants' cultural practices that do not violate the law. Liberal democracy is non-negotiable.

For sure, Western societies do not always live up to these lofty ideals: gays have fewer rights than straights in most countries; many countries practise positive discrimination; tolerance only goes so far; smokers (of which I am not) are the latest persecuted minority, while car drivers' right to poison the air remains largely unquestioned. But they are still the framework on which society is broadly based and the basis for our peaceful coexistence. So regardless of whether an immigrant feels a primary allegiance to his country of origin or to God, regardless of his citizenship status, regardless of whether he is in a country for a year or a lifetime, he must accept these principles – or at the very least the laws that have been built upon them.

Salman Rushdie argues:

> Societies, too, must retain the ability to discriminate, to reject as well as to accept, to value some things above others, and to insist on the acceptance of those values by all their members. This is the question of our time: how does a fractured community of multiple cultures decide what values it must share in order to cohere, and how can it insist on those values even when they clash with some citizens' traditions and beliefs?[13]

The answer is that society's values are based on liberal democracy and reflected in laws that can be changed only through peaceful negotiation and compromise.

But as I said earlier, integration is a two-way street. If we expect immigrants to abide by the rules of society, we must also make them feel welcome. Xenophobic rhetoric aimed at potential immigrants certainly does not make existing ones feel at home: attacks on asylum seekers elide easily into hostility towards ethnic minorities, and the argument that tough immigration controls are needed for 'good race relations' is a quasi-racist canard. Making citizenship readily available to those who settle is an important step to making them feel like they belong, and it is a prerequisite for exercising a political voice through voting. But the legal rights that citizenship grants are not enough: the French riots highlighted that if people do not feel part of society, their alienation can easily turn to rage. As I argued in Chapter 11, we also need to redefine nationhood in a way that reflects reality rather than trying to deny it: by embracing diversity rather than excluding some. What's more, we must make good on our pledge that immigrants are full and equal members of society by tackling issues of racism, poverty and social exclusion with renewed vigour; not by divisive positive discrimination, but by helping poor people of all backgrounds, strictly enforcing laws against discrimination and making a reality of equality of opportunity for all. This is not just in immigrants' interests; it is in wider society's interests, too. The alternative is to remain stuck in a trap of mutual resentment and misunderstanding where immigrants might ultimately form a hostile and isolated underclass.

Some people worry that it is a particular problem if immigrants live in separate communities. Indeed it is, if they do so because they are not welcome elsewhere, rather than out of choice. But it is only natural that immigrants congregate together at first. After all, they are strangers in a foreign land. Most of Britain's Jews, for instance, huddled together in impoverished east London when they arrived over a century ago. They spoke foreign languages, had their own religion and habits, and were often disliked by the natives, some better-off and long-established Jews included; the government also did little to turn them into Britons. Yet now, the Hasidim apart, they are fully integrated into society. 'At first, people want to live with people who are similar,' points out Uzma Shakir, the Canadian activist whom we met in Chapter 3, 'but people are afraid when immigrants live together, though not when rich whites live together.' Such geographical segregation makes political sense too, because it allows members of minority groups to elect their own local representatives if they so desire. The problem is not that immigrants may choose to live apart – although it is desirable that people mix eventually – but that they may be trapped in ghettoes and that they do not interact with the rest of society through work. Miriam Mejia, remember, lives in a predominantly Dominican-American area, but she is plugged into mainstream American life through her job. The real issue here is not the perceived failings of multiculturalism but the social and economic exclusion of some immigrants. The way out surely lies with policies that bolster social mobility for everyone.

Denmark has a long and admirable history of accepting political refugees, but it has now enacted hamfisted and racist new laws that illustrate how not to go about integrating immigrants. Playing to the gallery of Danish xenophobia, the government has made it almost impossible for new immigrants to enter the country legally. Even foreign spouses cannot easily get in, so many Danes who want to marry a foreigner and live with them now choose to do so in Sweden instead. Such draconian measures are hardly likely to make Denmark's existing immigrants feel welcome. Furthermore, any immigrants who do make it in must wait seven years for permanent residency and nine for citizenship, and then only after they pass a battery of tests, including a Danish language and history exam that, according to one Danish newspaper, many Danes would struggle to pass.[14] For sure, the extra money that the government is devoting to job counselling for immigrants is to be applauded. Newcomers also have to sign up to compulsory courses in civics and language, and, if necessary, compulsory work placements. But while helping people improve their language, social and work skills is good for the individuals involved as well as for society as a whole, compelling immigrants to do things that other residents do not have to do, and foisting local culture on them, is very different from offering them a helping hand, especially in the context of a broader clampdown on immigration. For a model of the future that works, Europeans would do better to look to Canada.

The Canadian model

Canada has gone furthest in embracing multiculturalism, although it does try to select immigrants that it deems more likely to fit in, by requiring that they be highly educated and speak English or French, for instance. Its Multiculturalism Act makes clear that Canada welcomes immigrants and respects their differences but is also committed to integrating them into Canadian society.

Consider Toronto – motto: 'Diversity Our Strength' – which is extremely multicultural even by Canadian standards: of its 2.5 million residents, nearly half (49 per cent) were born outside Canada, in over 200 different countries. One in five Torontonians immigrated in the last ten years. The city is home to 8 per cent of Canada's population, but 22 per cent of all immigrants. Some 43 per cent of Toronto residents are from racial minorities. Over a hundred languages and dialects are regularly spoken in Canada's biggest city, while over ninety religious groups congregate there. The number of Buddhists, Sikhs, Hindus and Muslims has doubled in a decade. And immigrants keep on coming: it has received over a third of the new arrivals in Canada since 2000 – an average of 82,000 immigrants and refugees a year, three-quarters of them from Asia and the Pacific, Africa and the Middle East.[15]

Yet visitors to Toronto expecting to find a city in the throes of ethnic conflict and cultural meltdown will be sorely disappointed. It is sedate rather than edgy, integrated not segregated, peaceful and prosperous not poor and violent. Hate crimes are rare. Deprived ethnic ghettoes such as those that scar American inner cities and the Parisian suburbs are virtually non-existent. The closest that Toronto gets to a ghetto is Thorncliffe Park, which is overwhelmingly South Asian and poor – but by American or British standards the area looks remarkably fine. 'Ghettoes? I don't think that is happening here,' says Jehad Aliweiwi, the Palestinian-born director of the Thorncliffe Neighbourhood Office, which provides social services to the local community. We chat while eating an Afghan kebab in a restaurant near his office. It's a cold, damp day, but his talk warms me up. 'There are no neighbourhoods in Toronto like the ghettoes in Leeds or Paris. Even middle-class suburbs are racially diverse. Canadians are comfortable with diversity. They have come to terms with it. There is an intolerance of segregation and closed doors.'

Jehad left his home town of Hebron in the West Bank in 1987 to study in Canada. 'I had finished high school and there was no university to go to,' he explains. 'I saw an ad about studying in Canada and I ended up applying for residency after I graduated.' He is certainly no government stooge: for six years he ran the Canadian Arab Federation, which he had joined at university during the first Gulf War, and he was the main spokesperson for the Muslim community after 9/11: 'Canada is not a la-la land,' he emphasises. 'There are incidents against Muslims: after 9/11, a temple was burned and a mosque was fire-bombed. But it doesn't compare to the US's racism against blacks.'

Why does multiculturalism appear to work so much better in Canada than elsewhere? Because Canadians do more than pay lip-service to it: they are genuinely committed to making a success of it. For instance, the City of Toronto translates all official documents into a dozen languages. The children of immigrants are encouraged to learn their parents' mother tongue at school. 'It allows you to be who you are in a greater Canadian society,' says Jehad. The Multiculturalism Act makes it official policy. The Canadian Charter of Rights and Freedoms gives legal substance to equal rights. The government invests heavily in social and cultural programmes: there is a Department of Canadian Heritage and Multiculturalism. Community dialogue is encouraged. But Jehad would like Canada to go even further to recognise the new reality of its diversity. 'Canadian institutions were created to serve a particular reality that was mainly Christian and white,' he explains. 'That is no longer true. We need to revisit Canada's institutions and founding principles to reflect the fact that we have the world's population within a country. Canada is a showcase experiment of what the world will be like in a hundred years.' He may be right. Canada certainly feels like it's in the vanguard of change, pushing the limits of what is possible and acceptable. 'We have a responsibility to be leading,' he insists. 'Even though it's a lot of work and a lot of pain.'

Jehad is totally committed to a political system based on 'plural, liberal, secular democracy', but he insists that the conservative vision of an Anglo-French, white, Christian Canada is unsustainable. 'If they aren't willing to renegotiate, they shouldn't bring in more immigrants,' he points out. 'They are actively pursuing immigrants. They should be pursuing a policy to integrate them into society's culture, economy and politics with equal zeal.'

Uzma Shakir agrees:

> Yes, Canada is a model: it acknowledges that it is an immigrant country. But no, it hasn't solved all its problems. The issue is no longer what Canada can do for immigrants, but how can we build a new country? The new Canada is pluralistic, multilingual, multi-racial and multi-faith. It's more than diversity. We are not just different. We need to renegotiate the power structures to

> reflect the pluralistic reality. The institutions need to change. For instance, we need coloured leaders and administration. Instead, there is a guild-like mentality where the establishment is trying to hold on to all the power.

Canada's overwhelmingly Anglo-French political elite is committed to making a virtue of diversity, if not yet to wholesale political change. 'Nobody has a clear notion of where this country is going,' says Uzma.

> We are an experiment in the making. But we have all bought in to something that is Canada. The new Canada could be defined by who its residents are, the laws they abide by, the institutions they govern themselves by and their respect for diversity. We are not the US: we may not have the vibrancy, but we have none of the belligerence either. Here in Canada we can create new relationships, a new reality where we negotiate our differences a lot better, in a non-hostile way. CASSA [Uzma's immigrant-support group in Toronto], for example, is creating a sense of community that doesn't exist in South Asia. I'm from Pakistan and I'd never met an Indian until I came here. I'm very hopeful. I think Canada is a good place to do it.

Most Canadians appear to appreciate its cultural mosaic. Three in four Canadians agree that 'It is better for Canada to have a variety of people with different religions' and 'Canada's multicultural make-up is one of the best things about this country', while two-thirds disagree with the statement that 'It is better for Canada if almost everyone shares the same customs and traditions'. But 56 per cent still say they think priority should be placed on encouraging minority groups 'to try to be more like most Canadians', while only 44 per cent would like 'Canadians as a whole to try and accept minority groups and their customs and languages'.[16] In short, Canadians increasingly make a virtue of their diversity, which refreshes, rather than dilutes, their sense of being Canadian – but they also feel immigrants must adapt to Canadian society as they embrace the newcomers' cultural differences.

It's not rocket science. Societies need to make every effort to ensure that everyone feels included and has an opportunity to participate fully in economic and social life. But they also need to accept the diversity of all their members – not just those of foreign descent – while insisting that all adhere to the fundamental principles on which they are based. The watchwords are tolerance and respect for the law. Learning the local language and how local institutions work, and promoting cultural understanding are also important, without seeking to impose a uniform culture or behavioural norms.

Yet Europe has found it particularly difficult to integrate its growing Muslim minority. Indeed, many people increasingly worry that Muslim immigrants will never fit in. Are they right?

15

Illiberal Islam?

Do Muslim immigrants threaten our security and our way of life?

This is not an Islamic country, it is a Christian country, and we should not be forced to accommodate Islam.

Walter Bosbach, spokesman for Germany's Christian Democratic Union party[1]

It is indispensable to recover our principles, the deepest roots of Europe – for example, our Christian roots. We must rediscover our cultural values and set aside the enormous error of multiculturalism . . . We should defend the notion that all citizens are equal before the law and that the law is the same for all. This is the true expression of tolerance: equality under the law. But we should also remember that the March 2004 terrorist attacks in Madrid and the more recent attacks in London were perpetrated by people who had lived for many years in our countries.

José María Aznár, former prime minister of Spain[2]

> Multiculturalism has always been an embattled idea but the battle has grown fiercer of late. In this, it is terrorism that is setting the agenda, goading us to respond: terrorism, whose goal it is to turn the differences between us into divisions and then to use those divisions as justifications. No question about it: it's harder to celebrate polyculture when Belgian women are being persuaded by Belgians 'of North African descent' to blow themselves – and others – up.
>
> Salman Rushdie[3]

'My mother wore the veil over everything but her eyes,' says Fatima Hennouch, whom we met in the previous chapter. 'But I've been in Spain for twelve years now and I've taken what I think is the best from each culture. There is good and bad in both; the important thing is how I feel.' Fatima is certainly forthright, but she also desperately wants to be accepted in Spain. 'I'm never looked at badly,' she says of her neighbours in the apartment block where she lives. 'But I can't just come here and say, "I'm Moroccan". People have to make efforts to be understood. If they disrespect others, they can't expect not to be treated badly. Integration is not about going to the supermarket, opening a Spanish bank account or taking the bus. It's about respecting yourself and respecting others.' She pauses for a second. 'If I had kids, I would educate them as Spaniards.'

'If only they were all like Fatima,' many Europeans will cry. 'And if only all Europeans were like the Spanish,' Muslims might respond. Andalusia, where Fatima lives, was for centuries ruled by Muslims from North Africa – indeed, Osama bin Laden often fantasises about recapturing it from Christian Europeans – yet the Spanish are surprisingly relaxed about Muslim immigration. In part, no doubt, this is because many Spaniards have recent first-hand experience of being immigrants themselves. But it is also because Spaniards are proud of their Islamic heritage:

witness the splendours of the Alhambra in Granada, or Córdoba's Mezquita, a mosque now embedded inside a church, the perfect metaphor for *convivencia*, peaceful coexistence between Christians and Muslims. Even though Moroccan immigrants were found to be responsible for the Madrid train bombings of 11 March 2004, the Spanish have not turned against Moroccans in general. 'It was okay,' says Ahmed Khalifa, a Moroccan student living in Malaga. 'People know how to distinguish between terrorists and other Moroccans. There are no far-right parties here and the new Socialist government made clear that Muslims are not the same as terrorists.'

But many other Europeans would disagree. In the previous chapter, for instance, we saw how the Dutch reacted to the murder of Theo van Gogh by lashing out at Muslims in general. It's not just a fear of terrorism that sets alarm bells ringing for many Europeans, though. It's the worry that many Muslim immigrants reject some of the most basic tenets of our society – that laws are made by people, not by God; that women are equal to men; that we must tolerate others' differences even if we disapprove of them. Gilles Kepel, a professor of Middle East studies at the Institute of Political Studies in Paris and the author of *The War for Muslim Minds: Islam and the West*, claims that Europe has become the 'primary battlefield on which the future of global Islam will be decided',[4] while Samuel Huntington warns that the global clash of civilisations between the West and Islam is in part being played out as a domestic clash of civilisations in European countries with Muslim minorities. Really?

Culture clash

There is plenty that many people would find shocking about El-Farouk Khaki. He is brashly and outspokenly gay, and acerbically critical of conventional society. But in many ways this tireless campaigner for women's equality, gay rights and justice for immigrants, who arrived in Toronto from Tanzania via Streatham in south London, is also profoundly reassuring: he is a devout Muslim who asserts that Islam is not incompatible with liberal values. He is fasting for Ramadan when I interview him, and although he claims that this is making it hard for him to think straight, in a few minutes he has no trouble dispelling many of the myths about Islam that most worry secular Westerners. 'I am a Muslim,' he asserts. 'It's part of my identity. It's a belief system. A humanist one. I believe that Mohammed was the last Prophet and that the Koran is the revealed word of God. But the image that mainstream Muslim groups project and others perceive, that Muslims should act in a certain way, is false,' he asserts. It has been hijacked by social convention: 'The only image that is fed to us is narrow, rigid, socially conservative, xenophobic.' But in fact, he argues, 'Islam embraces great diversity and different ways. I don't believe the Koran is misogynist. It's not frozen in time and space, it's contextual. It asserts that all human beings are equal: God speaks to both women and men. There is nothing in the Koran that says women can't lead prayer. Even alcohol was not forbidden at first: just at time of war and prayer.' Muslims in the West are told that they should practise Islam in a certain way and they don't know any better: 'they haven't grown up in the homeland and seen the variety, plurality and shades of Islam. They feel detached from their Pakistani roots, a sense of inadequacy.'

It is certainly chilling to hear the hatred that someone like Hassan Butt feels towards British, and by extension Western, society. A twenty-five-year-old British Pakistani from Manchester who was a spokesman for the extremist group al-Muhajiroun and helped recruit people to fight against the coalition forces in Afghanistan, he has gone from frustration and rootlessness to radical Islam. Asked if he felt any allegiance to Britain, he said, 'I feel absolutely nothing for this country. I have no problem with the British people . . . but if someone attacks them I have no problem with that either.' He was speaking before the London bombings in July 2005. 'My allegiance is to Allah, his sharia, his way of life. Whatever he dictates as good is good, whatever as bad is bad.' Asked whether many Muslims in Britain shared his opinions, he replied, 'I would say the majority of Muslims in this country care about neither moderate nor radical Islam; they care about living their day-to-day life. But of those people who are practising, the majority of them hold my views. The difference is that some people come out publicly and others keep quiet.' He reckoned a quarter of British Muslims have an interest in Islam and that around 80 per cent of those were over the moon about 9/11.[5]

There are reckoned to be around fifteen million Muslims living in western Europe, although nobody knows the precise figure. What is certain is that Islam is now the largest minority religion in Europe. There are more Muslims than Catholics in Protestant northern Europe and more Muslims than Protestants in the Catholic south. Europe's Muslims far outnumber European Jews. Some say there are as many as 6 million Muslims in France, a whopping 10 per cent of the population, while others put the figure as low as 2.5 million. There are said to be 3.1 million Muslims in Germany, 3.7 per cent of the population, and 1.5 million in Britain (2.5 per cent), 1.4 million in Italy (2.4 per cent) and 500,000 in Spain (1.2 per cent). The 870,000 Muslims in the Netherlands account for 5.4 per cent of the Dutch population, while Muslims are said to make up 3.6 per cent of Belgium's population, 3.1 per cent of Sweden's and Switzerland's and 3 per cent of Denmark's. Outside Europe, there are supposedly 6 million Muslims in the US, or 2.1 per cent of the population, 620,000 in Canada (2 per cent) and 280,000 in Australia (1.5 per cent). That Muslim immigration is not perceived to be as problematic in those countries suggests that the difficulties in Europe are not intrinsic to Islam.[6] One big difference is that whereas Muslims account for most immigrants in Europe, they are only a small minority of immigrants in the US, Canada and Australia, so broader fears about foreigners in general that are projected on to Muslims in Europe are projected on to others elsewhere: Latinos in the US, for instance. Moreover, whereas most Muslim immigrants in Europe are poor, working class and from former European colonies – three more sources of tension and prejudice – those in the US tend to be prosperous and middle class.

Muslims started arriving in Europe in large numbers in the 1950s and 1960s, mostly as guest-workers from Turkey and Morocco. Turks were recruited to work in German factories; France admitted immigrants from its ex-colonies in North Africa; the Netherlands brought in Turks, Moroccans, Indonesians and people from Surinam; Britain's Muslims came mostly from India and Pakistan. They came to work and were expected to leave eventually. They made little effort to fit in, living apart and not bothering to learn the local language, while Europeans largely ignored them. But when Europe tried to put a stop to immigration in the early 1970s, many decided to stay put, fearing that they might never be able to return to work. Then they brought over their families, while the manufacturing jobs they came to do disappeared. Often poor, isolated and discriminated against, many became resentful of a European society that made no place for them. More recently, they have been joined by a new wave of Muslim immigrants: refugees from the Middle East and Somalia, illegal immigrants crossing from Morocco to Spain, and Albanians making the short boat trip over to Italy.

Europeans might have continued ignoring Muslims, but in the late 1980s they were suddenly forced to take notice. It was Salman Rushdie's book, *The Satanic Verses*, that set the fires alight. His work had previously been emblematic of the creative blending of East and West; but now it set East and West apart. Although few bothered to read it, Muslims everywhere were outraged by what they saw as the book's blasphemous depiction of the Prophet Muhammad. Many British Muslims were incensed too. Fair enough – many Christians also object to art they find blasphemous, such as the film *The Last Temptation of Christ*, or Robert Mapplethorpe's photography – but then in January 1989, in a chilling echo of Hitler's Germany, the book was ceremonially burned in the predominantly Muslim town of Bradford. A month later, when Iran's spiritual leader, Ayatollah Khomeini, called on all 'zealous Muslims' to execute Rushdie, the Anglo-Indian writer was forced to go into hiding under police protection. (Similar outrage erupted in early 2006 over the publication in European newspapers of cartoons of the Prophet Muhammad that many Muslims considered blasphemous. In London, hundreds of Muslims marched from the Regent's Park mosque, one of the biggest Islamic centres in Europe, to the heavily protected Danish embassy, bearing placards declaring, 'Behead the one who insults the Prophet' and 'Free speech go to hell'.)

The book-burning, ironically, underlined the fact that the cultural divide cuts both ways. It would have been just as hard for Muslims with roots in the Indian sub-continent to understand why this was such a horrifying act to Europeans as it was for secular Europeans to comprehend the depth of Muslim revulsion at the insult to the Prophet. But it was not just the bonfires that caused alarm. Conflict soon erupted over many of the immigrants' religious and cultural practices. Europeans objected to the ritual slaughter of animals in urban streets and apartment blocks, while Muslims railed that governments denied them permission to build mosques. Many were shocked when they learned that female circumcision was still practised by some Muslims. The Westerners labelled it genital mutilation, while the immigrants asserted it was part of their cultural heritage, just as male circumcision is to Jews (and Muslims). Muslims complained that workplaces wouldn't accommodate prayer times, religious holidays and the wearing of Muslim dress. Europeans worried that many 'arranged' marriages between local Muslim girls and foreign Muslim men were in fact forced. Muslims complained that government made no provision for Muslim cemeteries, pastoral care for Muslims in prisons or the teaching of their religion in public schools. Governments responded that religion must not intrude on public life.

9/11 and Osama bin Laden's justification of terrorism in the name of Islam sharpened fears about the clash between the Western and Muslim worlds. That several of the terrorists had apparently lived for years in Western countries raised further worries about the enclosed societies that seemed to exist within the West, societies in which hate could be preached and treachery plotted while all around non-Muslims remained utterly unaware. The Dutch were shocked when a poll in late 2001 found that although 61 per cent of Muslims thought the 9/11 attacks had been a bad thing, 39 per cent did not. They are 'not like us', many native Dutch concluded.[7] Before his murder in 2002, Pim Fortuyn not only declared the Netherlands 'full up', but attacked Islam as a 'backward religion', intolerant of homosexuals and women's rights. The murder in November 2004 of Theo van Gogh by a Dutch-born Muslim seemed to confirm Fortuyn's claims.

The 11 March 2004 bombings in Madrid and the 7 July 2005 attacks in London caused new waves of alarm. While Moroccan immigrants planted the Madrid train bombs, the London tube and bus bombings were perpetrated by four British-born Muslims. Evidence piled up that terrorist networks were embedded in mosques throughout Europe. One of the 9/11 terrorists, Mohammad Atta, had attended the al-Quds mosque in Hamburg. German police found a tape featuring the imam of the mosque raging that 'Christians and Jews should have their throats slit'. The British 'shoe-bomber', Richard Reid, and the suspected twentieth 9/11 hijacker, Zacarias Moussaoui, were both linked to the Finsbury Park mosque, where the hooked cleric Abu Hamza al-Masri, later charged with inciting terrorism, used to preach.

Fouad Ajami, a respected Middle East expert, argues that Europe's new Muslim groups are fronts for Islamic militants from the Muslim Brotherhood and other banned organisations.[8] He claims that Islamic radicals expelled from the Middle East who came to Europe as political refugees have gained power in the wider Islamic community and are influencing European governments. Certainly, some radical Islamists – such as Omar Bakri Mohammad, a London-based cleric and leader of the militant group al-Muhajiroun, who was granted asylum in 1985 after he was deported from Saudi Arabia – have settled in Europe. But that hardly proves that most Muslims share his views – still less that they have broader political influence. Only 3 per cent of Britons are Muslims, remember.

Jytte Klausen, a Danish-American politics professor at Brandeis University, strongly disagrees with Ajami. In *The Islamic Challenge*, having interviewed over three hundred Muslim activists in Europe, she argues that 'Europe's Muslim political leaders are not aiming to overthrow liberal democracy and to replace secular law with Islamic religious law, the sharia. Most are rather looking for ways to build institutions that will allow Muslims to practise their religion in a way that is compatible with social integration.'[9] Despite a clash of values, Islam, Christianity and a secular state can coexist peacefully in Europe, Klausen argues.

Yet Europe's governments seem confused about what to do. The Dutch veer between declaring war on Islam and trying to force Muslims to come into the fold. Germany has eased its citizenship laws, allowing its Turkish Muslim residents to become citizens, but some German states have banned the Islamic headscarf and mandated the crucifix in public schools, declaring that Germany is a Judaeo-Christian state. France has banned girls from wearing the headscarf at school, on the grounds that church and state must remain wholly separate, while also announcing the creation of a foundation to fund 'French Islam'. It has also set up a single national Islamic council to act as an interlocutor with the authorities, which many say empowers unrepresentative traditionalist voices, while threatening to deport imams who challenge republican values (like freedom of speech, perhaps?). Britain has passed anti-terrorist laws that target Muslims while promising to allow sharia law to be used in court.

Disentangling the issues

Amid all this panic and confusion, Europeans are losing sight of the real issues. First, to what extent should Western societies accommodate the cultural and religious practices of Muslim immigrants? Second, how far can liberal societies tolerate illiberal views and behaviour? Third, what leads some European Muslims to become extremists and some even to become terrorists, and what can be done to prevent this?

Undeniably, Muslims force Europeans to confront a number of delicate issues. One is the role of religion in public life. Whereas many people insist that Europe is fundamentally secular, with a strict separation between church and state, in practice its Christian traditions are still influential, and some Europeans still assert the primacy of Christianity. Queen Elizabeth II is the head of the Church of England as well as Britain's head of state; Christmas and Easter are official holidays as well as religious ones; many European governments fund Christian schools and give churches various tax breaks and subsidies. When Muslims demand equal treatment, secularists respond that religion should be kept out of public life, while others reply that European countries should remain fundamentally Christian. Other Christians see Muslims as potential allies in their efforts to grab a bigger role for religion in public life, in asserting traditional family values, for instance, or curbing free speech they deem blasphemous.

Centuries of religious wars between Catholics and Protestants have surely taught Europeans that secularism is the only way that people of different beliefs – religious or not – can live together peacefully while maintaining their freedom of belief. Moreover, except where religious beliefs violate fundamental liberal principles of individual freedom, equality and tolerance, a liberal society should surely tolerate them. So pragmatism and principle both argue in favour of accommodating religious differences as far as possible while trying to keep church and state as separate as possible. In areas where links between the Christian church and state still remain, it would be best if they were broken; but if that is impossible, Islam – as well as Judaism, Hinduism, Buddhism and other faiths and belief systems – should as far as possible be granted equal treatment. To assert, as Walter Bosbach, a spokesman for Germany's ruling Christian Democrats did, that Germany 'is a Christian country, and we should not be forced to accommodate Islam' is not only factually incorrect but should send alarm bells ringing among Jews, atheists and secularists as well as Muslims.

Tolerant, liberal, multicultural societies can adapt to most religious differences. If there is no problem with Jews taking a day off work to celebrate their religious holidays, there should be no problem with Muslims doing likewise. If smokers are allowed to take time off work to nip out for a cigarette, or have a designated smoking room allocated to them, Muslims should surely be entitled to stop work to pray, in a separate prayer room where practical. They should also be free to build mosques and prayer halls where there is a demand for them. If state-owned airlines can dish out kosher, vegan and halal food to whoever asks for it, then surely so can state-run schools. Land should be set aside for Muslim cemeteries in France (which currently has only one) and Germany (which has none) or space should be allocated for them within municipal ones. At present, 90 per cent of Germany's Muslims are flown 'home' – that is, abroad – to be buried. And while the Islamic ban on coffins is problematic, because it conflicts with public-health laws, ingenious ways could doubtless be found of limiting the health risks.

The ritual slaughter of sheep at the annual feast of Eid may be deeply shocking to many Westerners, but this could surely be done out of sight of non-Muslims, just as animals are killed in abattoirs or shot by hunters away from the eyes of the squeamish or animal-lovers. Indeed, that is precisely what is starting to happen in France. In Evry, a town south of Paris that is home to some 15,000 Muslims (a third of the population) and the country's biggest mosque, the slaughter of sheep for Eid, which used to take place in living rooms, is now run by the council. Some 4,000 sheep are assembled under a huge marquee the size of a football pitch by the grassy banks of the Seine. Each family identifies and tags its own sheep, an official Muslim sacrificer dispatches it, and each family then takes its animal home for the feast. 'The French must understand that France is changing,' says a local official. 'Islam has its place here now.'[10]

France has traditionally been wedded to a particularly strict form of secularism, known as *laïcité*. Instituted in 1905 as a bulwark against the previous dominance of the Catholic church, this dictates that the state should protect individuals against pressure from any religious group by barring religion from public life, while respecting their right to practise their faith in private. Even the 'So help me God' intoned by incoming American presidents would be unthinkable in France. Yet the involvement of Evry town hall in sheep slaughter shows that secularist principle is starting to give way to multicultural pragmatism and accommodation.

But only up to a point. In 2004 France banned children from wearing the Islamic headscarf as well as other 'conspicuous' religious symbols, such as large crucifixes, Sikh turbans or the Jewish *kippa*, in state schools. Foreigners were baffled, many Muslims outraged. On the surface, the ban does not discriminate against Muslims, but few schoolchildren – save perhaps those who copy the bling jewellery of their favourite rap stars – turn up to class wearing crucifixes of a 'manifestly excessive dimension'. 'It's not the crucifix or the *kippa* that is targeted,' insists Khalil Merroun, the rector of the Evry mosque, 'but Islam.'[11]

Patrick Weil, an expert on immigration who sat on the presidential commission that recommended the ban, argues that it was necessary because Muslim girls were being forced to wear the headscarf. 'Either we left the situation as it was, and thus supported a situation that denied freedom of choice to those – the very large majority – who do not want to wear the headscarf; or we endorsed a law that removed freedom of choice from those who do want to wear it,' he argues. 'We decided to give freedom of choice to the former during the time they were in school, while the latter retain all their freedom for their life outside school.' He adds:

> In schools where some Muslim girls do wear the headscarf and others do not, there is strong pressure on the latter to 'conform'. This daily pressure takes different forms, from insults to violence. In the view of the (mostly male) aggressors, these girls are 'bad Muslims', 'whores', who should follow the example of their sisters who respect Koranic prescriptions . . . We received testimonies of Muslim fathers who had to transfer their daughters from public to (Catholic) private schools where they were free of pressure to wear the headscarf . . . The reason was plain: the wearing of a headscarf or the imposition of it on others is much more than an issue of individual

> freedom: it has become a France-wide strategy pursued by fundamentalist groups who use public schools as their battleground.[12]

Indeed, whereas a majority of Muslim men in France opposed the ban, a poll showed that 49 per cent of Muslim women supported it, while only 43 per cent were against it.[13]

But, while the ban was widely seen as striking a blow against the racist National Front as well as against fundamentalist Islamists, it is also deeply flawed. Not only is it illiberal to curtail people's freedom to display their religious beliefs but it may be counter-productive, since extremism feeds off Muslims' feeling that they face unfair discrimination. If the worry was that girls were being bullied into wearing the headscarf when they preferred not to, then it would surely be better to deal with that intimidation directly, by taking measures, through a criminal court if necessary, to stop it happening. This would allow those who wish to wear the headscarf to do so, while protecting the rights of Muslim girls who would rather not.

The principle of respecting cultural and religious differences does not imply that anything is acceptable. While Western societies should go a long way to accommodate Islam, both in order to remain true to their principles as well as to keep the peace, Muslims must in return agree to abide by, even if they do not share, the fundamental principles on which our societies are based, as well as the particular laws in which they are embodied. A liberal society must tolerate illiberal views but not illiberal behaviour. After all, nobody can legislate for hearts and minds – but we can insist that the law be obeyed. Even men who do not believe that women are their equals must treat them as such. Even those who think homosexuality is immoral must tolerate gays. Ultimately, the principles on which Western societies are based are in their Muslim minorities' interests too: even Christians who dislike Islam must tolerate Muslims.

Of course, it would be better if everyone really did believe in the values of individual freedom, equality, tolerance and democracy. But many non-Muslims do not – there are Christian fundamentalists as well as Muslim ones, not to mention ultra-Orthodox Jews, revolutionary communists and anarchists. Indeed, Olivier Roy, a leading French expert on Islam, points out that fundamentalist Muslims have much in common with US evangelical Protestants: both believe that

> Faith is the fault-line between the good people and the wicked. Religious norms should be the core of human life and are not linked to any culture. Life should be reconstructed upon these norms, because wider society is secular-minded, even if it pays lip-service to religion. Culture (novels, films, music) may bring about the dereliction of mores. Religious norms and creeds can apply to anybody anywhere: there is no need for 'cultural sensitivity'. The divide is between believers and non-believers within so-called cultures and not between different cultures.[14]

The Catholic Church does not admit women priests, while the Church of England wrestles with the issue of women bishops; neither condones homosexuality. It is right and proper that liberal values be enforced in the public sphere, but people are entitled to their private views, however abhorrent. The problem only arises when they act on those beliefs and break the law: if people discriminate against women in the workplace, if people not only hate gays but beat them up, if people go beyond loathing abortion to bombing abortion clinics. So if a Muslim girl objects to an arranged marriage, the state must intervene to protect her: her right to choose her husband must take precedence over a group's right to enforce its illiberal cultural traditions. As Uzma Shakir says: 'We have developed certain fundamental values, not just

Western values. Values that ought to be universal, such as racial and women's equality. I learned my feminism in Pakistan. They were not all educated women like me. We need to negotiate a middle ground where you can be Muslim and respect universal values.' She is adamant that governments cannot tolerate the oppression of women: 'The Canadian and Pakistani governments should intervene to prevent forced marriage. The girls are Canadian citizens, I don't care what the parents say. Older people stop me in grocery stores and say, "I saw you on TV, you make a lot of sense."' If civic law conflicts with sharia law, the law of man must take precedence over the law of God. In return for a broad acceptance of their cultural and religious differences, all Muslims must in turn accept the fundamental principles on which our societies are based.

Most do. We should not fall into the trap of thinking that Muslims are a uniform and separate community whose identity is wholly defined by their religion, still less an inevitably hostile or violent one. Muslim leaders have a vested interest in asserting that they represent a large minority community, encompassing all descendants of immigrants from Muslim countries, when this is not in fact the case. The Muslim Council of Britain is scarcely seen as representative, according to Muslims interviewed by Jytte Klausen. Muslims rarely vote as a block, for instance, as Olivier Roy points out: 'Political Islam is a dream or a nightmare, but not a sociological reality.'[15] Muslim immigrants originate in a variety of countries, each with their own cultural traditions that are not Islamic but Somali, Turkish or Moroccan. Muslims born in Europe have very different views to those of their foreign-born parents. Muslims in each European country confront different problems and have absorbed different local ways. Many Muslims are not religious at all. Many religious Muslims are secular and liberal; others are not, but accept that they must respect that Europe is. There are feminist Muslims, gay Muslims and Muslims who reject their faith.

It is also nonsense to suggest that all Muslims are socially conservative, displaying respect for their elders, close family ties and antiquated views about women. Muslims born in Europe tend to have fewer kids, live in nuclear not extended families and disrespect their parents – much like other Westerners do. Even arranged marriages are often merely a ruse to bypass immigration restrictions. 'As usual, cultural values are more preached than implemented,' says Olivier Roy. 'But this imaginary culture is too often taken at its own word by observers and politicians. With a slight time-lag, Muslim populations are entering the same patterns of sociological modernisation as the West, but this can occasionally be carried out through religious revivalism.'[16]

Most conservative, religious Muslims advocate integration without assimilation: being part of society without jettisoning their cultural heritage and religious practices. Groups such as the Union of Islamic Organisations in France and Milli Görüs in Germany strive to organise Muslims into a visible and active community, with institutions and establishment figures, involved in education and social services. 'They may evolve into a sort of Muslim church in Europe, which will pose little or no security threat but will push for conservative moral and social values,' argues Roy.[17] Only a small minority of Muslims are fundamentalist, and they are split between those who seek to isolate themselves from European society and those who seek confrontation with it. Only a tiny minority of the confrontational fundamentalists support terrorism, and an even smaller group aid or practise terrorism.

Terrorism

For years I lived in Finsbury Park and traipsed past its now-infamous mosque on the way to work. It looked innocuous enough at the time – this was before Abu Hamza had been expelled from it and had started preaching to large crowds in the street – an ugly, modern building quite in keeping with the desolation of Seven Sisters Road, which separates the mosque from the tube station. For sure, Finsbury Park has always had an edge to it, and the streets are filled with swarthy types chatting in foreign languages. But most of London is like that – and it's mostly a good thing. Where I live now, near Caledonian Road, there is a large Turkish community – you could hear the roars and then see the fireworks as Turkey progressed to the World Cup semi-finals in 2002 – and the shopkeepers are invariably friendly. So it came as a huge shock to hear that Londoners were plotting terrorism on my doorstep in Finsbury Park.

It was even more terrifying when London was rocked by four suicide bombers on 7 July 2005. I was safely at home that day, having just started to write this book the day before, but I had taken those tube lines and the number 30 bus many times before. The Piccadilly Line is my quickest route into town. It was truly shocking to find out that the terrorists were born and raised in Britain and had led apparently normal lives until that point. One was a teacher of kids with special needs – he hardly fitted the profile that one might expect of a terrorist. When it seemed as if London might be struck again two weeks later, I briefly descended into paranoia. On 22 July, on a bus home from an interview, my heart started racing uncontrollably and sweat began pouring out as I sat down next to an Asian-looking man holding a rucksack. I thought of getting off, or of asking the man to show me what was in his bag. I decided I was overreacting, and that he would rightly be offended by my behaviour. I said nothing, sat tight and wondered whether I was about to die.

It is understandable that people overreact when facing the possibility that a stranger might want to kill them. We spend our lives among strangers and assume for the most part that they mean us no harm, or that they will be deterred from any wrongdoing by the threat of punishment. It is terrifying to be confronted with our vulnerability and our helplessness. Short of going to live somewhere remote, there is no escaping the threat of terrorism. So once you stop and think, you decide to get on with your life as before. If your number's up, your number's up; if not, why worry about a risk you can't control? While we all need to be vigilant, the burden of preventing terrorism lies with the police and the government.

This is not a book about terrorism or Islam, and I do not pretend to be an expert on either. But it is illogical, unfair and counter-productive to blame or suspect immigrants in general or Muslims in particular for the activities of an extremist minority. The fact that we do it in the case of Muslims also betrays the unconscious colour-racism of European society. When the IRA was carrying out its terrorist attacks in the name of Irish nationalism, Britons did not blame or suspect everyone with an Irish accent and Irish citizens were still allowed to travel freely to Britain. British Muslims in general are not responsible for what extremists do in the name of Islam, any more than white Britons are all to blame for the noxious racism of the flag-waving British National Party. The United States has produced home-grown terrorists – think of the Oklahoma bombing and the Unabomber – who have nothing to do with Islam, and all societies produce serial killers and other mass murderers. European anarchists were suicide bombers a century ago, long before Islamists first started using the tactic in 1983. The overwhelming majority of Muslims, even those who feel alienated and discriminated against in Britain, abhor terrorism. Blaming them will only serve to increase their feelings of alienation.

Research on the attitudes of British Muslims, published by the London-based Islamic Human Rights Commission at the end of 2004, showed that 'There has been a radicalisation of the British Muslim community – but in the sense of a raising of consciousness about issues which Muslims feel strongly about. The biggest expression of this has been the participation of British Muslims in demonstrations against the war in Iraq. But this doesn't mean that you now have large numbers of British Muslims prepared to blow people up.' Massoud Shadjareh, the IHRC's main spokesman, says firebrands such as the Syrian-born Bakri Mohammed, who moved to the UK in 1985 and was the leader of the radical al-Muhajiroun group, have been 'politically demonised' but have negligible backing among British Muslims: he had 'between 50 and 100 supporters' turning up for his meetings.[18]

An Amsterdam taxi driver explained to me: 'The Dutch treat me like a foreigner, even though I was born here, I speak Dutch perfectly, I pay my taxes like everybody. All because I am dark. My parents are from Turkey, but I'm from here.' His views are actually more liberal than those of the supposedly liberal Dutch: 'I don't see why we can't all live together. It doesn't matter whether you are Muslim, Christian, black, white, gay or whatever, we should just get on with our lives and respect other people's differences. Things have got worse since van Gogh's murder. People blame Islam or all Muslims for the actions of a few extremists. The killing of van Gogh has nothing to do with Islam and most Muslims are not extremists.'

Uzma Shakir, who describes herself as 'a Canadian and an immigrant Muslim woman in a post-9/11 North American environment', is a worried mother as well as a political activist. 'I don't feel guilty for 9/11,' she says.

> The entire Muslim faith is not guilty. But I am a Muslim and I'm raising a Muslim son aged sixteen. You think I don't worry about who he hangs around with, whether he will become a terrorist? He is angry at racism and the pathologising of Muslims. Yesterday Ramadan started. We are both fasting. My son said I should pray. I rolled my eyes. 'Why are you rolling your eyes?' he asked me.

> 'You think I may be becoming a terrorist?' I replied: 'If you are praying for spiritual solace, OK. But if you are going to tell me to wear the veil, no.'

Blaming Muslim Europeans or Americans en masse for the actions of a few will only serve to increase their feelings of alienation. A proper response to terrorism has to be targeted at the culprits and the extremists who support them. We need to make sure that Muslims who are not extremists feel fully part of society and put in place policies that ensure their social and economic integration. But at the same time, Muslims themselves must fully cooperate with the efforts of the police and others to root out terrorism and win the debate against those who preach extremism and violence. If some Muslims want to kill Westerners in the name of Islam, other Muslims must make clear that their concept of Islam is different.

The first problem, therefore, is to understand why a handful of people become extremist. Hamayun Ansari argues:

> Younger generations of British Muslims are less prepared to fit in to the space they are allotted. They want to shape that space for themselves . . . Perhaps alienated from their family backgrounds as well as from mainstream society, some of them are attracted to an alternative vision of 'belonging'; one that connects to a collective identity that does not depend on where you live or even who you are. Instead, they can claim a Muslim identity that is as authentic as any in the world. Rather than perceiving themselves as second-class citizens in the west, they become as good as – if not, in their own minds, better than – any other Muslim. This can greatly empower a person. It is this knowledge that they can make an impact on events that persuades a small proportion of radical Islamists to sacrifice their lives for their objectives . . . For

> this tiny minority, theological understanding based on selective literal readings of the Koran legitimises the killing of innocent people as global jihad . . . Rather than succumbing to a state of denial, Muslim communities need to expose and reject those who preach and practise intolerance in the name of religion. A more robust critique of what young Muslims are taught is required. Local initiatives – challenging, if necessary, the views of leaders, elders and religious scholars – that give young Muslims a firmer stake in their communities and wider society might help channel their anger and sense of injustice into more peaceful and democratic activities.[19]

Abul Rizvi, the Indian-born Muslim in charge of developing and implementing Australia's immigration policy, admits there is some concern about Muslims in the government. Prime Minister John Howard meets community leaders and has set up a Muslim reference group to address concerns. Rizvi emphasises the importance of economics: 'it's a problem if people feel they're not getting a fair go'. Although there has been some debate about the headscarf, 'we won't tell people what to wear'. But the government does recognise the potential for home-grown Islamic terrorism. 'We are combating this with a hard edge – intelligence and appropriate laws – as well as a soft one: listening to the Muslim community and respecting their views.'

The soft edge should include making alienated young people feel like they belong. As I argued in Chapter 11, European countries need to redefine their notion of nationhood, so that it no longer excludes people from ethnic and religious minorities. We cannot expect people to feel allegiance to their country if we treat them as outsiders – or if we deny them the right to citizenship. Declarations in Germany that it is a Christian country, or by leading Dutch politicians that Holland is at war with Islam, clearly do a lot of damage. As Gilles Kepel acknowledges, 'neither the blood spilled by Muslims from North Africa fighting in French uniforms during both world wars nor the sweat of migrant labourers, living under deplorable living conditions, who rebuilt France (and Europe) for a pittance after 1945, has made their children . . . full fellow citizens'. No wonder, then, that a radical leader of the Union of Islamic Organisations of France, a group associated with the Muslim Brotherhood, curses his new homeland: 'Oh sweet France! Are you astonished that so many of your children commune in a stinging *naal bou la France* [fuck France], and damn your Fathers?'[20] There is only one Muslim member of parliament in France, and there are just two in Germany and four in Britain.

Governments must also do more to combat racism and social exclusion. Poverty, unemployment and discrimination are not just harmful in themselves but are breeding grounds for resentment, anger and potentially violent rejection of host countries. As Olivier Roy argues in *Globalised Islam: The Search for a New Ummah*, 'A second and third generation of Muslim migrants may recast their feelings of being excluded by importing a psychological frontier to their spaces of social exclusion in suburbs or inner cities. Islam is cast as the "otherness" of Europe and thus may be cast as an alternative identity for youngsters in search of a reactive identity.'[21] Islam becomes a form of radical protest, much as revolutionary communism once was. Indeed, Roy claims that 'The Islamisation of the French suburbs is largely a myth: youngsters are fascinated by Western urban youth subculture (baseball caps, hamburgers, rap or hip hop, fashionable dress, consumerism) and they speak an old French slang (*verlan*); Islamisation works at a very parochial, often ghettoised level, around one mosque and one imam.'[22] The surest way to undercut extremist voices is to root out social exclusion.

But Muslims must also do more to isolate the extremists, so that they can more readily be dealt with by the police and security services. Hikmat Mahawat Khan, the moderate Dutch Muslim whom we met in the previous chapter, advocates five steps that Muslim leaders should take in the short term to show that they are changing and so they can demand change in return. First, he wants a ban on foreign imams. He says all imams should be trained locally instead, and be instructed in Dutch civic values. Most imams in Europe are trained and paid for by foreign governments: some 90 per cent of France's 900 or so official and self-proclaimed imams are foreign-trained and sponsored, for instance.[23] That may be fine if they are trained in secular Turkey, less so if they come from Saudi Arabia. Soheib Bencheikh, the grand mufti of Marseille, says, 'Muslims must become immunised against outside radicalisation.' Like many others, they believe it essential that imams should be trained in Europe, not in the Middle East, the Maghreb or Pakistan.[24] Providing the money to build and run the training colleges may be a problem in secular France, where the government is constitutionally forbidden to give state money to religions, but ways could be found to bend the rules: after all, Christian churches and their Jewish counterparts receive tax benefits. I'm not so sure that Khan or Bencheikh is right, though: it is akin to banning all foreign priests or teachers because some are found to be fascists. Surely only imams who incite hatred and violence are a problem? By all means, set up schools to train local imams, but an absolute ban on foreign ones seems unjustified.

In the wake of the Madrid bombings, Spain has set up a board for the Foundation of Pluralism and Peaceful Coexistence, based on accords signed between the government and Islamic, Jewish and Protestant representatives in 1992. 'It is very important that the Muslim community is not put under suspicion,' says Mercedes Rico Carabias, director-general of religious affairs and member of the board. Instead, she hopes to give Islam the same status as other religions. 'In Spain, the problem is plurality. We have now changed from being a totally Catholic country, and we have to respect that.'[25] The foundation aims to bring Islam into mainstream society by paying for social programmes and encouraging imams to learn Spanish. Groups such as the Moroccan Immigrant Workers' Association had complained that financing of mosques was in the hands of Saudi-backed imams who preached radical Islam. The government wants public financing of mosques, but this is against the law. 'We must find another way, either with private or international money, to finance mosques in the future,' she says.

The second of Khan's five ideas is that mosques and Islamic organisations need to be more open, more outward-looking and more involved in their communities. Most mosques do good work, organising programmes for women about healthcare or child welfare. But what is taught by their imams, both in the mosque and in the school (or madrassa) that is generally attached, is often unknown to outsiders. Islamic organisations also do good work, such as helping immigrants find housing and jobs – but they may also teach that integration into Western societies is a betrayal of their faith. Chris Huinder of Forum, the Dutch Institute for Multicultural Development, says that foreign-born Muslims must make room for Dutch-born ones in Muslim institutions. 'Only one mosque in four hundred is controlled by fundamentalists, but only ten are run by the second generation,' he says. 'The first generation is often illiterate, badly educated, speaks bad Dutch, is poorly informed about our culture.' The second generation, the Muslims born in the Netherlands, are the ones who interact with the Dutch state: they fill in the forms, take their parents to the doctor, and so on, and thus have control over them.

Third, Muslim leaders must publicly acknowledge women's equality. 'We need to empower, educate and liberate women and girls through schools,' explains Khan. 'We need to create a network of female role models. There is no basis in Islam for telling women to wear hijab or burqa [the veil]. Men should stop telling women what to do. We need to seek a middle ground: pray and fast, be a good Muslim, but also adopt liberal values.'

Fourth, there should be more emphasis on Muslim pastoral care, especially in hospitals and prisons. Fifth, Islamic schools must be open to all. 'They need to teach tolerance, liberal values and equality,' insists Khan. 'We need to get parents more involved, to influence them too, so that they understand what their kids are being taught at school.' At the same time, non-Muslims need to be educated about Islam. In Germany, for instance, where the constitution says all children have the right to religious education, Jewish children receive teaching overseen by the Central Council of Jews, but Muslims receive no Islamic education from the state – leaving the field wide open to the unsupervised madrassas.

In addition, Chris Huinder believes that the Dutch government needs to 'foster the process of mixing different communities in neighbourhoods and schools'. He says that 'Radicalisation takes place in communities that are overwhelmingly immigrant. So we build middle-class housing next to migrants, as has happened near where Mohammed Bouyeri [Theo van Gogh's murderer] lived.' We also need to 'maintain contact with the sixteen- to twenty-one-year-old boys in the radicalisation process. We ask them, "Why are you so frustrated? Why are you so anti-Western? Have you really read the Koran? Why don't you talk to another imam?" We try to build lines of dialogue and trust, promote a different way of looking at things. So far, we have reached one hundred and fifty to two hundred out of an estimated total of one to two thousand. But as long as they are attacked and stigmatised, some will be driven to radicalise.'

Along with this soft edge, a hard edge is needed too. Anti-terrorist forces need to be boosted, international cooperation against terrorism enhanced, new laws enacted to help them do their job more effectively, surveillance of extremist groups and efforts to infiltrate them stepped up.

American worries

The fear that Islamic immigrants are a terrorist fifth column is not limited to Europe. In the US, people like Pat Buchanan have since 9/11 shamelessly sought to exploit these fears to further their anti-immigration agenda. But there is no evidence of a terrorist threat from American Muslims. Buchanan's real objection is to non-Western immigrants in general, but he latches on to fears about what a handful of them might do in order to try to discredit immigration more generally.

Americans are also worried that terrorists could enter their country from Mexico concealed among illegal immigrants. 'Terrorism is our top priority,' says Doug Mosier of the El Paso Border Patrol, whom we met in Chapter 1 – even though he acknowledged that he wasn't aware of any terrorists having been caught. Of course, it is possible that terrorists will try to sneak across porous borders, but they are much more likely to enter through a legal port of entry. 'Even the best visa and border inspection systems cannot prevent such entries because the intelligence on which a state's frontline officials make decisions about whom to allow in will never be foolproof,' says Demetrios Papademetriou of the US-based Migration Policy Institute. But he points out that 'This is not an "immigration" issue; it is an issue of trying to make error-free decisions about the billions of international travellers who cross borders each year.'[26]

The valid fear that foreign terrorists may enter our countries to plan and launch their attacks from within is not a reason to restrict immigration in general; rather, it requires better intelligence and police work and closer international cooperation to identify potential suspects. Visa applicants may need more careful vetting. But although known criminals or terrorists should be denied entry, we cannot rightly exclude the overwhelming majority of other immigrants, who may have in common with these terrorists only their country of origin, their religion, the colour of their skin, or indeed merely their foreignness.

A bigger threat, argues Robert Leiken, the author of *Bearers of Jihad? Immigration and National Security after 9/11*, is of 'passport-carrying, visa-exempt mujahideen coming from the United States' western European allies. In smoky coffeehouses in Rotterdam and Copenhagen, makeshift prayer halls in Hamburg and Brussels, Islamic bookstalls in Birmingham and "Londonistan", and the prisons of Madrid, Milan, and Marseilles, immigrants or their descendants are volunteering for jihad against the West.'[27] A study of 373 mujahideen in western Europe and North America between 1993 and 2004 by the Nixon Center, where Leiken heads the immigration and national security programme, found more than twice as many French citizens as Saudis and more British citizens than Sudanese, Yemenites, Emiratis, Lebanese or Libyans. A quarter of the jihadists it listed were citizens of western European countries eligible to travel without visas to the US.

Leiken is no soft touch on terrorism – yet he does not think the US should scrap its visa-waiver programme with European countries. He advocates instead more targeted measures, such as insisting that airlines require US-bound travellers to submit passport information when buying tickets to give the new US National Targeting Center time to check potential entrants without delaying flight departures, as well as stationing officers at check-in counters to weed out suspects. In short, the threat of Islamic terrorism is a reason for increased vigilance, surveillance and scrutiny; it is not a reason for limiting immigration.

Integrate, not alienate

Aristide Zolberg, of the New School University in New York, notes that when the Catholic Irish began to arrive in America in the 1830s, their religious loyalties were assumed to be to a foreign potentate who deplored the liberalism and republican values for which the United States stood: 'Everything now said in Europe about the unsuitability of Muslims for life in a liberal democracy was then said about the Irish.'[28] Hostility to Islam is often just a cover for a more general xenophobia: Patrick Weil, the French Socialist Party's guru on immigration, points out that even long-established Catholic immigrants from France's overseas territories are discriminated against.

Most Muslims have no problem in reconciling their faith with secularism and other liberal values. As El-Farouk Khaki pointed out, and many other Muslims' lives demonstrate, there is nothing in Islam that prevents Muslims becoming more liberal over time, as indeed have Western societies, where fifty years ago homosexuality was a crime and women were second-class citizens. Only a minority of Muslims refuses to accept the rules of Western societies. Indeed, devout Muslims are often good, law-abiding citizens, their faith a source of strength and a discipline on bad behaviour. Since they abstain from alcohol, for instance, they don't go on drunken rampages on the weekend. Only a tiny minority sympathises with terrorism, and an even smaller number is actually involved with it. While European governments should certainly crack down on those who plot and support terrorism, it is wrong and counter-productive to alienate the vast majority of Muslims who have no truck with it. Europe should not have a problem with Islam; the real problem is with extremism of any kind.

16

Open Borders

Let them in

The ingenuity and diversity of arguments against immigration and immigrants are impressive. Like the proverbial hydra, no matter how many heads are cut off, the monster instantly grows new ones. It suggests that the arguments do not matter. It is the state of mind producing the arguments which is important – blaming foreigners . . . If immigrants did not exist, it would be necessary to invent them, to create scapegoats.

Nigel Harris, *Thinking the Unthinkable*[1]

The accusation is merely part of the standard litany of complaints against foreigners, made in every country for a certain time after a new batch of people arrives from elsewhere, unless they are manifestly wealthy: they are dirty, they are noisy, they steal, they will not work but just want to live on welfare, they fill up the hospitals, they crowd out the schools, they will not adopt our ways,

> they live in overcrowded houses, they run down the neighbourhood, the government does more for them than it does for us. If they are wealthy, a new set of stock complaints is made: they are buying everything up, they make prices rise, they look down on us, they think they're too good for us, they've got the ear of government. These are not observations of reality: simply expressions of unthinking resentment.
>
> Michael Dummett, *On Immigration and Refugees*[2]

> The static state that emerged from the nineteenth century wanted stable populations, with immigrants either here or elsewhere, as long as they were settled permanently. The state in the twenty-first century will have to get used to managing the rights and status of nationals who are outside its territory, and aliens who are in its territory – in other words, to dealing with populations on the move.
>
> Patrick Weil, 'Populations on the move'[3]

When Elias Inbram was just seven years old, he walked for forty days and forty nights, over mountains and across deserts, on his way to the promised land. It was an exodus of truly biblical proportions: hundreds and then thousands of people on the move, carrying only a few worldly possessions. They paused briefly to celebrate Passover. As they trekked on from Ethiopia to Sudan, Elias's father fell sick, they ran perilously short of water, robbers attacked them, some of their guides turned out to be thieves. Many people died.

The remainder finally reached Sudan. The promised land it was not. But they were stuck there for two years, while Israel tried to organise their airlift out. Elias's father, a musician, played the piano and accordion to scrape by, his meagre income supplemented by donations from the Jewish diaspora. Elias went to Arabic school. 'I had to study on Saturday, but I couldn't because it's the Jewish Sabbath,' he explains. 'But I didn't admit I was Jewish. I got punished a lot for missing class.' Even Sudan was a culture shock. In Khartoum, the capital, he saw a white person for the first time. 'I thought he was an Ethiopian with a skin problem,' he says. 'I grew up thinking Ethiopia was the only place on earth. Then I saw Sudan. I realised there were two countries. When I arrived in Jerusalem, I expected to see only Ethiopian Jews.' Eventually, they were flown out to Israel via Greece. 'Israel was full of white people,' he recalls. 'It didn't make sense.'

Elias spent four years with his family in an 'absorption centre', a state-run halfway house to help ease immigrants' transition into Israeli society. 'We were mostly Ethiopian there,' he remembers. 'An old man taught me English. We studied Hebrew and learned how to cope with Israeli life, basic things like what public services were available, how to budget, and so on.' Initially his friends were only Ethiopians, but then he moved into a regular class with other Israelis and made new friends. Gradually, he came to feel Israeli. 'In Ethiopia I felt Jewish,' he says. 'In Israel I felt Ethiopian. But now Israel is my homeland. I understand and like Ethiopian culture but I have absorbed another one. I'm not confused or looking for an identity. I'm Jewish, Israeli, with an Ethiopian influence.

'In my wave of immigration, we had no role models. We were told to be good, quiet, respectful and determined. But there was nobody to guide us. Parents couldn't speak Hebrew and assumed the school was looking after us; the school never communicated with parents and assumed parents were supervising us.' Many Ethiopians ended up losing their way. But times are changing. 'More and more Ethiopians are going to university. Our vision is to be part of Israeli society. We want to work alongside other Israelis, not live apart. If someone discriminates against me or is racist to me, it is their problem. I know what I want to do.'

Elias is now thirty-two. Like most Israeli men, he has served in the army; unlike most, he has completed several degrees, spent a year in Germany learning German and worked as a mentor to kids. When I met him, he was just completing yet another degree, in law, at Kiryat Ono University near Tel Aviv and had passed the very tough entry exam to work for the Israeli foreign ministry.

I have met many inspiring people during the research for this book: Lasso, Inmer and Uzma, to name but three. Their lives bear witness to the power of hope and determination to overcome adversity and the immense liberating potential of migration. But there is something particularly moving about the story of a young boy plucked from the Ethiopian wilderness and thrust into the bustle of modern Israeli society who has found serenity, fulfilment and a place for himself. He grew up without role models, but now he is a role model to others.

Israel too is a role model of successful immigration. Although this tiny country, scarred by the conflict with the Palestinians, has many problems, both Europe and America could learn a lot from it. Israel's door is wide open to immigrants, albeit of one particular group: anyone of Jewish origin is free to settle there; most Israelis were born abroad. And although they have in common their Jewishness, in practice the immigrants are a disparate lot: some religious, some not; some highly educated, others scarcely so; from countries as diverse as Germany, Morocco, Russia, Ethiopia, the United States and Iran. A recipe for disaster, many might think.

Not so. Israel's flexible economy not only absorbed a huge influx of immigrants in the 1990s relatively painlessly; it soon thrived on it. It blazed a trail in internet entrepreneurship and its new workforce fuelled a long economic boom. And it has successfully integrated the newcomers into Israeli society. Immigrants automatically and almost immediately become citizens, so they feel like they belong and have a stake in society. Israel therefore has every incentive to help them fit in. Newcomers are offered language lessons, housing, help finding a job and, initially at least, a hand up from the government. This welcome package helped Leonid Dinevich, whom we met in Chapter 4, make the transition from defending the Soviet Union to protecting birds. And while Israel helps immigrants integrate socially, it respects their individual freedom. They are not expected to conform culturally: Leonid watches TV in Russian, while Elias speaks Tigric and Amharic (along with Hebrew, English and German).

A world away

Yemisrach Benalfew – Yemi to her friends – was born in Ethiopia around the same time as Elias. In another life, their paths might have crossed. Instead, they have ended up thousands of miles apart. Yemi was a journalist for an English-language newspaper in Addis Ababa, the Ethiopian capital, but when she was twenty-five she won a scholarship to Antwerp University in Belgium. From there she secured a six-month internship at the United Nations, which brought her to New York City. She fell in love with the city and applied for asylum, on the grounds that as a journalist her life would be at risk if she returned home.

Yemi has had a tough time during her five years in the Big Apple. She has had a string of badly paid jobs and is still waiting for her green card granting her permanent residency in the US. In an effort to get back into journalism, she interned for two days a week at a news agency, while spending the other five working in a furniture store. She took out a $60,000 loan to do a masters degree in international relations at Columbia University, and now she has graduated, she is looking for a job in humanitarian affairs or political risk analysis.

When I ask her what immigrants bring to America, she replies: 'They bring different perspectives. We have to struggle. We have no one to depend on. It's a very tough life. If you survive, you are a very strong person. In this country, everything is just given. People don't have to worry if they will be able to eat dinner.' The diversity and dynamism that immigrants bring are continually enriching and rejuvenating America, keeping complacency at bay and stimulating new and better ways of doing things.

America has brought Yemi a lot too: 'I love New York City because it gives you the freedom to be you. I can do the things I want in my own time. I like big cities, the diversity, people from different countries. Compared to other countries, America treats refugees well: you aren't detained, you are among society, it's easier to integrate and adapt.' Freedom, opportunity, a richer life in the broadest sense: migration has an exceptional potential to change people's lives for the better.

So does Yemi now feel Ethiopian or American? 'I don't see myself as Ethiopian or just as an American. I'm stranded between the two. Ethiopians say, "You don't sound Ethiopian. You are so Americanised"; Americans say, "You are not from here." I want to belong, but I don't want to be defined. I just want to be me.' And why not? While immigrants often wrestle with this conundrum more acutely than most, people everywhere are torn between the desire to be themselves and the urge to fit in. They have multiple, overlapping identities that vary according to circumstances. So it is neither feasible nor desirable to squeeze people's individuality into the straitjacket of a single national identity: if we are one, we are also many. The way forward lies with a Canadian style of national identity that embraces our diversity rather than seeking to deny it.

People on the move

The world has changed dramatically over the past fifty years. Technology has brought distant people closer, while individualism has set neighbouring people apart. Together, they have undermined the tyranny of geography which tied people to a place and loosened the shackles of nationalism which dictated that people in one place should all be alike. Rejoice: people can increasingly break free from the stifling confines of cloistered uniformity. Yet even as we roam our newly open world more freely than before, we cling tenaciously to some boundaries. Mental boundaries – Them and Us, poor and rich, black and white – as well as physical ones: barbed-wire fencing, fortified walls, gunships on patrol. The world is Our oyster, but it is gritty for Them.

Our new mobility, and that of products, money and information, jars with our efforts to hold people in poor countries in place. We sun ourselves on their beaches, peddle them aspirations to a better life through a soft drink or a baseball cap, broadcast alluring images of our munificent Eldorado – and then expect them to stay put. 'It's impossible to enter Europe legally,' says Eduard Nazarski of the Dutch Refugee Council. 'The Iron Curtain to keep people in has been replaced by an electronic curtain to keep people out.' America offers a mere 5,000 visas a year to low-skilled foreigners with no relatives in the country. No wonder they break in. 'I thought Europe was the promised land,' says Lasso, who fled the civil war in Côte d'Ivoire and almost died trying to reach Spain. And for many, it is. 'Back in Ukraine, it was next to impossible to be gay,' recalls Stephan. 'Then I came to London and all of a sudden I felt free.' And America too has an irresistible pull. 'If I had an opportunity, I would want to be an American,' says Inmer, who tore himself away from his family in Honduras and risked death to reach the US border.

Our efforts to keep poor people out while the rich and the educated circulate freely are a form of global apartheid. And like apartheid, they look increasingly unsustainable. The sheer weight of numbers is against us; and if our conscience is not sufficient to persuade us to change course, then our self-interest surely ought to. Already, over a million immigrants manage to enter Europe and North America illegally each year by hook or by crook. To stem the flow would require not only a new degree of ruthlessness – shooting people who try to cross our borders, for instance, as East Germany used to do – which even hard-hearted voters might have trouble stomaching, and which would violate our domestic and international commitments to human rights. It would also entail a costly isolationism – a clampdown on the vast majority of people who cross borders briefly for tourism or business, to visit friends or to study – as well as rigorous internal checks on people's right to be there. In effect, the land of the free would have to become a police state. By trying to keep out foreigners, we would lose ourselves. And even then, some migrants would get through: documents can be forged, people smuggled, officials bribed. So long as there is work to be done in rich countries for wages many times higher than in poor ones, they will come.

So why not make a virtue of it? After all, we need them. We need them to do the jobs we won't do. We need them to do the jobs we can't do. We need them to square our lofty aspirations to opportunity for all with the dismal reality of drudgery for some. We need them to care for the old and to look after the young, to allow mothers back to work and free up time in our busy lives. We need them even more because every talented foreigner we recruit adds to the demand for people willing to do menial work. We need them because they are more willing to move within a country to where the jobs are, and more willing to change jobs as conditions in the economy change. Indeed, because low-skilled workers are in relatively short supply in rich countries, while highly skilled workers in general are not, we potentially have most to gain from letting in people like Inmer.[4] Perhaps most importantly, in a world where different perspectives and new ideas are at a premium, immigrants stimulate innovation and economic growth. Just look at flourishing cosmopolitan cities like London and New York. They are the future.

Allowing people to come and work in rich countries legally would have other big benefits too. It would save lives: more migrants have died trying to cross the US–Mexico border since 1995 than were killed in the 9/11 attacks. It would put the people smugglers out of business. It would reduce tax evasion, labour-law dodges and other manifestations of the grey and black economies. It would shrink the shadow world where illegal immigrants live in fear and isolation; illegal immigrants who are already in rich countries should be allowed to regularise their situation. It would shore up respect for law and order that misguided prohibition corrodes. It would bolster faith in government and improve perceptions of immigrants' character. It would remove the perverse incentive for immigrants to settle permanently when many would rather work in a rich country for a while and then go home, much like people commute back and forth between the suburbs and the city. And it would reduce the incentive for people who want to work to masquerade as asylum seekers. So governments could relax the draconian measures they have imposed to try to deter such subterfuge, which are not only ineffective (because it is often impossible to distinguish between economic and political migrants) but cause immense suffering to refugees, besmirching our commitment made in the aftermath of the Second World War to help those fleeing terror.

Make it free and legal

If you caught sight of Hanna in the streets of London, you might think she was Swedish. With her blonde hair, good looks and fashionable clothes, she certainly doesn't look out of place. But Hanna is Polish – and she was until recently working in Britain illegally. 'My husband first came to London in 2001,' she recalls.

> He had lost his job in Poland and his sister, who had moved to London two years earlier, invited him to stay. She had come on a student visa and then married a gay British friend in order to be able to stay and work legally. He came on a tourist visa, but started working doing up houses. It was easy for him to find work: other Poles helped him out and there is a huge demand for builders and decorators in London. Then I came and joined him and started working as a cleaner. It was easy for me to find work too, and even though I was working illegally, I was making six pounds an hour, which is much more than I could make in Poland.

Now Hanna's situation has changed. In May 2004, Poland and seven other relatively poor ex-communist countries in central and eastern Europe joined the European Union. One of the fundamental principles of the EU is that the citizens of one country are entitled to live and work freely in any other, a freedom from which British builders in Frankfurt, Portuguese waiters in London and German pensioners on the Costa del Sol have all amply benefited. Even so, most existing EU member states chose to impose temporary restrictions on east European workers. But Britain, Ireland and Sweden opened their borders to them (although Britain required them to register with the Home Office and denied them the right to claim welfare benefits during their first two years in the country). And in May 2006, Finland, Greece, Spain and Portugal followed suit.

'I have now registered to work here,' Hanna declares proudly. 'I have my own national insurance number and my own company. I declare all my income and pay taxes like everyone else. Before 2004, I couldn't because I didn't have the right to work here. It's not like I didn't want to; I just couldn't. Now I do everything by the book.'

Opponents of immigration claim that allowing in foreign

workers freely would cause all manner of ills: they would steal our jobs, place an unsustainable burden on the welfare state, overrun our country. In short, they see immigrants as a drain on our resources and a threat to our way of life. I have argued that these fears are largely unfounded, but you don't have to take my word for it. By allowing anyone in the eight relatively poor new members of the EU to come and work freely, Britain, Ireland and Sweden are putting these claims to the test. All seventy-five million people in Poland, Hungary, the Czech Republic, Slovakia, Slovenia, Estonia, Latvia and Lithuania are now free to move to Britain and work. Since wages in Poland are typically only a fifth of those in Britain, Poles have a big incentive to come and work here. If opponents of immigration are right, Britain should now be deluged with East Europeans and unemployment should be soaring.

But it isn't. In fact, only 427,000 East Europeans have so far applied to work in Britain (many of whom were already in the country illegally) – and most stay only briefly: net migration from eastern Europe was only 48,000 in 2004.[5] Unemployment remains at thirty-year lows, tax receipts are up and jobs that British people no longer want to do are being filled. The newcomers are working in factories and on farms, in kitchens, warehouses and packing plants, as cleaners and as waiters. John Monks, the British head of the European Trade Union Confederation, says fears that cheap workers from the east would drive out local workers had so far proved unfounded. 'I've not been aware of any cases where Brits have been forced to make way for cheap Czechs and Poles,' he says. 'There's a genuinely welcoming atmosphere.' In contrast, France issued only 1,600 work permits to Poles in the eleven months after EU enlargement; and, during the French referendum campaign on the EU constitution in spring 2005, the 'Polish plumber' became a demonised figure, a symbol of how 'open Europe' posed a threat to French jobs.[6]

Closed borders don't create jobs: France's unemployment rate is double Britain's. Open borders work: Hanna is the proof of that. And they could work for the US too. As Miriam Mejia of the Alianza Dominicana says, 'If the US opened the door, many people would come. But not everybody. Not everyone can afford the flight and anyway people enjoy living in the Dominican Republic. Many people would move back and forth. After they legalised alcohol again, not everybody had a drink or became a drunk. It's the same with legalising migration: not everyone would come or stay for good.'

Helping the poor

'Make Poverty History' is the rallying cry for a new generation of campaigners for global justice, led by the now-familiar faces of Bob Geldof and Bono. Their key demands include fairer trade, debt relief, more and better aid, and action against AIDS and corruption. Yet one thing that is not on their list could make a bigger dent in global poverty than all of those combined: freer international migration. Critics of globalisation argue that 'another world is possible'. Indeed it is – but do campaign groups have the courage of their convictions? As Dani Rodrik points out, if we were trying to create an alternative globalisation designed to bring maximum benefit to poor countries, 'relaxing restrictions on the international movement of workers . . . would produce the largest possible gains for the world economy, and for poor countries in particular. Nothing else comes close to the magnitude of economic benefits that this would generate.'[7] It is time for those who want to make poverty history to confront the entrenched prejudices of Western voters – and doubtless many of their supporters – and lobby the US and EU governments to 'Let Them In'. It is a cause for our time.

Rodrik calculates that a temporary-work-visa scheme that would boost rich countries' labour forces by a mere 3 per cent by allowing workers from poor countries, skilled and unskilled, to work in rich countries for three to five years, and then replaced by a new wave of inflows upon returning home, would 'easily yield $200 billion annually' for the citizens of poor countries – two and a half times more than rich governments' current paltry overseas aid. 'The positive spillovers that the returnees would generate for their home countries – the experience, entrepreneurship, investment, and work ethic they would bring back with them and put to work – would add considerably to these gains,' he says. 'What is equally important, the economic benefits would accrue directly to workers from developing nations.' And the biggest gains would go to the poorest countries: while the typical immigrant would see her living standards treble, those from sub-Saharan Africa could see them increase more than sevenfold, because their wages in Africa are so much lower.[8] Likewise, the money that migrants from Africa send home gives the biggest boost to the desperately poor people there.

Think about it: letting people come to work in rich countries would help children in poor countries stay in school. It would help pay for life-saving medicines for the old and the sick. It would help people escape poverty, start their own businesses, build a better future. 'I think the United States should give an opportunity to those who need it,' says Inmer. 'Because life is hard. The US is one of the most developed countries. I know that some people come with bad intentions but I don't have any vices. The US should give us permits to come and work from Honduras. We come to work hard, not to destroy.' Inmer just wants to earn a living so his kids can study and don't have to suffer like him.

'Let Them In' is a cry that should unite the free-market right, who oppose the dead hand of government controls on domestic labour markets, and the internationalist left, who believe that solidarity for our fellow-human beings should not stop at the border. And if immigration is mostly temporary, nationalists, social conservatives and the communitarian left ought to have fewer objections to it: the foreigners will be coming to work for a while, not to settle permanently.

Towards flexibility and fairness

How do we get from here to there? There are a variety of options. We could open our borders at the stroke of a pen, as Britain, Ireland and Sweden have done for East Europeans. We could negotiate bilateral agreements, as the Philippines has done with several rich countries. We could set up an international organisation through which governments could negotiate broader agreements and try to resolve issues that arise. We could open our markets to foreign service-providers at the WTO, allowing national or international recruitment companies to match cleaners from Kenya, say, with hospitals in Britain, or chambermaids from Guatemala with hotels in Miami.

It would be best if our borders were completely open. But if that is deemed impossible for now, let them at least be more open. And if even that is not acceptable, let them at least be better regulated. Immigration policy nowadays is 'piecemeal, incoherent and non-transparent', as Stephen Castles of Oxford University rightly points out.[9] Rich-country governments need to be honest about their policies, clear about their aims and work more closely with poor-country governments to help achieve them. In particular, they should stop trying to micromanage the movement of people across borders in a way reminiscent of the Soviet Union's failed attempts to match workers to jobs domestically. Governments are simply incapable of knowing which workers are needed when and where. They should move instead to a policy that does not discriminate arbitrarily between different types of worker. And if they are to regulate inflows of workers, they should do so through taxes rather than quotas.

They could, for instance, charge a set fee for prospective migrants, pitched higher or lower according to the desired restrictiveness of the policy. The fee could be raised or lowered at will. Alternatively, the government could impose an extra payroll tax on migrant workers. Such a scheme would have several advantages: it would be transparent; it would be flexible; it would raise revenue that could be spent, for instance, on retraining domestic workers, highlighting the contribution to the economy that immigrants make. In the case of skilled workers, the revenue could be used to compensate developing countries for their investment in training them. The tax would also give companies an incentive to hire and/or train domestic workers. Even if the tax were set relatively high, it would undercut people smugglers. And over time, if natives became more relaxed about immigration, the tax could be gradually lowered – or raised again, if immigration provoked unexpected problems.

Making the best of it

Inevitably, if we open our borders, some people will end up settling – and there is no denying that this can cause friction. When different people are thrown together, our tribal instincts tell us to view the foreigners with suspicion. The unknown is potentially a threat. But fears about being swamped are unjustified: most people do not want to leave their homes temporarily, let alone for ever. Most of the temporary workers who ended up staying in Europe in the 1970s did so because Europe shut its borders, forcing them to remain if they wanted the option to continue working there. All 75 million East Europeans in the EU could potentially come and live in Britain now, yet fewer than one in 175 of them have – and most have already returned home.

In any case, rich countries already are countries of immigration. We must tackle the social and cultural issues that it throws up regardless of whether we let in more newcomers. But once we have dealt with them, we should have far less difficulty admitting more. We are not destined to repeat the mistakes of the past.

A more open immigration policy, and one that is seen to be transparent, fair and effective, would do wonders for defusing tensions. Israel's example shows that vigorous efforts to integrate newcomers into society are compatible with a respect for their cultural distinctness. Canada's example shows that diversity can be a source of strength, not of weakness; a reason to belong, not an excuse to exclude. America's long tradition of immigration testifies to the power of newcomers to forge a dynamic economy and society.

Our Open World is riven between those who are free to move and those who are still tied to one place. This is morally wrong, economically stupid and politically unsustainable. Opening our borders offers huge opportunities for all. Our rallying cry for a better world must be 'Let Them In'.

Notes

Introduction: Migration Isn't Just for the Birds

1 J. K. Galbraith, *The Nature of Mass Poverty*, Harvard University Press, 1979

2 'The victim: Cashier at bank had all to live for', *Guardian*, 14 July 2005

3 Pew Hispanic Center, *Size and Characteristics of the Unauthorized Migrant Population in the US*, March 2006

4 The estimated numbers of illegal immigrants are from 'Decapitating the snakeheads', *The Economist*, 6 October 2005

5 The figures for legal immigration are from OECD, *International Migration Outlook*, 2006, Tables A.1.1 and A.1.2, pages 233 and 234

6 *Ibid.*

7 Interview with Abul Rizvi

8 International Organization for Migration, *World Migration Report*, 2005, Tables 23.3 and 23.6, updated with OECD, *International Migration Outlook*, 2006, Table A.1.4, page 262

9 Peter Brimelow, *Alien Nation: Common Sense about America's Immigration Disaster*, HarperPerennial, 1996

10 *Ibid.*, page xvii

11 *Ibid.*, page xix

12 Patrick J. Buchanan, *The Death of the West: How Dying Populations and Immigrant Invasions Imperil Our Country and Civilization*, Thomas Dunne, 2002, page 2

13 *Ibid.*, page 3

14 Samuel P. Huntington, *Who Are We? America's Great Debate*, The Free Press, 2005, page xvii

15 See www.minutemanproject.com

16 'Come hither', *The Economist*, 1 December 2005

17 Richard B. Freeman and Remco H. Oostendorp, *Wages around the World: Pay across Occupations and Countries*, Working Paper 8058, National Bureau of Economic Research, 2000
18 http://www.rand.org/education/projects/crip.html
19 Steven Glover *et al.*, *Migration: An Economic and Social Analysis*, RDS Occasional Paper 67, 2001
20 World Bank, *Global Economic Prospects*, 2006, Table 2.3, page 34
21 There are around 1 billion people in rich countries, so overseas aid of $79 billion a year is equivalent to $79 a year per person, or around $1.60 a week.
22 The Global Commission on International Migration, *Migration in an Interconnected World: New Directions for Action*, 2005, page 85
23 World Bank, *Global Economic Prospects*, 2006, Table 4.2, page 88
24 Personal calculation, assuming Mexican GDP of $676 billion in 2004, according to the United Nations Statistics Division

1 War on Our Borders

1 Nigel Harris, *Thinking the Unthinkable: The Immigration Myth Exposed*, I. B. Tauris, 2002, page 3
2 Peter Brimelow, *Alien Nation: Common Sense about America's Immigration Disaster*, HarperPerennial, 1996, page 241
3 Médecins Sans Frontières, *Violence and immigration: Report on illegal sub-Saharan immigrants (ISSs) in Morocco*, http://www.msf.org/source/countries/africa/morocco/2005/morocco_2005.pdf
4 'Spain heightens fence at African enclave', *Guardian*, 22 September 2005
5 'Immigrant death toll surges', *Guardian*, 6 January 2005
6 No border network, http://www.noborder.org/dead.php
7 'The last frontier', *The Economist*, 22 June 2000
8 Nigel Harris, *Thinking the Unthinkable: The Immigration Myth Exposed*, I. B. Tauris, 2002, page xvi
9 http://www.united.non-profit.nl/pdfs/DEATHLIST_7182.pdf Deaths are listed if they can be put down to 'Fortress Europe' (border militarisation, asylum laws, accommodation, detention policy, deportations, carrier sanctions, etc.)
10 'Decapitating the snakeheads', *The Economist*, 6 October 2005

11 Human Rights Advocates, *Violations of Migrants Rights at the Border*, September 2002
12 'Deaths of immigrants uncover makeshift world of smuggling', *New York Times*, 29 June 2003
13 http://www.wsws.org/articles/2001/may2001/ariz-m28.shtml
14 Wayne Cornelius, 'Evaluating enhanced US border enforcement', 1 May 2004, Migration Information Source: http://www.migrationinformation.org/Feature/display.cfm?ID=223
15 'Refugee boat survivors traumatized; hundreds die', Associated Press, 23 October 2001, http://sievx.com/articles/disaster/20011023_Oakridger.html
16 Pew Hispanic Center, *Size and characteristics of the unauthorized migrant population in the US*, March 2006, http://pewhispanic.org/reports/report.php?ReportID=61
17 http://www.aflcio.org/issues/civilrights/immigration/ns09062001.cfm
18 'By a back door to the US: A migrant's grim sea voyage', *New York Times*, 13 June 2004
19 'Decapitating the snakeheads', *The Economist*, 6 October 2005
20 Wayne A. Cornelius, *Controlling 'Unwanted' Immigration: Lessons from the United States, 1993–2004*, The Center for Comparative Immigration Studies, Working Paper 92, December 2004
21 'Come hither', *The Economist*, 1 December 2005
22 *Ibid.*
23 Peter Brimelow, *Alien Nation: Common Sense about America's Immigration Disaster*, HarperPerennial, 1996, page 259
24 *Ibid.*, page 236
25 Wayne A. Cornelius, *Controlling 'Unwanted' Immigration: Lessons from the United States, 1993–2004*, The Center for Comparative Immigration Studies, Working Paper 92, December 2004
26 'From sea to shining sea', *The Economist*, 14 January 2006

2 Border Crossing

1 Francis A. Walker, 'Restriction of immigration', *Atlantic Monthly*, June 1896
2 See www.ellisisland.com for more information
3 David Held *et al.*, *Global Transformations*, Polity, 1999, page 322
4 Dhananjayan Sriskandarajah and Francesca Hopwood, 'United

Kingdom: Rising numbers, rising anxieties', May 2005: http://www.migrationinformation.org/Profiles/display.cfm?ID=306

5 Eric Hobsbawm, *The Age of Empire*, Abacus, 1987, Table 3, page 344

6 Jeffrey G. Williamson, *The Political Economy of World Mass Migration: Comparing Two Global Centuries*, AEI, 2005, page 1

7 Eric Hobsbawm, *Age of Extremes: The Short Twentieth Century 1914–1991*, Abacus, 1994

8 Stephen Castles and Mark J. Miller, *The Age of Migration: International Population Movements in the Modern World*, third edition, Palgrave Macmillan, 2003, page 64

9 International Organization for Migration, *World Migration Report*, 2005, Table 23.3

10 G. Jasso and M. Rosenzweig, 'Labor immigration, family reunification, and immigration policy: The US experience', paper presented at the Conference on Migration and International Cooperation, 1993, quoted by Peter Stalker, *The No-Nonsense Guide to International Migration*, New Internationalist/Verso, 2001, page 45

11 International Organization for Migration, *World Migration Report*, 2005, Table 23.1

12 The total number of international migrants rose from 81.5 million in 1970 to 99.8 million in 1980, 154 million in 1990 and 174.9 million in 2000. Excluding the former Soviet Union, the total rose from 78.4 million in 1970 to 96.5 million in 1980, 123.7 million in 1990 and 145.4 million in 2000: *ibid.*

13 Excluding the Soviet Union, the total number of international migrants rose by 18.1 million in the 1970s, of whom 9.3 million went to rich countries, and 21.7 million in the 1990s, of whom 21.5 million went to rich countries: *ibid.*

14 The total number of international migrants in rich countries rose from 35.2 million in 1970 to 44.5 million in 1980, 59.3 million in 1990 and 80.8 million in 2000: *ibid.*

15 In 1970–5, net migration accounted for 1 per 1000 and the natural increase for 6.8 per 1000 of the 7.8 per 1000 population growth rate in developed countries. In 1995–2000, net migration accounted for 2.2 and the natural increase for 1.2 of the 3.4 per 1000 population growth rate: *ibid.*, Table 23.4

16 Three-fifths of the world's migrants live in thirteen countries: the United States 35 million (20 per cent), Russia 13.3 million (7.6 per

cent), Germany 7.3 million (4.2 per cent), Ukraine 6.9 million (4 per cent), France 6.3 million (3.6 per cent), India 6.3 million (3.6 per cent), Canada 5.8 million (3.3 per cent), Saudi Arabia 5.3 million (3 per cent), Australia 4.7 million (2 per cent), Pakistan 4.2 million (2.4 per cent), Great Britain 4 million (2.3 per cent), Kazakhstan 3 million (1.7 per cent), Hong Kong 2.7 million (1.5 per cent): *ibid.*, Table 23.3

17 *Ibid.*, page 382; updated with OECD, *Trends in International Migration 2004*, 2005, Table II.1

18 *Ibid.*, Overview, page 19, updated with OECD, *International Migration Outlook*, 2006, Table A.1.4

19 *Ibid.*, Table B.1.4

20 International Organisation for Migration, *World Migration Report*, 2005, Table 23.6. The US received 993,000 immigrants a year on average in 2000–2, of whom 81 per cent were from developing countries, 11 per cent from countries in transition, and 8 per cent from developed countries; 30 per cent were from Asia and 42 per cent from Latin America and the Caribbean.

21 *Ibid.* Canada received 236,000 immigrants a year on average in 2000–2, of whom 78 per cent were from developing countries, 12 per cent from countries in transition, and 10 per cent from developed countries; 54 per cent were from Asia and 8 per cent from Latin America and the Caribbean.

22 OECD, *Trends in International Migration 2004*, 2005, Table B.1.4

23 International Organization for Migration, *World Migration Report*, 2005, Table 23.6. Australia received 92,000 immigrants a year on average in 2000–2, of whom 53 per cent were from developing countries, 6 per cent from countries in transition, and 41 per cent from developed countries; 40 per cent were from Asia.

24 Migration Information Source, http://www.migrationinformation.org/Profiles/display.cfm?ID=86

25 Europe is European Economic Area plus Switzerland: OECD, *Trends in International Migration 2004*, 2005, Overview, page 19

26 OECD, *International Migration Outlook*, 2006, Table A.1.4, page 262, and Chart 1.4, page 45. Figure for Spain is derived from *Boletín Estadísitico de Extranjería e Inmigración*, Número 7, January 2006. The figure for France is for 1999.

27 OECD, *Trends in International Migration 2004*, 2005, Figure I.7

28 OECD, *International Migration Outlook*, 2006, Table A.1.1

29 *Ibid.*, Table A.1.2

30 OECD, *Trends in International Migration 2004*, 2005, Figure I.2
31 OECD, *International Migration Outlook*, 2006, Table A.1.1
32 International Organization for Migration, *World Migration Report*, Table 23.5
33 *Ibid.*, Table 23.7
34 Michael Dummett, *On Immigration and Refugees*, Routledge, 2001, page 45
35 OECD, *International Migration Outlook*, 2006, Table A.1.3
36 *Ibid.*, Chart 1.2, page 35

3 Why We Need the Huddled Masses

1 Alan Winters, Terrie Walmsley, Zhen Kun Wang and Roman Grynberg, *Negotiating the Liberalisation of the Temporary Movement of Natural Persons*, University of Sussex, DP 87, October 2002
2 C. Hamilton and J. Whalley, 'Efficiency and distributional implications of global restrictions on labour mobility: Calculations and policy implications', *Journal of Development Economics*, 14(1–2), 1984: 61–75
3 Jonathon W. Moses and Bjørn Letnes, 'The economic costs to international labor restrictions: Revisiting the empirical discussion', *World Development*, 32(10), 2004: 1610
4 George Borjas, *Heaven's Door: Immigration Policy and the American Economy*, Princeton University Press, 1999, page 181
5 Peter Stalker, *The No-Nonsense Guide to International Migration*, New Internationalist/Verso, 2001, page 65
6 George Borjas, *Heaven's Door: Immigration Policy and the American Economy*, Princeton University Press, 1999, page 114
7 US Census Bureau, Current Population Survey, 2004. Calculations from Foreign-Born Population of the United States, Table 1.1: 52.1 per cent of non-US citizens are aged 20–39, while 26 per cent of natives are: http://www.census.gov/population/socdemo/foreign/ppl-176/tab01-1.pdf. Table 2.1: 57.6 per cent of foreign-born people who arrived in the USA since 2002 are aged 20–39: http://www.census.gov/population/socdemo/foreign/ppl-176/tab02-1.pdf. The UK figures are from Home Office, 'Accession Monitoring Report May 2004–June 2006', 2006
8 *Sunday Times* Rich List 2005

9 London First, 'A passion for success', *Business London*, 1 March 2004: http://www.london-first.co.uk/feature_articles/fa_2349.pdf

10 George Borjas, *Heaven's Door: Immigration Policy and the American Economy*, Princeton University Press, 1999. Estimated from Table 2.1, page 21

11 US Census Bureau, Current Population Survey, 2004. Calculations from Educational Attainment in the United States, Table 5: http://www.census.gov/population/socdemo/education/cps2004/tab05-01.pdf

12 UK National Statistics, *Social Trends*, 35:2005 edition, Table 3.16

13 OECD, *Education at a Glance 2005*, Table A1.3a

14 US Census Bureau, Occupations: 2000, Table 1: Selected Occupational Groups and Subgroups by Sex for the United States: http://www.census.gov/prod/2003pubs/ c2kbr-25.pdf

15 Nigel Harris, *Thinking the Unthinkable*, I. B. Tauris, 2002, page 78

16 R. Wilson, K. Homenidou and A. Dickerson, *Working Futures: New Projections of Occupational Employment by Sector and Region, 2002–2012*, Volume 1, national report, Institute for Employment Research (University of Warwick), January 2004, Table 4.1: http://www.ssda.org.uk/ssda/pdf/wf-national.pdf

17 *Ibid.*, Table 4.2

18 RSA Migration Commission, *Migration: A Welcome Opportunity: A New Way Forward*, 2005

19 'Hey, big-spender', *The Economist*, 1 December 2005

20 Atsushi Kondo, 'Development of immigration policy in Japan', *Asia and Pacific Migration Journal*, 11(4), 2002: 415–36

21 'Insular Japan needs, but resists, immigration', *New York Times*, 24 July 2003

22 Nigel Harris, *Thinking the Unthinkable*, I. B. Tauris, 2002, page 62

4 The Global Talent Contest

1 'Strong management turns Chalmers around', *Ontario Business Report*, March 2001

2 The quotes about Chalmers are from an interview he gave in 2001, not the interview he gave me in October 2005

3 OECD, *International Migration Outlook*, 2006, Chart I.2, page 35

4 OECD, *Trends in International Migration 2004*, 2005, Table III.1,

page 148; Table I.1, page 32

5 Home Office, *Controlling Our Borders: Making Migration Work for Britain, Five Year Strategy for Asylum and Immigration. 2005*: http://www.archive2.official-documents.co.uk/document/cm64/6472/6472.pdf

6 OECD, *Trends in International Migration 2004*, Table III.32, page 284

7 OECD, *Education at a Glance 2005* – Tables 2005, Table C3.7a

8 OECD, *Trends in International Migration 2004*, Table I.4, page 37

9 9,923,000

10 Frédéric Docquier and Abdeslam Marfouk, 'International migration by education attainment, 1990–2000', in Çaglar Özden and Maurice Schiff, eds, *International Migration, Remittances, and the Brain Drain*, World Bank and Palgrave Macmillan, 2006, Tables 5.6.A and 5.6.B

11 G. Chellaraj, K. E. Maskus and A. Mattoo, *The Contribution of Skilled Immigration and International Graduate Students to US Innovation*, World Bank manuscript, 2005

12 AnnaLee Saxenian, 'Brain circulation: How high-skill immigration makes everyone better off', *The Brookings Review*, 20(1), Winter 2002: 28–31

13 OECD, *A New Economy? The Changing Role of Innovation and Information Technology in Growth*, 2000

14 Econtech, *The economic impact of 2000/01 migration program changes, 12 February 2001*: http://www.immi.gov.au/research/publications/econimpact_2000_01.pdf

15 'Costello signals switch to unskilled immigrants', *Sydney Morning Herald*, 17 October 2005

16 RSA Migration Commission, *Migration: A Welcome Opportunity*, 2005, Web Annex A: 4 sectoral reports – A scarcity of labour?

5 Cosmopolitan and Rich

1 Joshua Reynolds, *Discourses on Art no.* 6, 10 December 1774

2 G. Pascal Zachary, *The Diversity Advantage: Multicultural Identity in the New World Economy*, Westview, 2003, page 68

3 Richard Florida, *The Rise of the Creative Class: And How It's Transforming Work, Leisure and Everyday Life*, Basic Books, New York, 2002

4 Richard Florida and Gary Gates, *Technology and Tolerance: The Importance of Diversity to High-Technology Growth*, Brookings Institution, Survey Series, June 2001
5 Peter Hall, *Cities in Civilization*, Weidenfeld & Nicholson, London, 1998
6 Census data April 2001: www.statistics.gov.uk
7 Edward L. Glaeser, *Urban Colossus: Why is New York America's Largest City?*, NBER Working Paper 11398, June 2005
8 George Borjas, *Heaven's Door: Immigration Policy and the American Economy*, Princeton University Press, 1999, page 98
9 John Stuart Mill, *Principles of Political Economy*, 1848, pp 581–2
10 Gianmarco Ottaviano and Giovanni Peri, 'The economic value of cultural diversity: Evidence from US cities', *Journal of Economic Geography*, 2005
11 Gianmarco Ottaviano and Giovanni Peri, 'Cities and cultures', *Journal of Urban Economics*, 2005
12 Edward Lazear, *Diversity and Immigration*, NBER Working Paper 6535, April 1998
13 Diane Coyle, *The Economic Case for Immigration*, Institute of Economic Affairs, London 2005
14 Quotes from: http://www.lanl.gov/orgs/dvo/sci_diversity/norm_bio.shtml
15 J. E. McGrath, *Groups: Interaction and Performance*, Prentice-Hall, 1984; P. L. McLeod and S. A. Lobel, 'Ethnic diversity and creativity in small groups', *Small Group Research*, 27(2), 1996: 248–64; W. E. Watson, K. Kumar and L. K. Michaelsen, 'Cultural diversity's impact on interaction process and performance: Comparing homogeneous and diverse task groups', *Academy of Management Journal*, 36(3), 1993: 590–602; S. E. Jackson, 'Team composition in organizational settings: Issues in managing an increasingly diverse work force', in S. Worchel, W. Wood and J. Simpson, eds, *Group Process and Productivity*, Sage, 1991, pages 138–71
16 Lu Hong and Scott E. Page, *Problem Solving by Heterogeneous Agents*, October 1998 and *Diversity and Optimality*, Santa Fe Institute, Working Paper 98-08-077
17 Quoted in *Fortune*, 19 July 1999
18 Edward Lazear, *Globalization and the Market for Teammates*, NBER Working Paper 6579, May 1998
19 'Arsène Wenger, a football coach for Europe', *The Economist*, 25

February 1999

20 Andrea Prat, *Should a Team Be Homogeneous?*, London School of Economics, 2000: http://econ.lse.ac.uk/staff/prat/papers/sharedeer2.pdf

21 Alberto Alesina and Eliana La Ferrara, *Ethnic Diversity and Economic Performance*, NBER Working Paper 10313, February 2004

22 G. Pascal Zachary, *The Diversity Advantage: Multicultural Identity in the New World Economy*, Westview, 2003, page 57

23 *Ibid.*, page 58

24 *Ibid.*, pages 61–2

6 Stealing Our Jobs?

1 Federation for American Immigration Reform: http://www.fairus.org/site/PageServer?pagename=iic_immigrationissuecenterslistc3fe

2 Sarit Cohen Goldner and Chang-Tai Hsieh, *Macroeconomic and Labor Market Impact of Russian Immigration in Israel*, October 2000

3 For evidence on the USA, see Robert J. LaLonde and Robert H. Topel, 'Economic impact of international migration and the economic performance of migrants', in Mark Rosenzweig and Oded Stark, eds, *Handbook of Population and Family Economics*, North-Holland 1997. See also Rachel M. Friedberg and Jennifer Hunt, 'The impact of immigration on host country wages, employment and growth', *Journal of Economic Perspectives*, 9, 1995: 23–44, which concludes that 'the effect of immigration on the labor market outcomes of natives is small'. Also, James P. Smith and Barry Edmonston, eds, *The New Americans: Economic, Demographic, and Fiscal Effects of Immigration*, National Academy Ptress, 1997, finds that 'the weight of the empirical evidence suggests that the impact of immigration on the wages of competing native workers is small'. And David Card, *Is the New Immigration Really So Bad?*, CReAM Discussion Paper Series 0204, University College London, 2004, finds that 'The evidence that immigrants harm native opportunities is slight.' For evidence on Europe, see Herbert Brücker, 'Can international migration solve the problems of European labour markets?' http://www.unece.org/ead/sem/sem2002/papers/Brucker.pdf

4 US Labor Force Survey 2005

5 Jorge Mora and J. Edward Taylor, 'Determinants of migration,

destination and sector choice: Disentangling individual, household and community effects', in Çaglar Özden and Maurice Schiff, eds, *International Migration, Remittances, and Development*, World Bank, 2005

6 Christian Dustmann, Francesca Fabbri, Ian Preston and Jonathan Wadsworth, 'The local labour market effects of immigration in the UK, 2003': http://repec.org/res2003/Dustmann.pdf

7 J. Haisken-DeNew, K. F. Zimmerman, *Wage and Mobility Effects of Trade and Migration*, CEPR Discussion Paper 1318, London, 1995

8 Dominique Gross, *Three Million Foreigners, Three Million Unemployed? Immigration and the French Labour Market*, IMF Working Paper 99/124, IMF, 1999

9 Jonathan Coppel, Jean-Christophe Dumont and Ignazio Visco, *Trends in Immigration and Economic Consequences*, Economics Department Working Paper 284, OECD, 2001

10 S. Castles, R. Iredale and E. Vasta, 'Australian immigration between globalization and recession', *International Migration Review*, 28(2), 1994

11 George J. Borjas, *The Labor Demand Curve is Downward Sloping: Reexamining the Impact of Immigration on the Labor Market*, NBER Working Paper 9755, June 2003

12 Gianmarco I. P. Ottaviano and Giovanni Peri, *Rethinking the Gains from Immigration: Theory and Evidence from the US*, NBER Working Paper 11672, September 2005

13 Peter Brimelow, *Alien Nation: Common Sense about America's Immigration Disaster*, HarperPerennial, 1996, page 162

7 Snouts in Our Trough?

1 Quoted in Peter Brimelow, 'Milton Friedman at 85', *Forbes*, 29 December 1997, page 52

2 Peter Brimelow, *Alien Nation: Common Sense about America's Immigration Disaster*, HarperPerennial, 1996, page 247

3 T. C. Boyle, *The Tortilla Curtain*, Bloomsbury, 2004

4 George Borjas, *Heaven's Door: Immigration Policy and the American Economy*, Princeton University Press, 1999, page 114

5 *Ibid.*

6 *Ibid.*

7 George Borjas, 'Welfare reform and immigrant participation in welfare programs', *International Migration Review*, Winter 2002: 1093–123. Borjas says, 'In 1997 the typical TANF household with two children in California could receive a maximum of $6,780 in cash benefits. This household probably qualified for food stamps worth another $3,132 annually. And if this household also participated in the Medicaid program, it received additional benefits valued at over $2,700.'

8 Personal Responsibility and Work Opportunity Reconciliation Act of 1996, § 401, 411, 432

9 Michael E. Fix and Laureen Laglagaron, *Social rights and citizenship: An international comparison*, Urban Institute, August 2002: http://www.urban.org/url.cfm?ID=410545

10 OECD, *Trends in International Migration*, Paris, 1997

11 J. Smith and B. Edmonston, *The New Americans: Economic, Demographic and Fiscal Effects of Immigration*, National Academy Press, 1997

12 Ronald Lee and Timothy Miller, 'Immigration, social security, and broader fiscal impacts', *American Economic Review Papers and Proceedings*, 90(2), 2000: 350–4

13 Alan J. Auerbach and Philip Oreopoulos, 'Analyzing the fiscal impact of US immigration', *American Economic Review Papers and Proceedings*, 89(2), 1999: 176–80

14 Access Economics, 'Impact of migrants on the Commonweath budget, summary report, 2001 update', 2001: http://www.immi.gov.au/research/publications/fiscal_impact_0301.pdf

15 C. Gott and K. Johnston, *The Migrant Population in the UK: Fiscal Effects*, RDS Occasional Paper 77, London, 2002

16 Dhananjayan Sriskandarajah, Laurence Cooley and Howard Reed, *Paying Their Way: The Fiscal Contribution of Immigrants in the UK*, Institute for Public Policy Research, 2005

17 Holger Bonin, Bernd Raffelhuschen and Jan Walliser, 'Can immigration alleviate the demographic burden?', *Finanz Archiv*, 57(1), 2000: 1–21

18 M. Dolores Collado, Inigo Iturbe-Ormaetxe and Guadalupe Valera, 'Quantifying the impact of immigration on the Spanish welfare state', *International Tax and Public Finance*, 11, 2004: 335–53

19 Hans Fehr, Sabine Jokisch and Laurence Kotlikoff, *The Role of Immigration in Dealing with the Developed World's Demographic*

Transition, National Bureau of Economic Research Working Paper 10512, 2004
20 The calculations assume migration had stopped in 1995.
21 United Nations Population Division, *Replacement Migration: Is It a Solution to Declining and Ageing Populations?*, 2000: http://www.un.org/esa/population/publications/migration/migration.htm
22 World Bank, *Global Economic Prospects*, 2006, page 29
23 Glenn Withers, 'Australia's need for a population policy', *Business Council of Australia (BCA) Papers*, 1(1), 1999
24 Survey on migration in 'A modest contribution', *The Economist*, 31 October 2002
25 World Bank, *Global Economic Prospects*, 2006, page 29

8 'Our Heroes'

1 Kevin O'Neil, 'Labor export as government policy: The case of the Philippines', 1 January 2004, Migration Information Source: http://www.migrationinformation.org/Feature/display.cfm?ID=191
2 Nigel Harris, *Thinking the Unthinkable: The Immigration Myth Exposed*, I. B. Tauris, 2002, page 89
3 International Organization for Migration, *World Migration Report*, 2005, page 239
4 Dean Yang, *International Migration, Human Capital, and Entrepreneurship: Evidence from Philippine Migrants' Exchange Rate Shocks*, Ford School of Public Policy Working Paper Series 02-011, University of Michigan, 2004
5 International Organization for Migration, *World Migration Report*, 2005, page 241
6 Peter Stalker, *The No-Nonsense Guide to International Migration*, New Internationalist/Verso, 2001
7 C. Dustmann and O. Kirchamp, 2001, *The Optimal Migration Duration and Activity Choice after Re-Migration*, IZA Discussion Paper 266, Institute for the Study of Labor
8 Kevin H. O'Rourke and Jeffrey G. Williamson, *Globalization and History: The Evolution of a Nineteenth-Century Atlantic Economy*, MIT, 1999, Table 7.2
9 *Ibid.*, Table 8.1
10 *Ibid.*, page 156

11 'Monetary lifeline', *The Economist*, 29 July 2004
12 World Bank, *Global Economic Prospects*, 2006, page 85
13 The Global Commission on International Migration, *Migration in an Interconnected World: New Directions for Action*, 2005, page 85
14 World Bank, *Global Development Finance*, Washington, DC, 2005
15 As a share of GDP, Tonga received 31.1 per cent, Moldova 27.1 per cent, Lesotho 25.8 per cent, Haiti 24.8 per cent, Bosnia 22.5 per cent, Jordan 20.4 per cent, Jamaica 17.4 per cent, Serbia and Montenegro 17.2 per cent, El Salvador 16.2 per cent, Honduras 15.5 per cent, Philippines 13.5 per cent, Dominican Republic 13.2 per cent, Lebanon 12.4 per cent, Samoa 12.4 per cent, Tajikistan 12.1 per cent, Nicaragua 11.9 per cent, Albania 11.7 per cent, Nepal 11.7 per cent, Kiribati 11.3 per cent and Yemen 10 per cent.
16 The twelve are Albania, Bosnia, Cape Verde, Gaza, Haiti, Jamaica, Kiribati, Lebanon, Nepal, Samoa, Serbia and Montenegro, and Tonga.
17 I. Adelman and J. E. Taylor, 'Is structural adjustment with a human face possible?', *Journal of Development Studies*, 26, 1992: 387–407
18 World Bank, *Global Economic Prospects*, 2006, Table 5.1, page 120. High-remittance countries are those where remittances are over 4 per cent of GDP; high-poverty-rate countries are those where over 20 per cent of the population are poor.
19 *Ibid.*
20 Richard Adams and John Page, 'Do international migration and remittances reduce poverty in developing countries?', *World Development*, 33(10), 2005: 1645–69
21 Richard Adams, *Remittances and Poverty in Ghana*, unpublished paper, World Bank, 2005
22 J. Edward Taylor, Jorge Mora and Richard Adams, *Remittances, Inequality, and Poverty: Evidence from Rural Mexico*, Research Program on International Migration and Development, DECRG Mimeo, World Bank, 2005
23 Richard Adams, *Remittances and Poverty in Guatemala*, Policy Research Working Paper 3418, World Bank, 2004
24 George Clarke and Scott Wallsten, *Do Remittances Protect Households in Developing Countries against Shocks? Evidence from a Natural Disaster in Jamaica*, unpublished paper, World Bank, Washington, DC, November 2004
25 Dean Yang and Hwa Jung Choi, *Are Remittances Insurance? Evidence from Rainfall Shocks in the Philippines*, Research Program

on International Migration and Development, DECRG Mimeo, World Bank, 2005

26 Dean Yang, *Coping with Disaster: The Impact of Hurricanes on International Financial Flows, 1970–2001*, unpublished paper, Gerald R. Ford School of Public Policy, University of Michigan, 2005

27 Edward Funkhouser, 'Migration from Nicaragua: Some recent evidence', *World Development*, 20(3), 1992: 1209–18

28 Dean Yang, *International Migration, Human Capital, and Entrepreneurship: Evidence from Philippine Migrant's Exchange Rate Shocks*, Research Program on International Migration and Development, DECRG, Policy Research Working Paper 3578, World Bank, 2004

29 Christopher Woodruff and Rene Zenteno, *Remittances and Microenterprises in Mexico,* unpublished paper, Graduate School of International Relations and Pacific Studies, University of California–San Diego, 2001

30 Richard Adams, 'The economic uses and impact of international remittances in rural Egypt', *Economic Development and Cultural Change* 39(4), 1991: 695–722

31 Richard Adams, 'Remittances, investment, and rural asset accumulation in Pakistan', *Economic Development and Cultural Change*, 41(1), 1998: 155–73

32 Richard Adams, 'Remittances, household expenditure and investment in Guatemala', in Çaglar Özden and Maurice Schiff, eds, *International Migration, Remittances, and the Brain Drain*, World Bank, 2005

33 Alejandra Cox Edwards and Manuelita Ureta, *International Migration, Remittances, and Schooling: Evidence from El Salvador*, NBER Working Paper 9766, June 2003

34 Peggy Levitt, *The Transnational Villagers*, University of California Press, 2001, page 180

35 Alejandro Portes, Cristina Escobar and Alexandria Walton Radford, *Immigrant Transnational Organizations and Development: A Comparative Study*, CMD Working Paper #05-07, August 2005

36 Richard Black, Savinna Ammassari, Shannon Mouillesseaux and Radha Rajkotia, *Migration and Pro Poor Policy in West Africa*, Working Paper C8, Sussex Centre for Migration Research, University of Sussex, 2004

37 Patricia Landolt, *Transnational Communities: An Overview of Recent Evidence from Colombia, Dominican Republic, and El Salvador*,

unpublished report, Program in Comparative and International Development, Department of Sociology, Johns Hopkins University, 1997

38 Stalker's guide to international migration: http://www.pstalker.com/migration/mg_emig_6.htm#

39 International Organization for Migration, *World Migration Report*, 2005

40 '3 por 1. Proyectos Compartidos', prepared for the seminar Migracion, remesas y el Programa 3 por 1 para Migrantes, Secretaria de Desarollo Social, Mexico and IADB, Washington, DC, June 2005

41 David Kyle, *The Transnational Peasant: The Social Structures of Economic Migration from the Ecuadoran Andes*, Ph.D. Dissertation, Department of Sociology, Johns Hopkins University, 1994

42 Alejandro Portes and Luis E. Guarnizo, 'Tropical capitalists: US-bound immigration and small enterprise development in the Dominican Republic', in S. Diaz-Briquets and S. Weintraub, eds, *Migration, Remittances and Business Development: Mexico and Caribbean Basin Countries*, Westview Press, 1990, pages 101–31

43 Alejandro Portes, William Haller and Luis E. Guarnizo, *Transnational Entrepreneurs: The Emergence and Determinants of an Alternative Form of Immigrant Economic Adaptation*, WPTC-01-05, February 2001

44 Prachi Mishra, *Macroeconomic Impact of Remittances in the Caribbean*, unpublished paper, International Monetary Fund, 2005

45 Paola Giuliano and Marta Ruiz-Arranz, *Remittances, Financial Development, and Growth*, IMF Working Paper, 2005

9 Brain Drain or Brain Gain?

1 'A nomad's life is hard', *The Economist*, 5 August 1999

2 AFFORD (African Foundation for Development), *Globalisation and development: A diaspora dimension*, May 2000: http://www.afforduk.org/resources/download/diaspora_dimension.pdf

3 'The view from afar', *The Economist*, 31 October 2002

4 Michel Beine, Frédéric Docquier and Hillel Rapoport, 'Brain drain and economic growth: Theory and evidence', *Journal of Development Economics*, 64, 2001: 275–89

5 Frédéric Docquier and Abdeslam Marfouk, 'International migration by education attainment, 1990–2000', in Çaglar Özden and Maurice

Schiff, eds, *International Migration, Remittances, and the Brain Drain*, World Bank and Palgrave Macmillan, 2006, Table 5.2, page 164

6 *Ibid.*

7 *Ibid.*, Table 5.6.B

8 Mario Cervantes and Dominique Guellec, 'The brain drain: Old myths, new realities', *OECD Observer*, May 2002

9 Frédéric Docquier and Abdeslam Marfouk, 'International migration by education attainment, 1990–2000', in Çaglar Özden and Maurice Schiff, eds, *International Migration, Remittances, and the Brain Drain*, World Bank and Palgrave Macmillan, 2006, Table 5.4

10 *Ibid.* High-skilled workers are those having some university or further education. The top thirty are Guyana 89.0 per cent, Grenada 85.1 per cent, Jamaica 85.1 per cent, Saint Vincent and the Grenadines 84.5 per cent, Haiti 83.6 per cent, Trinidad and Tobago 79.3 per cent, Saint Kitts and Nevis 78.5 per cent, Samoa 76.4 per cent, Tonga 75.2 per cent, St Lucia 71.1 per cent, Cape Verde 67.5 per cent, Antigua and Barbuda 66.8 per cent, Belize 65.5 per cent, Dominica 64.2 per cent, Barbados 63.5 per cent, the Gambia 63.3 per cent, Fiji 62.2 per cent, the Bahamas 61.3 per cent, Malta 57.6 per cent, Mauritius 56.2 per cent, Seychelles 55.9 per cent, Sierra Leone 52.5 per cent, Suriname 47.9 per cent, Ghana 46.9 per cent, Mozambique 45.1 per cent, Liberia 45.0 per cent, Marshall Islands 39.4 per cent, Lebanon 38.6 per cent, Kenya 38.4 per cent and Micronesia 37.8 per cent.

11 *Ibid.*

12 World Bank, *Global Economic Prospects*, 2006, page 68

13 B. L. Lowell, A. Findlay and E. Stewart, *Brain Strain: Optimising Highly Skilled Migration from Developing Countries*, Asylum and Migration Working Paper 3, Institute for Public Policy Research, London, 2004

14 'Devastating exodus of doctors from Africa and Caribbean is found', *New York Times*, 27 October 2005

15 Fitzhugh Mullan, 'The metrics of the physician brain drain', *New England Journal of Medicine*, 27 October 2005: http://content.nejm.org/cgi/reprint/353/17/1810.pdf

16 Rupa Chanda, *Trade in Health Services*, paper prepared for the Working Group on Health and International Economy of the Commission on Macroeconomics and Health, World Health Organization, Geneva, 2001

17 Tikki Pang, Mary Ann Lansang and Andy Haines, 'Brain drain and health professionals', *British Medical Journal*, 324(7336), 2 March 2002: 499–500
18 International Organization for Migration, *World Migration Report*, 2005, page 173
19 Peter Stalker, *The Work of Strangers: A Survey of International Labour Migration*, International Labour Office, 1994.
20 Kimberly Hamilton and Jennifer Yau, 'The global tug-of-war for health care workers', 1 December 2004, Migration Information Source: http://www.migrationinformation.org/Feature/display.cfm? ID=271
21 Tim Martineau, K. Decker and P. Bundred, 'Briefing note on international migration of health professionals: Levelling the playing field for developing health systems', International Health Division, School of Tropical Medicine, Liverpool, 2002
22 Fitzhugh Mullan, 'The metrics of the physician brain drain', *New England Journal of Medicine*, 27 October 2005: http://content.nejm.org/cgi/reprint/353/17/1810.pdf
23 Article 13 says that everyone has the right to leave any country, but it does not offer the right to offer another country except as a refugee.
24 'Exodus of medical staff hampers aids programmes,' *Financial Times*, 16 July 2004, based on a report by Physicians for Human Rights, presented at the International Aids Conference in Bangkok
25 David Ellerman, *Policy Research on Migration and Development*, World Bank Policy Research Working Paper 3117, 2003
26 Jagdish Bhagwati, 'Borders beyond control', *Foreign Affairs*, January/February 2003
27 Ross Herbert and Trish Guy, 'Reversing the brain drain, harnessing the diaspora', *eAfrica*, 1, September 2003: http://www.braingain-instruments.nl/docs/governance-innovation-09-2003.pdf
28 James E. Rauch and Victor Trindade, *Ethnic Chinese Networks in International Trade*, NBER Working Paper 7189, National Bureau of Economic Research, June 1999
29 Asian Development Bank, 'Developing the diaspora', 2004: http://www.un.org/esa/population/publications/thirdcoord2004/P12_AsianDevBank.pdf
30 Brett Johnson and Santiago Sedaca, 'Diasporas, émigrés, and development: Economic linkages and programmatic responses', study conducted for the Trade Enhancement Service Sector (TESS) Project

under contract with the US Agency for International Development, Carana Corporation, January 2004

31 Mercy Brown, 'South Africa shows the value of the diaspora option', 22 May 2003, SciDev.Net: http://www.scidev.net/Opinions/index.cfm?fuseaction=readOpinions&itemid=154&language=1

32 Caroline Sorgho, 'Making a difference back home', *eAfrica*, 1, September 2003: http://www.braingain-instruments.nl/docs/governance-innovation-09-2003.pdf

33 M. Cervantes and D. Guellec, 'The brain drain: Old myths, new realities', *Observer*, 7 May 2002: www.oecdobsever.org

34 AnnaLee Saxenian, 'Transnational communities and the evolution of global production networks: The cases of Taiwan, China and India', *Industry and Innovation*, special issue on global production networks, Fall 2002

35 *Ibid.*

36 Kevin O'Neil, 'Brain drain and gain: The case of Taiwan', 1 September 2003, Migration Information Source: http://www.migrationinformation.org/Feature/ display.cfm?ID=155

10 It Needn't Be Forever

1 Philip Martin, *Managing Labor Migration: Temporary Worker Programs for the Twenty-first Century*, International Institute for Labour Studies, 2003

2 *Ibid.*

3 Martin Ruhs, 'Designing viable and ethical labour immigration policies, in United Nations', *World Migration Report*, 2005

4 'Be my guest', *The Economist*, 6 October 2005

5 Lant Pritchett, *Labor Mobility and the Development Policy Agenda in the 21st Century* (22 November 2002 draft), Center for Global Development, page 20

6 Dani Rodrik, *Feasible Globalizations*, NBER Working Paper 9219, September 2002

7 L. Alan Winters, *GATS Mode 4: The Temporary Movement of Natural Persons*

11 Alien Nation

1 Peter Brimelow, *Alien Nation: Common Sense about America's Immigration Disaster*, HarperPerennial, 1996, page xxi
2 Mario Vargas Llosa, 'The culture of liberty', *Foreign Policy*, February 2000
3 Peter Brimelow, *Alien Nation: Common Sense about America's Immigration Disaster*, HarperPerennial, 1996, page 203
4 *Ibid.*, pages 206 and 205
5 Nigel Harris, *Thinking the Unthinkable: The Immigration Myth Exposed*, I. B. Tauris, 2002, page 64
6 Gaston Kelman, *Je suis noir et je n'aime pas le manioc*, Max Milo, 2004
7 Peter Brimelow, *Alien Nation: Common Sense about America's Immigration Disaster*, HarperPerennial, 1996, page 216
8 *Ibid.*, page 19
9 *Ibid.*, page 66
10 *Ibid.*, pages 263–4
11 *Ibid.*, page 232
12 *Ibid.*, page 57
13 Joe Volpe, speech to the tenth International Metropolis Conference, Toronto, Ontario, October 2005: http://www.cic.gc.ca/english/press/speech-volpe/metropolis2005.html
14 Ipsos Reid, 'Canadian immigration and ethnicity – Where do voters stand?', 11 January 2006: http://www.ipsos-na.com/news/pressrelease.cfm?id=2934
15 *Toronto Globe and Mail*, 4 November 1995, page D6; all of the above is from a discussion on the Fraser Institute website: http://oldfraser.lexi.net/publications/forum/1998/august/identity.html

12 Huntington and Hispanics

1 Samuel P. Huntington, *Who Are We? America's Great Debate*, The Free Press, 2005
2 Patrick J. Buchanan, *The Death of the West: How Dying Populations and Immigrant Invasions Imperil Our Country and Civilization*, Thomas Dunne, 2002, pages 125–6
3 Quoted in Peter Brimelow, *Alien Nation: Common Sense about*

America's Immigration Disaster, HarperPerennial, 1996

4 *Ibid.*

5 Samuel Huntington, 'The Hispanic Challenge', *Foreign Policy*, March/April 2004. All of the subsequent Huntington quotes in this chapter are from this article.

6 The Pew Research Center of the People and the Press, 'The 2004 political landscape, Part 8: Religion in American life', November 2003: http://people-press.org/reports/display.php3?PageID=757

7 Commentary on 'The Hispanic Challenge'. *Foreign Policy*, May/June 2004: http://www.foreignpolicy.com/story/cms.php?story_id=2530&page=3#19

8 Quoted in Peter Brimelow, *Alien Nation: Common Sense about America's Immigration Disaster*, HarperPerennial, 1996

9 Commentary on 'The Hispanic Challenge', *Foreign Policy*, May/June 2004

10 *Ibid.*

11 *Ibid.*: http://www.foreignpolicy.com/story/cms.php?story_id=2530&page=4#8

12 Pew Hispanic Center/Kaiser Family Foundation, 2002 'National survey of Latinos, summary of findings', December 2002, Chart 2.5, page 33: http://pewhispanic.org/files/reports/15.pdf

13 US Census Bureau 2000, 'Overview of race and Hispanic origin', C2KBR/01-1, Table 1: http://www.census.gov/prod/2001pubs/c2kbr01-1.pdf

14 US Census Bureau, 'Census 2000', Table 1a: United States Ability to Speak English by Language Spoken at Home for the Population 5 Years and Over, 2000: http://www.census.gov/population/cen2000/phc-t37/tab01a.pdf

15 According to US Census Bureau, 'Census 2000', Summary File 3, Table PCT12, <www.census.gov/population/cen2000/phc-t20/tab06.xls>, of the 28.1 million people who speak Spanish at home, 14.8 million were born in the USA and 13.34 million were born abroad. Among those foreign-born people who speak Spanish at home, 29 per cent (or 3,869,000) speak English 'very well', 21 per cent (or 2,801,000) speak English 'well', 31 per cent (or 4,135,000) speak English 'not well' and 19 per cent (or 2,535,000) speak English 'not at all': http://www.census.gov/population/www/socdemo/foreign/slideshow/fbprofile/txtSlide13.html

16 Pew Hispanic Center/Kaiser Family Foundation, '2002 National

survey of Latinos, summary of findings', December 2002, Chart 3.6, page 45: http://pewhispanic.org/files/reports/15.pdf

17 *Ibid.*, Chart 3.4, page 44

18 Commentary on 'The Hispanic Challenge', *Foreign Policy*, May/June 2004: http://www.foreignpolicy.com/story/cms.php?story_id=2530&page=2#4

19 *Ibid.*: http://www.foreignpolicy.com/story/cms.php?story_id=2530&page=4

20 *Ibid.*: http://www.foreignpolicy.com/story/cms.php?story_id=2530&page=1#2

21 Patrick J. Buchanan, *The Death of the West: How Dying Populations and Immigrant Invasions Imperil Our Country and Civilization*, Thomas Dunne, 2002, page 140

22 Victor Davis Hanson, *Mexifornia: A State of Becoming*, Encounter Books, 2003

23 Pew Hispanic Center/Kaiser Family Foundation, '2002 National survey of Latinos, summary of findings', December 2002, Table 2.1, page 25: http://pewhispanic.org/files/reports/15.pdf

24 Barry Edmonston, Sharon M. Lee and Jeffrey S. Passel , 'Recent trends in intermarriage and immigration and their effects on the future racial composition of the US population', in *The New Race Question: How the Census Counts Multiracial Individuals*, Russell Sage Foundation and the Levy Institute of Bard College, 2003

25 Commentary on 'The Hispanic Challenge', *Foreign Policy*, May/June 2004: http://www.foreignpolicy.com/story/cms.php?story_id=2530&page=2#4

13 Stranger, Can You Spare a Dime?

1 David Goodhart, 'Too diverse?', *Prospect*, February 2005

2 *Ibid.*

3 Alberto Alesina, Edward Glaeser and Bruce Sacerdote, *Why Doesn't the US Have a European-Style Welfare System?*, NBER Working Paper 8524, October 2001

4 The research paper is Stuart Soroka, Keith Banting and Richard Johnston, 'Immigration and redistribution in the global era', in Pranab Bardham, Samuel Bowles and Michael Wallerstein, eds, *Globalization and Social Redistribution*, Princeton University Press and Twentieth

Century Fund, Princeton, NJ, and New York, in press. The quote is from Keith G. Banting, *Canada as counter-narrative: Multiculturalism, recognition and redistribution*, paper presented to the Panel on Canada's Contribution to Understanding Rights and Diversity, Canadian Political Science Association, University of Western Ontario, 2 June 2005.

5 The research papers are Keith Banting and Will Kymlicka, 'Are multiculturalism policies bad for the welfare state?', *Dissent*, Fall 2003: 59–66; and 'Do multiculturalism policies erode the welfare state?', in Philippe van Parijs, ed., *Cultural Diversity versus Economic Solidarity*, Deboeck Université Press, 2004. The quote is from the same paper as in the previous footnote.

6 Stuart Soroka, Richard Johnston and Keith Banting, 'Ethnicity, trust and the welfare state, in Philippe Van Parijs', ed., *Cultural Diversity versus Economic Solidarity*, Deboeck Université Press, 2004

7 Keith G. Banting, 'Canada as counter-narrative: Multiculturalism, recognition and redistribution, paper presented to the Panel on Canada's Contribution to Understanding Rights and Diversity', Canadian Political Science Association, University of Western Ontario, 2 June 2005

14 Learning to Live Together

1 John Stuart Mill, *Principles of Political Economy*, 1848, pages 581–2

2 Salman Rushdie, 'What this cultural debate needs is more dirt, less pure stupidity', *The Times*, 10 December 2005

3 Junot Díaz, *Drown*, Faber and Faber, 1996

4 'Dim drums throbbing in the hills half heard', *The Economist*, 8 August 2002

5 'We hate France and France hates us', *Guardian*, 9 November 2005

6 'Liberté, égalité et fraternité but only for some', *Financial Times*, 8 November 2005

7 Stepan Kerkyasharian, *The Concept of Citizenship in a Globalised World*, Community Relations Commission for a Multicultural New South Wales, 2001

8 Joanne van Selm, 'The Netherlands: Death of a filmmaker shakes a nation', Migration Information Source: http://www.migrationinfor-

mation.org/Profiles/display.cfm?ID=341

9 'The war of the headscarves', *The Economist*, 5 February 2004

10 Amartya Sen, 'Solution to cultural confusion is freedom and reason', *Financial Times*, 29 November 2005

11 Salman Rushdie, 'What this cultural debate needs is more dirt, less pure stupidity', *The Times*, 10 December 2005

12 Sarfraz Manzoor, 'We pass the Tebbit test', *Observer*, 21 August 2005

13 Salman Rushdie, 'What this cultural debate needs is more dirt, less pure stupidity', *The Times*, 10 December 2005

14 Sasha Polakov-Suransky, 'Denmark: Rebuffing immigrants', *World Press Review*, 49(8), August 2002

15 City of Toronto, 'Diversity our strength: Perspectives and experiences from the City of Toronto', presentation to the Dutch Ministry of Health delegation, 4 October 2005

16 Ipsos Reid, 'Canadian immigration and ethnicity. Where do voters stand?', 11 January 2006: http://www.ipsos-na.com/news/pressrelease.cfm?id=2934

15 Illiberal Islam?

1 Quoted in Jytte Klausen, *The Islamic Challenge: Politics and Religion in Western Europe*, Oxford University Press, 2005, page 10

2 José María Aznár, 'Not too late to cast off Europe's pessimism', *Financial Times*, 17 October 2005

3 Salman Rushdie, 'What this cultural debate needs is more dirt, less pure stupidity', *The Times*, 10 December 2005

4 Gilles Kepel, *The War for Muslim Minds: Islam and the West*, Harvard University Press, 2004, page 241

5 Interview with Hassan Butt, *Prospect*, August 2005

6 http://www.islamicpopulation.com

7 'Forget asylum-seekers: it's the people inside who count', *The Economist*, 8 May 2003

8 Fouad Ajami, 'The Moor's last laugh: Radical Islam finds a haven in Europe', *Wall Street Journal*, 22 March 2004

9 Jytte Klausen, *The Islamic Challenge: Politics and Religion in Western Europe*, Oxford University Press, 2005, page 3

10 'The war of the headscarves', *The Economist*, 5 February 2004

11 *Ibid.*

12 Patrick Weil, 'A nation in diversity: France, Muslims and the headscarf', *Open Democracy*, 25 March 2004
13 Poll quoted in *ibid.*
14 Olivier Roy, *Globalised Islam: The Search for a New Ummah*, C. Hurst, 2004, page 329
15 *Ibid.*, page 80
16 *Ibid.*, page 143
17 *Ibid.*, page 276
18 Stephen Fidler, Jimmy Burns and Roula Khalaf, 'The UK foment of Islam's radical fringe', *Financial Times*, 14 July 2005
19 Hamayun Ansari, 'Identity struggle leads to radicalism', *Financial Times*, 21 July 2005
20 Gilles Kepel, *The War for Muslim Minds: Islam and the West*, Harvard University Press, 2004
21 Olivier Roy, *Globalised Islam: The Search for a New Ummah*, C. Hurst, 2004, page 45
22 *Ibid.*, page 50
23 'The war of the headscarves', *The Economist*, 5 February 2004
24 'Dim drums throbbing in the hills half heard', *The Economist*, 8 August 2002
25 'Al-Andalus revisited', *The Economist*, 28 July 2005
26 Demetrios G. Papademetriou, 'The global struggle with illegal migration: No end in sight', Migration Information Source, 1 September 2005: http://www.migrationinformation.org/Feature/display.cfm?ID=336
27 Robert S. Leiken, 'Europe's angry Muslims', *Foreign Affairs*, July/August 2005
28 'Feeling at home', *The Economist*, 31 October 2002

16 Open Borders

1 Nigel Harris, *Thinking the Unthinkable: The Immigration Myth Exposed*, I. B. Tauris, 2002, pages 74–5
2 Michael Dummett, *On Immigration and Refugees*, Routledge, 2001, pages 67–8
3 'Populations en mouvement, Etat inerte', in Roger Fauroux, Bernard Spitz (eds.), *Notre Etat, le livre vérité de la Fonction publique*, Robert Laffont, 2000, pages 413-433.

4 T. L. Walmsley and L. A. Winters, *Relaxing the Restrictions on the Temporary Movements of Natural Persons: A Simulation Analysis*, CEPR Discussion Paper 3719, CEPR, London, 2003. According to Alan Winters of the University of Sussex and Terrie Walmsley of Purdue University, rich countries stand to gain $75.5 billion a year from allowing in an extra 8 million skilled and 8.4 million unskilled workers on temporary work permits – an increase in their workforce of only 3 per cent – of which $57.5 billion would come from freer unskilled migration and only $18 billion from freer skilled migration. This calculation does not include many of the benefits from migration, such as greater diversity, more women working, and so on.

5 The figure of 427,000 is from Home Office, 'Accession Monitoring Report May 2004–June 2006,' 2006; the figure of 48,000 is from the Office for National Statistics. http://www.statistics.gov.uk/cci/nugget.asp?id=260

6 'London's allure', *Financial Times*, 27 October 2005

7 Dani Rodrik, *Feasible Globalizations*, NBER Working Paper 9129, September 2002

8 World Bank, *Global Economic Prospects*, 2006, chapter 2

9 GCIM Migration Futures Workshop 10 December 2004, St Antony's College, Oxford

Index

9/11: 5, 10, 30, 94, 112, 168, 285, 293, 296, 297, 308, 315, 316, 326

AFL-CIO 37
Afghanistan 50, 60, 185, 240, 292
agriculture, role of immigrants in 82
aid, overseas 20–1, 164, 168, 330
AIDS and brain drain 181, 187
Ajami, Fouad 297
Akosa, Agyeman 186
al-Muhajiroun 292, 297, 308
Albania 57, 181, 274, 294
Alesina, Alberto 130, 252
Algeria 48, 57, 167, 265
Algerian immigrants 35, 49, 57, 274
Alianza Dominicana 173, 228–32, 329
Aliweiwi, Jehad 285–6
Amnesty International 27
Amsterdam 6, 270, 308
Andorra 55
Angola 184
Ansari, Hamayun 309–10
Antigua 184
Argentina 46–7
Arizona 236
Arizona desert 11, 33–4, 237
Arsenal 13, 129–30, 213
asylum seekers 6, 34, 49–50, 59–60, 208, 326
Atta, Mohammed 296
Auerbach, Alan 153
Australia
  Afghan refugees 6, 34, 208
  anti-immigrant riots in Sydney 5
  asylum seekers 59–60
  border deaths 34–5
  brain gain 95
  education improvements 73
  emigrants to Britain 57
  foreign university students 95
  immigrant detention centres 34
  immigrants' access to welfare benefits 149
  immigrants and the government budget 153–4
  immigrants and unemployment 139–40
  immigration before First World War 46–7
  immigration points system 92–3, 108–9
  immigration policy 15, 92–3, 107–9, 111–12
  immigration since Second World War 48, 53
  immigration statistics 9, 55, 56
  multiculturalism 267–9
  Muslim immigration 293, 310
  national community 221
  'Populate or Perish' 53
  population ageing 159–60
  role of immigration in 2001 election 6, 208
  skilled immigration 15, 83–5, 92–3, 95, 107–9, 111–2, 115, 183, 186, 187, 191
  Standard Classification of Occupations 92–3

'White Australia' policy 53, 108
Austria 50, 60
Aznár, José María 289

Bahamas 184
Bakri Mohammad, Omar 297, 308
Bangladesh 168, 170, 264, 274
Banting, Keith 254–5
Barbados 184
Barbuda 184
Belarus 55
Belgium 48, 59, 253, 278, 293, 322
Belize 184
Benalfew, Yemisrach 36–7, 322–3
Bencheikh, Soheib 312
Berlin Wall 34, 40
Berton, Pierre 223
Bhatia, Sabeer 100
bin Laden, Osama 227, 290, 296
bird tracking by radar 110–11
Black Hawk Down 179
Blair, Tony 42, 267
Bono 329
book-burning 295
border deaths 42–3
  Australia 34–5
  Europe 27–9
  US 31–4
Borjas, George 7
  economic impact of immigration 65, 120
  immigrants and the labour market 140–1
  immigrants and welfare benefits 68–9, 145–6, 147, 149
Bosbach, Walter 289, 299
Botswana 189
Bouyeri, Mohammed 270, 314
'Bowie Bonds' 177
Boyle, T. C. 144
Bracero programme 200, 203–4
Bradford 275
'brain circulation' 193–6
'brain drain'
  benefits of 182–3, 190–3
  blame for 189–90
  costs of 181–2
  medical staff 186–9
  optimal rate 186
  statistics 183–5
brain-gain rates 95–6
brain-loss rates 96
Brazil 46–7, 50, 58, 77, 82, 167, 178
Brimelow, Peter 10, 23–4, 40–1, 143, 144, 207, 210–1, 217–21
Brin, Sergey 68
Britain
  asylum seekers 59–60
  backlash against immigration 12
  border controls 42, 45
  brain-loss rate 96
  Britishness 212–4, 216, 256, 275, 278, 279
  Chinese immigrants 28–9, 35–6
  Church of England 298
  citizenship ceremony 1–2
  cockle pickers 35–6
  East European immigrants 6, 326–8, 332
  education improvements 73–4
  emigration to New World 46–7
  foreign university students 95
  healthcare 113–16, 186, 188
  Home Office 35, 115, 154, 327
  hotel staff 76–7
  illegal immigration 35–6
  immigrants' access to welfare benefits 148–9
  immigrants' contribution to the government budget 154
  immigrants' effect on employment 137–8, 139
  immigration and the welfare state 145, 146, 148–9, 245–7, 249, 252
  immigration from the 'New Commonwealth' 49
  immigration since Second World War 48–51
  immigration statistics 55–7
  Jewish immigration 282

Britain – *continued*
job aspirations higher 73–4
job market 75–6
July 7 bombings 2–5, 276, 279, 296, 306, 307
multiculturalism 274–9, 282–3
Muslim immigrants 273–6, 292–3, 294, 296, 298, 304, 305–8, 311
national community 210, 211, 213, 216
national identity 212–4, 216, 256, 275, 278, 279
Pakistani immigrants 49, 71, 264, 274, 275, 279, 292, 294,
population ageing 156–9
proposed points system 93
seasonal agricultural migration 200
skilled immigrants 183–4
skilled immigration policy 93
British National Party 307
Brown, Mercy 192
Buchanan, Pat 10–11, 226–7, 236, 242, 315
Burkina Faso 192–3
Burnley 275
Bush, George 39, 153, 201, 234, 243, 259
Butt, Hassan 292–3

California 6, 11, 13, 33, 46, 51, 82, 100, 104, 144, 146, 200, 230, 235–7, 241–3
Cambodia 51
Canada
brain gain 95
diversity as a virtue 221–5, 250, 253–5, 276, 278, 287
education improvements 73
foreign university students 95
hometown associations 174
immigrants' access to welfare benefits 149
impact of diversity on welfare state 247, 253–5
immigration before First World War 46–7
immigration since Second World War 48, 52
immigration statistics 9, 55–6, 60
Muslim immigration 285–7, 291–2, 293, 294, 303–4, 308–9
multiculturalism 222, 255, 284–8
national identity 221–5
seasonal-farmworker scheme 201
skilled immigrants 15, 83–4, 89–92, 95, 111–2, 115, 180, 181, 183–4, 186, 187
skills-based immigration policy 91, 112
Cape Verde 184
cartoons of prophet Muhammad 295
Castles, Stephen 331
Catholic Church 300, 303
Catholics 233, 269, 293, 299, 301, 312, 316, 317
Ceuta 15, 24–7, 41
Chile 50
China 18–19, 97, 102, 193, 196
Chinese diaspora 191
Chinese emigrants 28–9, 55–6, 60, 82, 94, 95, 166–7, 182, 184
Chirac, Jacques 260
Cisneros, Henry 227
Ciudad Juárez 29–30, 32, 62
Clinton, Bill 227
clusters 13, 16, 97–100, 181
Cohen Gouldner, Sarit 134
Colombia 57, 146, 174, 176
Conexión Colombia 174
Contrera, Jaime 37
Coolidge, Calvin 217
Cornelius, Wayne 38–9, 41
Cortes, Edgar 163
cosmopolitan cities 3, 118–120, 122, 325
Costello, Peter 109
Côte d'Ivoire 24–6, 55, 324
Coyle, Diane 125
'coyotes' 32

Crash 260
creativity and immigration 123, 131–2
Cuban emigration 32, 55, 166, 182, 185, 187, 189, 237, 238
Cubanisation of Florida 226, 235, 240–1, 260
Cullingworth, Jane 84
cultural integration 258–288
culture 11, 210, 215–6, 218–20, 222, 223, 229, 232–4, 240, 242, 244, 303, 305, 320
cultural benefits of immigration 6, 8, 87, 91, 103–4, 108, 118, 120–3, 129–32, 195, 258, 290, 322, 333
cultural friction 88, 129, 226–7, 229, 236, 238, 241, 246, 289, 291–3, 295
cultural understanding 279–80, 302, 304
Czech Republic 6, 54, 57, 328

Daniels, Roger 240
democracy 242, 280–1, 286, 297, 303, 317
Denmark 12, 59, 283–4, 293
dependency ratios 156–60
developing countries
  baby boom in 17
  benefits of emigration to 16, 19, 161–78
  benefits of returning emigrants 163, 164, 192–3
  brain drain 180–2, 184–90
  highly-skilled workers encouraged to emigrate 182–3
  medical staff problems 186–8
  remittances to 20–1, 161–2, 165–73
'Devil's Path' 33
diaspora, benefits of 190–3, 196–7

Díaz, Junot 259
Dincvich, Lconid 109–11, 134
discrimination 5, 10, 218, 231, 267, 274, 277, 281–2, 302, 311
diversity
  economic benefits of 117–32
  innovation 124–5
  limits to 260–1
  impact on social solidarity 245–57
  political fears 246–7
  problem-solving 125–130
  seen as virtue in Canada 221–5, 250, 253–5, 287
Doha Round 206
Dominica 184
Dominican Republic
  Alianza Dominicana 173, 228–32, 329
  benefits of return migration 176–7
  brain-drain 185
  emigration to US 228–32, 235, 259, 283, 329
  hometown associations 173–4
  Miraflores Development Committee 173
Duffy, Malcolm 118
Dummett, Michael 59, 319
DTPM 117–8
Dustmann, Christian 137

East European immigration 6, 326–8, 332
eBay 100
Ecuador 57, 176
education improvements in richer countries 73
Egypt 172
El Paso 29–32, 33, 62, 315
El Salvador 37, 55, 172–3, 175, 176, 178, 185, 238
Ellerman, David 190
Ellis Island 45–6, 55, 144–5
emigration, impact on developing countries 161–97
employment, immigrants' impact on 133–43
entrepreneurship, immigrants and 14, 90–1, 94, 100–6, 164, 194–6, 321, 330

equality before the law 222, 234, 266, 280, 289, 299, 303
equality of women 262, 267, 276, 292, 304, 313, 314
Estefan, Gloria 259
Estonia 6, 230, 328
Ethiopia 186, 322–3
Ethiopian Jews 319–21
ethnicity 10, 11, 125, 131, 212, 220, 224, 225, 228, 234, 250, 256, 268
Europe
  backlash against immigration 11–12
  border controls 15, 41–2
  border deaths 26–9
  controls on low-skilled immigration 15
  education improvements 73–4
  emigration before First World War 46–7
  guest-worker programmes 48–50
  illegal immigration 9, 35
  immigrants and unemployment 138–9
  immigration since Second World War 47–51, 263–4
  immigration statistics 9, 54, 56
  'job-seeker's permit' 94
  Muslim issues 289–305
  population ageing 156–9
EU Single Market 51
exclusion, social 71, 282–3, 311

Fabregas, Cesc 130
family values, diverse 277–8
Federation for American Immigration Reform (FAIR) 133–4
Fiji 184
Finland 6, 48, 56
Finsbury Park mosque 305–6
Flamini, Mathieu 130
Florida 32, 51, 226, 237, 241
Florida, Richard 118–9, 122
foreign direct investment 20, 167
foreign worker levies 203
foreigners, fear of 5, 8, 9–12, 42–3, 256, 294, 332
Fortuyn, Pim 270, 271, 296
France 5, 12
  asylum seekers 59–60
  backlash against immigration 12
  closed border to east Europeans 328
  education improvements 73
  foreign university students 95
  Frenchness 215, 265
  headscarf ban 298, 301–2,
  immigrants' access to welfare benefits 149
  immigrants' effect on employment 138–9
  immigration before First World War 46
  immigration between the Wars 47
  immigration after Second World War 48–51
  immigration statistics 55–7
  integration 259, 260, 261, 264–6, 278
  Muslim immigration 293, 294, 298, 300–2, 305, 311, 312, 317
  national community 211, 215–16
  national identity 215, 265
  OSIMs 174
  population ageing 156–9
  seasonal agricultural migration 200
  secularism 300–1
  skilled immigrants 93, 95, 183
  suburban riots 5, 12, 265–6
Frattini, Franco 94
Freeman, Lee 118
Friedman, Milton 144
Fuerteventura 25, 28

Galbraith J. K. 1
Gallas, William 129
Galliano, John 99
Gambia 184

Gardner, Howard 131
gays 119, 210, 213, 250, 262, 263, 277, 280–1, 292, 302, 303, 304, 308, 324
Geldof, Bob 329
General Agreement on Trade in Services (GATS) 205–6
Germany
asylum seekers 59–60
bilateral subcontracting schemes 205–6
ethnic German immigration 50
foreign university students 95
'guest-workers' 6, 48–50, 200, 264
immigrants' access to welfare benefits 149
immigrants' impact on wages 138
immigration before First World War 46
immigration since Second World War 48–51
immigration statistics 55–7
integration 264
Muslim immigrants 289, 293, 297–8, 299, 300, 305, 311, 314
national community 212, 216
pensions crisis 154–5
population ageing 156–9
skilled immigrants 94, 95, 106, 183
Turkish immigrants 12, 164, 264
Ghana 170, 184, 186
Giuliano, Paola 178
Glaeser, Edward 120, 252
global cities
cosmopolitan diversity 48, 118–20
diversity 120–2
Global Commission on International Migration 166
global justice campaigners 20–1, 329
globalisation
benefits of 18–20
clusters 97–9
from below 175–7
migration as part of 12–17, 54
impact on national identity 213, 217
small companies 103–4
transnational businesses 175–7
Goodhart, David 245–6, 247, 250–3
Google 68, 100
Gouldner, Alvin 132
Greece 6, 28, 29, 44, 50, 53, 320,
'green card' 37, 202, 322
Greenspan, Alan 139
Grenada 184, 186
Griswold, Daniel 237
Gross, Dominique 138
group decision-making 125–8
Grove, Andy 100
Guadeloupe 49
Guam 55
Guatemala 62, 167, 170, 172, 185
Gulf states 49
Guyana 184

Haine, La 260
Haiti 32, 177, 184, 190, 228
Hall, Peter 119
Hamilton, Bob 64
Hamza, Abu 297, 305–6
Hanson, Pauline 267
Hanson, Victor Davis 242
Hargeisa University 179–180, 183
Harris, Nigel 23, 86, 211, 318
Hausman, Ricardo 241
Hennouch, Fatima 279–80. 290
Henry, Thierry 130
Hleb, Alexander 130
Hollywood 99
Holy See 55
hometown associations 173–5
homosexuality 280, 302, 303, 317
Honda, Mioko 83
Honduras 7, 15, 62–3, 70, 146–7, 167, 185, 324, 330
Hong, Lu 128
Hong Kong 55, 111, 162, 185

Hotmail 100
Howard, John 6, 208, 209, 221, 267, 310
Hsinchu Science Park 196
Huinder, Chris 269–71, 313–4
human rights 34, 163, 188, 209, 223, 280, 325
Huntington, Samuel 11, 225–44, 291

illegal immigrants 35–43, 59, 83, 146, 148, 152, 200, 202, 210, 243, 294, 315, 326
illegal immigration 15, 30, 39–41, 144, 235
illiberal behaviour 302–3
illiberal views 302
Illinois 51
imams 312–3
immigrants
  enterprising 8, 69–70
  hard-working 8, 69–70
  innovators 96–7, 123–8
  integration 258–88
  scapegoats 136, 270, 318–9
  self-selected minority 69
  separate communities 282
  situation if none 81
  worldwide need 16–17
immigration
  benefits, international trade analogy 79–80
  controls 23–43
  economic benefits of 18–9
  global debate 12–17
  impact on labour market 133–43
  impact on government finances 150–5
  impact on population ageing 155–60
  impact on welfare state 144–9
  low-skilled 61–88
  pattern 44–60
  political requirements 256
  potential global gains 64–5
  restrictions taken for granted 63–4
  skilled 13, 83–5, 89–116
  temporary 198–206
Inbram, Elias 319–21
India 55, 162, 166, 167, 181, 182
Indian emigrants 14, 55–7, 71, 84, 88–90, 94, 100–6, 108, 164, 184, 187, 189, 192, 193–6, 260, 268, 274, 279, 287, 294–5
Indonesia 34–5, 49, 56, 57, 208, 294
Indus Entrepreneur, The (TiE) 100–2, 192
innovation 96–7, 123–8
Institut Montaigne 265
Institute for Employment Research 76
integration 258–88
Intel 100
Iran 31, 50, 56, 60, 321
Iraq 34, 60, 153, 208, 240, 269, 308
Ireland 6, 44, 48, 50, 56, 164–5, 223, 247, 327, 331
Islam, see Muslim immigration
Islamic Human Rights Commission 307–8
Islamic terrorism 2–5, 296–7, 305–16, 316
Israel
  absorption of Soviet Jews 109–111, 133–5, 136, 321
  Ethiopian Jews 319–21
  role model 321–2, 333
Italy
  border deaths 28
  emigration 44, 46, 47, 52, 53, 55
  illegal immigration 28–9
  immigration statistics 56–7
  population ageing 156–9
  shift from emigration to immigration 50

Jackson, Peter 182
Jacobs, Mark 99
Jacoby, Tamar 15, 233–5
Jamaica 171, 184, 186
Jandl, Michael 38

Japan
cohesion and economic growth 125–6
effect of very limited immigration 77–8, 82–3, 253, 256
Filipino immigrants 162
foreign students 95
immigration statistics 58
population ageing 156
trainees and technical interns system 82–3
Jews 233, 240, 269, 293, 296, 299, 303, 312, 314
Jewish immigration 46, 68, 111, 134, 282, 319–22
jihadists 316
'job-seekers permit' 94
jobs, immigrants' impact on 133–43
Johnson, Norman 125–7

Kassovitz, Mathieu 260
Kazakhstan 55, 178
Kelman, Gaston 215
Kenya 184, 189, 191
Kepel, Gilles 291, 310–1
Kerkyasharian, Stepan 85, 266, 268–9
Khaki, El-Farouk 291 2, 317
Khalifa, Ahmed 291
Khan, Hikmat Mahawat 272–3, 312–4
Khomeini, Ayatollah 295
Khosla, Vinod
Klausen, Jytte 297, 304
Kondo, Atsushi 83
Korea, North 15, 184
Korea, South 97, 102, 184, 193, 204, 253
Korean immigrants 51, 55, 266
Kourouma, Lasso 7, 15, 24–6, 28, 42, 68, 321, 324
Kymlicka, Will 254–5

La Ferrara, Eliana 130
labour market, immigrants' effect on 133–43
Lacerda, Jander 7
laïcité 212, 300
language and language tests 261–2, 278
Lani, Remzi 181
Laos 51, 184
Last Temptation of Christ, the 295
Lauren 129
Lazarus, Emily 61
Lazear, Edward 123, 129
Le Pen, Jean-Marie 12
LeBoeuf, Michelle 29–32
Lee, Ronald 153
legislation
Aliens Act 1905 (UK) 45–6, 145
Asylum and Immigration Act 1999 (UK) 148
Multiculturalism Act 1988 (Canada) 222, 284, 286
Personal Responsibility and Work Opportunity Reconciliation Act 1996 (USA) 147–8
Welfare Reform Act 1996 (USA) 147–8
Lehmann, Jens 129
Leiken, Robert 316
Leshem, Yossi 110–1
'Let Them In' 329–31, 333
Letnes, Bjørn 65
liberal democracy 280–1, 297, 317
liberal values 260, 276, 280–1, 292, 298, 299, 302, 303, 308, 314
Liberia 184
Linares, Guillermo 120
Livingstone, Ken 2
Ljungberg, Fredrik 130
London
cosmopolitan city 1–3, 7, 48, 51, 118–20, 121, 123, 132, 198, 213, 247, 259, 261, 263, 324, 325
benefits of clustering 13, 14, 16, 18, 97–9, 106
illegal immigration 36
immigration 49, 71, 77, 275, 282, 326–7

London – *continued*
need for low-skilled immigrants 77, 78
July 2005 1–5, 276,279, 289, 295, 296, 306
'Londonistan' 316
London School of Economics 14
Los Angeles 119, 176, 227, 235, 239, 243, 260
low-skilled immigrants
allow natives to do different jobs 80–1
competition with native workers 67
controls on 15
created jobs invisible 66–7
demand for workers 39, 74–8
misconceived fears 66–7
need for 16–7, 61–88
pride in jobs 80
role of temporary workers 85–6
unpopular jobs 72
visible jobs 66
welfare scroungers 68–9
Lyon, Richard 77

Macao 55
machines replacing people 77–8
Madonna 198
Madrid bombings 289, 291, 296, 312
'Make Poverty History' 329
Málaga Acoge 37, 279, 290
Malave, Alejandra 231–2
Malawi 187
Mali 27
Malta 28, 29, 184
Mapplethorpe, Robert 295
Martin, Philip 204
Martinique 49
mass migration, 19th century 46–7
Mauritius 184
Médecins sans Frontières 27
medical doctors 113–16
Mejia, Miriam 227–31, 283, 329
Melilla 15, 24–5, 41
Merroun, Khali; 301
Mexico
Bracero programme 200, 203–4
Canadian seasonal-farmworker scheme 201
emigration to US 52, 55, 62, 137, 147, 226–7, 235–44
'heroes' 164
high-skilled emigration 184
hometown associations 175
remittances 20, 166–7, 170, 172, 177–8
3-for-1 programme 175
US border 5, 11, 29–32, 34, 39, 40–1, 315, 326
Miami 228, 235, 239, 240–1, 260
Michaeli, Sonia 133, 134
migrants, see immigrants
migration, see immigration
migration patterns
before First World War 46–7
current 53–8
since Second World War 47–53
migration reasons
asylum seekers 58–60
economic 58–9
family reunification 58, 60
political refugees 58–60
migration statistics 53–8
Mill, John Stuart 121, 258
Miller, Jonathan 153
Milli Görüs 305
'Minutemen' 11
Miraflores Development Committee 173
Monaco 55
Monks, John 328
Morecambe Bay 35–6
Moroccan immigrants 49, 57, 270–2, 278, 279, 291, 294, 296, 304, 313
Morocco 15, 24–6, 27–8, 57, 166, 294, 321
Moses, Jonathon 65
Mosier, Doug 31–2, 315
Moussaoui, Zacarias 297

Mozambique 184
Mugabe, Robert 189
multiculturalism
  and segregation 283–3
  Australia 267–9
  Britain 274–5, 279
  Canada 222, 255, 284–8
  criticisms of 275–7, 289–90
  different approaches 267–9
  impact on welfare state 255
  Netherlands 12, 269–74, 278
  Toronto 284–5
  US 218, 219, 228, 283
Muñoz, Elena 37
Muslim Council of Great Britain 304
Muslim immigration
  Britain 2–5, 274–6, 292–8, 305–8, 311,
  circumcision 295–6
  Europe 289–98
  forced marriages 261, 270, 271, 296, 303–4
  France 293, 294, 298, 300–2, 305, 311, 312, 317
  fundamentalist groups 302, 303, 305, 313
  halal food 299
  headscarf ban 298, 301–2, 310
  hostility 263
  imams 296, 298, 311–3, 314
  multiculturalism 274–7
  Muslim burial 300
  issues surrounding 289–317
  Netherlands 6, 269–73, 291, 293, 294, 296, 308, 312–4
  prayer rooms 299
  religious holidays 299
  ritual slaughter of animals 295, 300
  sharia law 293, 297, 298, 304
  Spain 289, 290–1, 293, 294, 296, 312–2
  statistics 293–4
  Toronto 291–2
  US 293, 315–7
nation 10, 11, 13, 207–225, 269, 275
National Academy of Sciences 152–3
national community
  diverse and divided 212–13
  extended family concept 210–12, 214
  immigration as opportunity 215, 216
  multiple identities 213–14
  myth that unchanged 210
national identity 6,8, 207–25, 299, 242, 260, 323
National Council of La Raza 243
National Health Service (NHS) 114–6, 214, 250
Nauru 34
Nazarski, Eduard 271–2, 273–4, 324
Netherlands
  asylum-seekers 59–60
  backlash against immigration 12
  emigrants to Canada 52
  foreign-born population 55–7
  immigration since the Second World War 49
  multiculturalism 12, 267, 269–74, 278
  Muslim immigration 6, 269–73, 291, 293, 294, 296, 297, 308, 312–4
  skilled immigrants 94
Nevada 236
New Jersey 51,
New Mexico 30, 33, 236
New York 7, 173, 174, 176, 239, 322–3
  cluster 97, 99
  diversity 247, 252, 261
  Dominican immigrants 228, 230, 235, 237, 259,
  global city 48, 118–23, 132, 325
  harbour 44
  illegal immigrants 37
  state 51

New Zealand 46–7, 48, 56, 58, 90, 96, 182, 191
Nicaragua 172, 185
Nicely,Michael 39
Nigeria 167
Noon, Sir Gulam 71, 111
Norway 188

O'Rourke, Kevin 165
OECD 106–7
Oldham 264, 275
Omidyar, Pierre 100
Operation Gatekeeper 33
Operation Hold the Line 31
Oreopoulos, Philip 153
Ottaviano, Gianmarco 121–2, 141–2
Owen, Sotero 163

Page, Larry 68
Page, Scott 128
Pakistan 55, 56, 84, 167, 172, 186, 189, 304, 312
Papademetriou, Demetrios 315
Papua New Guinea 34, 185
Paris 12, 97, 99, 100, 106, 119, 215, 260, 265, 285
'pateras' 15
pension crisis 154–5
people mobility 323–6
people smugglers
  encouraged by system 42–3
  Mexico–US 32
  size of criminal operations 38
Peri, Giovanni 121–2, 141–2
Peru 58, 82, 178
Petrusiak, Stephan 7
Philippines
  child labour 172
  diaspora benefits 192, 193
  emigrants 51, 55, 56, 82, 146, 184
  emigration encouraged 161–3, 181, 182, 187, 331
  migrant-recruitment agencies 204
  Migrant Workers Day 161
  Overseas Workers Welfare Administration (OWWA) 163
  remittances 21, 162, 165–6, 171, 177
Pinochet, Augusto 50
polleros 32, 63, 147
Polanco, Griselidys 230–1
Poland 6, 7, 57, 166, 184, 326–8
population ageing 155–60
Portes, Alejandro 176
Portugal 6, 47, 50, 56–7
poverty 5, 253, 282, 311, 329, 330
poverty alleviation 1, 164, 166, 168–73
Prat, Andrea 130
Premji, Azim 195
Pritchett, Lant 204
problem-solving 125–7, 128–30
'progressive dilemma' 247
Protestants 11, 120, 221, 227–8, 232–4, 244, 252, 261, 266, 269, 293, 299, 303, 312

Qatar 55
Quebec 225

race 9, 10, 11, 125, 209, 228, 236, 248, 252, 256, 268, 275, 277, 282
racism 12, 108, 132, 144, 231, 246–8, 262, 282, 283, 285, 302, 307, 308, 311, 320
  'good race relations' 248, 282
Rammohan, Seshan 101–2
Ramp Networks 104–5
'rampant individualism' 277
refugees 6, 34, 49–50, 59–60, 326
Reid, Richard 297
religion in public life 298–9, 302–3
religious fundamentalists 302, 303, 305, 313
remittances
  definition 162
  developing countries 20–1, 165–8
  international totals 165–8
  macroeconomic impact 177–8

poverty relief 168–73
retirement age 159
Réunion 49
Reynolds, Joshua 117
Rico Carabias, Mercedes 312–3
Rio Grande 29–30
Ritchie, Guy 198
Rivera, Inmer Omar 7, 15, 62–3, 70, 87, 146–7, 324, 330
Rizvi, Abul 107–9, 267–8, 310
Rodriguez, Katherine 42
Rodrik, Dani 204–5, 329–30
Romania 57
Rosicky, Tomas 130
Roy, Olivier 303, 304, 305, 311
RSA Migration Commission 76–7, 114–5
Ruhs, Martin 203
Ruiz-Arranz, Marta 178
Rushdie, Salman 258–9, 276–7, 281, 290, 294–5
Russia 55, 321
Russian emigrants 68, 134–5, 237
Ruto, Cecilia 191
Rwanda 185

Saint Kitts and Nevis 184
Saint Lucia 184
Saint Vincent and the Grenadines 184
Samoa 184
Sarkozy, Nicolas 12
Satanic Verses, the 294
Saudi Arabia 49, 55, 162, 163, 272, 297, 312
Saxenian, AnnaLee 101–3, 104, 193–5
Schröder, Gerhard 106
Schwarzenegger, Arnold 11
Scott, Ridley 179, 184
seasonal migration 46, 77, 200, 201
secularism 212, 215, 280, 297, 298, 299–300, 317
securitisation 178
Seidenberg, Ivan 129
Sen, Amartya 276
Senderos, Philippe 129
Senegal 27
Senni, Aziz 266
Serbia and Montenegro 167
Seychelles 184
Shadjareh, Massoud 308
Shakir, Uzma 84–5, 282–3, 286–7, 303–4, 308–9, 321
Shalala, Donna 234
sharia law 293, 297, 304
Sierra Leone 184, 187,
Sierra Leonean Women's Forum 174
Silicon Valley
  global cluster 14, 16, 97, 99–107, 193–6
  immigrant successes 100–1
  US-Asia links 102–5, 164, 182, 193–6
Silva, Gilberto 129
Singapore 162, 203
skilled immigration 13, 83–5, 89–116
Somalia 60, 179–80, 185, 197, 294
Somaliland 180, 183, 197
South Africa 56, 57, 186–8, 189, 192
Soviet Union 50, 54, 68, 110, 116, 134, 190, 264, 322, 331
Spain
  amnesty for illegal immigrants 35, 200
  border controls 15
  border deaths 27–9
  Canary Islands 25–6
  Ceuta 15, 24–7, 41
  cultural integration 279–80
  East European immigration 6, 327
  emigration 47
  foreign university students 95
  immigration and government budget 155
  immigration through Morocco 24–6, 27–8, 290
  immigration statistics 56–7
  Malaga 7, 37, 279, 290, 324
  Melilla 15, 24–7, 41

Spain – *continued*
  Muslim immigration 289, 290–1, 293, 294, 296, 312–3
  national community 210–1
  reaction to terrorism 312–3
  shift from emigration to immigration 5, 50–1
Sri Lanka 167, 182, 185
Stalker, Peter 66
Statue of Liberty 45, 61
Sudan 316, 319–20
Sun Microsystems 100
Surinam 49, 57, 184, 294
Suro, Roberto 242, 244
Sweden
  benefits of emigration 164–5
  brain-gain rate 96
  East European immigration 6, 283, 327, 328, 331
  immigration since Second World War 48, 50
  Muslim immigration 293
  refugees 56, 59–60
  welfare state 246, 247, 248, 251, 253,
Switzerland 48, 56–7, 59–60, 95, 278, 293
Sydney 5, 48, 84, 92–3, 118, 120
synergy from diversity 127–8

Taiwan 102–5, 162, 193, 195–7
Takhar, Harinder 89–91, 96, 106, 180
Tampa, the 208
temporary migration
  Bush proposal 201–2
  economic benefits 198–206
  case for 329–30
  global schemes 204–6
  illegal immigration 199
  impact on welfare state 151–2
  seasonal labour 200–1
terrorism 2–5, 31, 296–7, 305–16, 316
Texas 29–32, 33, 51, 62, 200, 236
Thailand 82, 192
tolerance of difference 2, 134, 223, 234, 272, 276, 280–1, 288, 289, 299, 303, 314
Tonga 167, 184
Toronto
  multiculturalism 284–5
  Muslim immigration 291–2
  skilled immigrants 84
Touré, Kolo 129
Trades Union Congress (TUC) 77
transnational entrepreneurs 195
Trinidad and Tobago 184
Tunisian immigrants 49, 57,
Turkey 28, 48, 57, 178, 241, 306, 312
Turkish immigrants 6, 12, 164, 264, 270, 272, 294, 297, 304, 306, 308

Uganda 168, 170, 184
Ukraine 55, 134, 324
unemployment, immigrants' impact on 133–43
Union of Islamic Organisations of France 305, 311
United 29
United Arab Emirates 55
United Nations 53, 322
United Nations Human Development Index 185
United Nations Population Division 156
United States 5
  affirmative action 9–10, 219–20, 266
  Anglo-Protestant culture 11, 221, 227–8, 232–5, 244, 252, 261, 266
  backlash against immigration 9–11
  bilingualism 218–9, 239–41, 243
  border controls 15, 29–32, 38–41
  border deaths 31, 33–4, 326
  Border Patrol 15, 29–32, 33–4, 39–41, 240, 315
  Bracero programme 200, 203–4

brain gain 95
Bush temporary-worker proposal 201–2
changing pattern of immigration 9–10
Christianity 232–5
Congress 40, 41, 52, 75, 147
Constitution 217, 233, 234, 242, 261, 266
contribution of immigration to technology boom 106–7
controls on low-skilled immigration 14–5
cost of people smuggling 38
Cuba 32–3
cultural components 232–4, 240
cultural diversity 259
Declaration of Independence 217, 228, 261, 266
developing-country doctors 188
education improvements 73–4
English language 234
evangelical Protestantism 303
foreign university students 94–5
Haiti 32
Hispanic immigration 5, 11, 31, 226–244
hometown associations 173–5
illegal immigrants 9, 35–7
illegal immigration from Mexico 9, 30–1, 52
immigrant amnesty 1986: 52
immigrant businesses 176
immigrants' access to welfare benefits 147–8
immigrants' perspective 322–3
immigration before First World War 19, 44–7
immigration from Honduras 62–3
immigration policy 14–5
immigration reform 1965: 51
immigration since Second World War 47–8, 51–2
immigration statistics 55
impact of immigration on labour market 137, 139–43
impact of immigration on welfare state 144–8, 152–3
impact of skilled migration on patents 97
integration 265
job aspirations higher 73–4
job market 75
Latino immigration 5, 11, 31, 226–44
'melting-pot' approach 266
Mexican immigrants 235–8, 238–44
Mexico border 29–32, 62–3
multiculturalism 218, 219, 228, 283
Muslim immigration 293, 315–7
national community 217–21
national identity 207, 211, 217–21, 232–5, 244
National Guard 5, 40
need for unskilled labour 75, 78
'open-door' immigration policy 45
population ageing 156–9
Presidential bilingual address 243–4
proposed temporary worker scheme 202–3
proposed border wall 39–41
remittances to developing countries 166
skilled migration 52, 92, 183–4
Spanish language 232, 238–44
Universal Declaration of Human Rights 188
Uruguay 46
Utah 236

Valentine, Jo 99
values 277–8, 280–1
van Gogh, Theo 6, 270, 291, 296, 308, 314
van Persie, Robert 130
Vargas Llosa, Mario 208
Veerina, Mahesh 104–5
Vietnam 50, 51, 55, 182, 184, 185

Volpe, Joe 221–2
von Bechtolsheim, Andy 100

Walker, Francis 44
Webster, Mark 84, 92, 111
Weil, Patrick 301, 317, 319
welfare benefits, immigrants' access to 147–9
welfare state
  illegal immigrants 147–9
  impact of immigration on 68–70, 144–55, 246–56
Wenger, Arsène 129–30
Westhenry, Mark 118
Whalley, John 64
Willetts, David 246, 247
Williamson, Jeffrey 165
Wilson-Smith, Anthony 223
Winters, Alan 61, 205
Wipro 195
Withers, Glenn 85, 112, 159–60
Wong, Agnes 37
World Bank 19, 147, 166, 168, 170, 190, 204
World Health Organisation 187
World Trade Organisation 88, 162, 205–6, 331
Wu, Miin 103

Yahoo! 100
Yang, Jerry 100
Yugoslavia 50, 53, 54, 57

Zachary, G. Pascal 117, 131
Zimbabwe 60, 189, 190
Zolberg, Aristide 316
Zongo, Sylvain 192–3